Autism

Information and Resources for Professionals and Parents

SECOND EDITION

Richard L. Simpson
and
Paul Zionts

pro·ed
An International Publisher
8700 Shoal Creek Boulevard
Austin, Texas 78757-6897
800/897-3202 Fax 800/397-7633
Order online at http://www.proedinc.com

pro·ed
An International Publisher

8700 Shoal Creek Boulevard
Austin, Texas 78757-6897
800/897-3202 Fax 800/397-7633
Order online at http://www.proedinc.com

Library of Congress Cataloging-in-Publication Data

Simpson, Richard L.
Autism : information and resources for professionals and parents / Richard L. Simpson, Paul Zionts.—2nd ed.
p. cm.
Prev. ed. pub. with subtitle: Information and resources for parents, families, and professionals.
Includes bibliographical references and index.
ISBN 0-89079-820-6 (pbk. : alk. paper)
1. Autistic children—Treatment—Popular works. 2. Autism—Popular works. I. Zionts, Paul. II. Title.
RJ506.A9S56 1999 99-13965
618.92′8982—dc21 CIP

This book is designed in Utopia and Goudy.

Production Director: Alan Grimes
Production Coordinator: Dolly Fisk Jackson
Managing Editor: Chris Olson
Art Director: Thomas Barkley
Designer: Jason Crosier
Print Buyer: Alicia Woods
Preproduction Coordinator: Chris Anne Worsham
Staff Copyeditor: Martin Wilson
Project Editor: Debra Berman
Publishing Assistant: John Means Cooper

Printed in the United States of America

1 2 3 4 5 6 7 8 9 10 03 02 01 00 99

Contents

Preface

We wrote this book primarily for professionals and parents who directly experience the frustration, concern, and uncertainty of living and working with a youngster with autism or an autism-related disorder such as Asperger syndrome. The information included is scientifically valid; however, it is presented in such a manner that professionals and parents with limited background in autism and behavioral sciences will find it beneficial. Moreover, for ease of reading and brevity's sake, we have chosen to provide supporting references only when absolutely necessary.

The book's focus is on answering common questions about autism and autism-related disorders, including issues posed to us by countless parents and family members of children and youth with autism. These individuals continually ask the same questions: What is autism? What causes autism? Did we do something to cause our child to develop autism? Is there a cure for autism? What can we do to help someone who has autism? What will become of a child with autism when he or she is an adult? Why does our child continually flap his arms and do bizarre things? These issues shape the content of this book.

A myriad of questions surround autism and autism-related disorders. For some of these questions, we have answers. For others, there are no definitive answers. In such cases, we have summarized and discussed what is known and reported progress being made to better understand and deal with a particular issue.

Autism was first described in the medical literature nearly 50 years ago. Since that time a great deal has been learned about the disorder. In fact, we have literally witnessed an explosion of knowledge and information about children and youth with autism. Although there is much debate as to the best methods for achieving desired outcomes with persons with autism and related disabilities, there is no question that continuing progress is more and more evident. As a result of this new information, many individuals with the disorder are now experiencing successes that earlier would have been considered nearly impossible. Children and adolescents with autism and autism-related disorders have also benefited from the commitment and perseverance of parents and families, as well as the willingness of schools, communities, and legislation to commit resources on behalf of these citizens. It is our belief that the future will continue to open doors for individuals with autism if professionals, parents, communities, and decision makers are well informed. It was with this mission in mind that this book was written.

Introduction to Autism

1

Children and youth diagnosed as having autism and pervasive developmental disorders have been given considerable attention in recent years. Dustin Hoffman skillfully portrayed Raymond, a high-functioning adult with autism in the movie *Rainman;* the National Football League Charities have established autism information libraries; magazines and newspapers have provided countless human interest stories about individuals with autism; and TV specials have brought the subject of autism into American homes. Such attention has created strong interest in autism and pervasive developmental disorders, yet the complexity of these disorders routinely leaves persons with questions (e.g., What exactly is autism? What are the best interventions for persons with autism?).

This book is for parents and family members of children with autism, and professionals who work and interact with children and youth with autism. We attempt to give readers an overview of characteristics of autism; background on the disorder; and alternatives and strategies for obtaining education, treatment, and support.

The book focuses primarily on children and adolescents. Although we recognize that autism affects individuals of all ages, and that families and professionals who are involved with adults with autism also need information and strategies for meeting the unique challenges they face, our focus in this book is on young people with autism.

Because there is no known cure for autism and because education and training are the cornerstones of the growth and development of children with autism, this book emphasizes educational considerations. Because children and youth with autism are receiving more and more services from schools and other educational agencies, these programs are increasingly being identified as responsible for children's gains. Accordingly, we give considerable attention to matters of education and training, while at the same time discussing issues related to noneducation professionals, disciplines, and treatments (e.g., mental health, medical interventions, transition).

Children and youth with autism are classified using different terms, including *pervasive developmental disorder*, *autistic-like*, *higher functioning autism disorder*, *Asperger syndrome*, and so forth. We identify these terms (and discuss the somewhat confusing and variable terminology used to describe children with autism); however, for purposes of brevity and convenience, we use the term *autism* to refer to children who demonstrate any one of a number of autism-related conditions.

CHARACTERISTICS OF AUTISM

Leo Kanner wrote in 1943 about 11 children he had seen in his psychiatric practice. These children demonstrated a variety of unique symptoms and behaviors, including desire for sameness (e.g., agitation and distress following changes in their routine or environment), abnormal speech and language development (e.g., speech delays, speech restricted to echoing what others say), and social withdrawal (e.g., extreme preference for aloneness). Kanner observed that these children's behavior generally differed from anything that psychologists and psychiatrists had previously reported. In his seminal article, Kanner used the word autistic to describe the children's inability to relate and their strong preference for being left alone. Previously, the term autistic had been used to refer to a thought-process disorder in persons with schizophrenia, a severe emotional disorder characterized by disturbances of thought, mood, and behavior. Some professionals currently use the term *pervasive developmental disorder* to refer to autism.

Information about autism has increased dramatically since the time of Kanner's article; however, a number of his observations about the characteristics of children with autism are still current, including (a) problems in relating normally to people and situations; (b) speech and language problems; (c) developmental delays; (d) problems in reacting to environmental changes; and (e) stereotypic, repetitive actions and other peculiar motor movements.

SORTING OUT THE TERMS: AUTISM AND PERVASIVE DEVELOPMENTAL DISORDERS

Definitions in the *Diagnostic and Statistical Manual of Mental Disorders*

A term commonly used by psychiatrists and psychologists to refer to children and adolescents with autism is pervasive developmental disorder. The term is taken from the *Diagnostic and Statistical Manual of Mental Disorders–Fourth Edition* (frequently referred to as DSM–IV) (American Psychiatric Association, 1994), a guide used by mental health professionals to classify, diagnose, and communicate about mental disorders.

The DSM–IV notes that the term pervasive developmental disorder is reserved for children who simultaneously show significant problems in a number of basic areas of psychological development, such as relating normally to people and situations, developing and using speech and language, and dealing with changes in the environment. Also these children often display nonuseful repetitive actions and other peculiar motor movements. Some children with autism also experience developmental delays (slowness in acquiring skills and developmental milestones).

Five forms of pervasive developmental disorder are identified in the DSM–IV: autism, Rett's disorder, childhood disintegrative disorder, Asperger syndrome, and pervasive developmental disorder–not otherwise specified. A description of each follows.

Autism

According to the DSM–IV, autistic disorder refers to persons with significant social interaction impairments, communication problems, and repetitive, stereotypic, and restricted interests and activities. Individuals diagnosed with autistic disorder show their symptoms prior to 36 months of age, and most children diagnosed with this form of pervasive developmental disorder are moderately to severely impaired, including having moderate to severe mental retardation. The DSM–IV diagnostic criteria for autistic disorder follow.

DSM-IV Autistic Disorder Diagnostic Criteria

Social interaction impairments, as shown by at least two of the following characteristics:

- Significant qualitative impairment in the use of nonverbal behaviors such as eye-to-eye gazc, facial expression, body postures, and social interaction gestures
- Failure to develop developmentally appropriate peer relationships
- Failure to spontaneously seek out others for the purpose of sharing enjoyment, interests, or achievements
- Poor social or emotional reciprocity

Qualitative communication impairments, as manifested by at least one of the following characteristics:

- Delay in, or total lack of, spoken language development (not accompanied by compensation attempts and alternative modes of communication such as gestures)
- Significant impairment in the ability to initiate or maintain a conversation with others, in persons with adequate speech
- Idiosyncratic, or stereotyped and repetitive language
- Lack of developmentally appropriate and varied spontaneous social imitative or make-believe play

Repetitive, restricted, and stereotyped interests, activities, and patterns of behavior, as shown by at least one of the following characteristics:

- Significant preoccupation with one or more stereotyped and restricted interests that is abnormal either in focus or intensity
- Inflexible adherence to nonfunctional, specific routines or rituals
- Repetitive and stereotyped motor movements such as hand or finger twisting or flapping, complex whole-body movements, and so forth
- Persistent preoccupation with object parts

Rett's Disorder

Rett's disorder is a relatively rare condition in females. Onset of the disability typically occurs by age 1 to 2, and is characterized by head growth deceleration; loss of previously acquired hand movements and other motor skills; stereotypic hand wringing or hand washing; various motor impairments; and social and communication impairments. Loss of previously acquired skills tends to be progressive and permanent, and prognosis (i.e., prediction about the course and outcome of the disorder) for individuals with Rett's disorder is poor.

Childhood Disintegrative Disorder

Children identified as having childhood disintegrative disorder (also known as Heller's syndrome, dementia infantilis, or disintegrative psychosis) have similar characteristics to those with autistic disorder, including social interaction, communication, behavioral, and other impairments. The difference between persons with childhood disintegrative disorder and those with autistic disorder relates to the age of onset of the disability. Children diagnosed with autistic disorder demonstrate symptoms of pervasive developmental disorder prior to 3 years of age, often from the time of birth. In contrast, children with childhood disintegrative disorder have a period of normal growth and development prior to manifesting social interaction, communication, and behavioral impairments. This apparently normal period of growth and development occurs for 2 to 10 years, after which time the child with childhood disintegrative disorder experiences a significant loss of previously acquired skills in expressive or receptive language, social skills, adaptive behavior, bowel or bladder control, play, or motor skills. According to the DSM–IV, the prognosis for children identified as having childhood disintegrative disorder is guarded.

Asperger Syndrome

Social interaction impairments are the primary difficulty experienced by individuals with Asperger syndrome. Indeed, children and youth with the disorder tend to have good language and cognitive skills, and are almost always referred to as high functioning. However, their social ineptness and generally poor social interactions create significant difficulties for them and the individuals with whom they interact.

Named for the German physician Hans Asperger, the term Asperger syndrome was first used in 1944 to refer to higher functioning children with autistic-like characteristics. Asperger syndrome was largely ignored in the United States until the 1990s, when professionals were becoming increasingly aware of the characteristics and needs of individuals with autism-related symptoms who are able to function at a relatively high level. Although the exact prevalence of Asperger syndrome is unknown, it appears to be a relatively common form of pervasive developmental disorder, and currently schools and clinics are reporting significant numbers of students with this diagnosis. A summary of the DSM–IV diagnostic criteria for Asperger's disorder follows.

DSM–IV Asperger Disorder Diagnostic Criteria

Social interaction impairments, as shown by at least two of the following characteristics:

- Marked qualitative impairment in the use of eye-to-eye contact, facial expression, body postures, social interaction gestures, and other nonverbal behaviors
- Significant inability to develop and maintain developmentally appropriate relationships with peers
- Significant inability to spontaneously seek social interaction opportunities with other people (e.g., by a lack of identifying objects of interest to others)
- Lack of emotional or social reciprocity

Repetitive and restricted stereotyped patterns of behavior, activities, and interests, as shown by at least one of the following characteristics:

- Significant preoccupation with one or more stereotyped and restricted patterns of interest that is abnormal either in focus or intensity
- Inflexible adherence to nonfunctional routines or rituals
- Stereotyped and repetitive motor movements, such as complex whole-body movements or hand or finger twisting or flapping
- Significant preoccupation with object parts

Clinically significant impairment in social, occupational, or other areas of functioning associated with the disorder:

- Absence of a clinically significant general language delay
- Absence of a clinically significant cognitive development delay, or in the development of age-appropriate adaptive behavior, self-help skills, and curiosity about the environment in childhood

Pervasive Development Disorder–Not Otherwise Specified

The final subtype of pervasive developmental disorder identified in the DSM–IV is pervasive developmental disorder–not otherwise specified. This somewhat vaguely defined diagnostic classification is used to refer to children who manifest "severe and pervasive impairment in the development of reciprocal social interaction or verbal and nonverbal communication skills, or when stereotyped behavior, interests, and activities are present" (American Psychiatric Association, 1994, p. 77).When pervasive developmental disorder–not otherwise specified is used as the classification, criteria for other forms of pervasive developmental disorder or other disabilities are not met.

Autism Society of America's Definition of Autism

Autism is also commonly defined in accordance with the definition adopted by the Autism Society of America (ASA) (1995). This definition encompasses the same general characteristics used in the DSM–IV.

According to ASA, autism is a severely incapacitating lifelong developmental disability that typically appears during the first 3 years of life. Autism is frequently called a *spectrum disorder*, meaning that the characteristics of the disability may present themselves in various combinations, from very severe to very mild. Thought to be the result of a neurological disorder that affects functioning of the brain, autism and its behavioral symptoms occur in approximately 15 out of every 10,000 births. Autism is four times more common in boys than girls. The disorder has been found throughout the world in families of all racial, ethnic, and social backgrounds. No known factors in a child's psychological environment have been shown to cause autism.

ASA's Behavioral Symptoms of Autism

- Delays and disruptions in the rate of appearance of various skills, including physical, social, and language
- Abnormal responses to sensations, including sight, hearing, touch, balance, smell, taste, reaction to pain, and the way a person holds his or her body
- Delays and aberrations of speech and language
- Abnormal ways of relating, including to people, objects, and events

According to ASA, autism occurs by itself or in association with other disorders that affect the function of the brain, such as viral infections, metabolic disturbances, and epilepsy. ASA also notes that it is important to distinguish autism from mental retardation or mental disorders because accurate diagnostic information is a key to the use of appropriate and effective treatment methods.

UNDERSTANDING THE CHARACTERISTICS OF AUTISM AND PERVASIVE DEVELOPMENTAL DISORDERS

Conceptualizations and definitions of autism and pervasive developmental disorders used in the DSM–IV and by ASA share several basic themes. That is, individuals diagnosed with autism and pervasive developmental disorder commonly experience problems in relating, speech and language difficulties, problems in responding to environmental changes, nonfunctional and repetitive motor movements, and developmental delays.

? *What is meant by problems in relating to people and situations?*

A characteristic of many children and youth with autism is their difficulty in relating to and interacting with people. These children may prefer to spend time in isolation, or may give the appearance of having little awareness of or interest in others, including family members. Some parents of children with autism may even wonder if their children can hear, based on observations that their children may be oblivious to the presence of others. In other instances, children with autism may attempt to interact with others in abnormal, socially clumsy, or unacceptable ways. For example, a child may attempt to interact by sniffing or licking the ankles or legs of people with whom he or she comes in contact, or an adolescent may repeatedly ask the same question of people (e.g., "What is your name?" "What are you doing?"), ignoring the answer and cues that it is inappropriate to repeat the same question over and over. Social interaction problems may also take the form of eye contact avoidance and reluctance to be near people, particularly strangers. Even higher functioning autistic persons (including children and adolescents) can be expected to have difficulty in developing and maintaining friendships and are frequently thought of as socially odd.

? *To what extent do children and youth with autism have speech and language problems, and how significant are these problems?*

As noted earlier, speech and language problems are common among children and youth with autism; in fact, a number of experts think that speech and language disorders are the most significant problems of children with autism. In this regard, *speech* refers to forming and using the sounds of oral language (i.e., problems in voice pitch, loudness, or quality disorders; making and using correct speech sounds; and stuttering), whereas *language*, a broader term, refers to a system or set of rules used by people to communicate. Language problems include absence or delays of verbal language development (i.e., ability to understand and use language); echolalia (parroting back whatever is heard); nonsense word and sentence use (use of "words" and phrases that have no meaning to others and that are not designed to communicate); ineffective use of communication gestures and affect (e.g., poor use of facial expression, gestures, and tone); pronoun reversals (e.g., use of *you* when *I* is intended); inability to name objects; and general difficulty in communicating. Speech and language problems and possible interventions are discussed in Chapter 7 of this book.

An estimated one half of individuals diagnosed as having classic autism (i.e., autistic disorder, per the DSM–IV criteria) fail to develop spoken language. Individuals diagnosed with Asperger syndrome and other higher functioning autism-related conditions will typically develop speech in an age-appropriate fashion; however, they too will experience communication problems, albeit in the form of poor social use of their language, nonverbal communication abnormalities, socially inappropriate comments, and so forth. Thus, even when persons with autism develop speech, they can be expected to experience communication difficulties. In fact, language problems are so pervasive that prognosis (prediction about the course and outcome of the disorder) has been related to whether or not persons with autism develop spoken language, and to their pragmatic (social) use of language.

? *What is meant by problems of reacting to environmental changes?*

This common characteristic of children with autism is related to their insistence on sameness. That is, some children with autism may become upset (e.g., have tantrums, withdraw, or become aggressive) if their environment is varied. For instance, some parents have reported that their children with autism will eat or drink only from one particular dish or cup; other children have been observed to become agitated if a road detour forces their school bus to take a different route. Every autistic child or adolescent is not adversely affected by environmental changes; however, such a pattern is common.

In a related manner, children and youth with autism may demonstrate strong attachment to unusual objects, preferring to maintain contact with the item at all times. For example, a child may keep a single blade of grass or piece of string and become agitated or aggressive if the item is removed. In comparison, children without this disorder spontaneously show affection and attachment toward toys and objects (e.g., teddy bears, dolls, blankets); however, the items to which they become attached usually have symbolic significance (e.g., a doll has human characteristics, a blanket serves to warm and comfort). The types of objects to which children with and without autism become attached, the degree to which they insist upon maintaining contact with an item, and the age of children engaging in such behavior differentiate "normal" from unusual object attachment.

? *What is meant by displays of nonfunctional repetitive actions and other peculiar motor movements?*

Among the most unusual and puzzling characteristics of children and adolescents with autism is their display of repetitive, stereotypic body movements that appear to have no useful function. These patterns, often referred to as *self-stimulatory behavior*, are designed to provide sensory stimulation. Examples of self-stimulatory behaviors are discussed in Chapter 4.

Self-stimulation can take a nearly infinite number of forms: body rocking, hand flapping, finger waving, light filtering (i.e., a child reflects light by moving his or her hands back and forth in front of his or her eyes), object twirling, hand rubbing, and a myriad of other behaviors that appear to have no functional value. Some children with autism would spend (if allowed) virtually every waking moment engaging in self-stimulatory behavior, thus interfering with the development of more functional skills. Moreover, self-stimulation is a solitary activity, making it difficult for children to appropriately interact with others at the same time. Decreasing self-stimulatory behaviors and replacing these responses with more functional behaviors is often a priority for children with autism.

? *What types of developmental delays do children and youth with autism experience?*

Children's development falls into three primary areas: cognition, social adaptation, and motor skills. Developmental delay refers to the tendency of children with autism to be slower in developing skills, compared with normally developing children; to fail to develop particular skills or functions (to experience arrests); or to develop and then lose a particular cognitive, social adaptive, or motor skill or function (to regress).

Cognitive delays (i.e., intellectual and learning deficits and problems) are typical of children and youth with autism. This does not mean that all children with autism are mentally retarded; on the contrary, some have average or above average intelligence and learning potential. However, the vast majority of children with autism have intellectual and learning problems.

Problems of social adaptation are typically characterized by social withdrawal, social deficits, and social ineptness. Thus, children and youth with autism can be expected to experience problems in relating to others. This form of developmental delay creates obvious problems for children, their families, and professionals.

Children and youth with autism also may show motor delays and deficits (*motor* refers to use of muscles of the body, such as in walking, crawling, writing, etc.). However, motor problems are not as common and pervasive as cognitive and social delays; thus some children with autism experience relatively normal motor development.

UNDERSTANDING AUTISM AND PERVASIVE DEVELOPMENTAL DISORDERS

Autism is the quintessential human enigma, even when compared to other disorders. Indeed, individuals with autism show highly unique characteristics. Thus, autism stands out as a condition that provokes a number of questions about the disorder. In this section we attempt to respond to some of these issues.

? *Is autism a form of emotional disturbance?*

Children with autism share some similarities with other groups of children with disabilities, including those with emotional disturbance and behavior disorders. However, *autism is not a form of emotional disturbance*. In fact, the Individuals with Disabilities Education Act of 1990, a federal law that has been described as a bill of rights for persons with disabilities and the primary enactment for structuring educational policy and guaranteeing the rights of students with disabilities, specifically excludes students with autism from being categorized as emotionally disturbed. Moreover, the problems experienced by the majority of children and adolescents with behavior disorders and emotional disturbance (e.g., defiance, impulsivity, poor social skills) are quite different from those of persons with autism.

The terms *schizophrenia* and *psychosis* (severe forms of mental illness characterized by thought, mood, and behavior disorders, and lack of contact with reality) were once used interchangeably with autism. However, research has clearly shown that autism is different from schizophrenia and psychotic conditions. Competent professionals no longer use the terms synonymously.

? *At what age do children develop autism?*

Autism is a lifelong disorder that begins in childhood. Most children with autism show signs of the disorder by 2 to 3 years of age. In fact many children with autism are described by their parents as "different" from other children from the time they are born. Parents have observed that even as infants their children were aloof and withdrawn and that often they displayed little concern for others.

Some children with autism appear to develop normally for several years, except perhaps for relatively minor problems such as language delays, before showing significant signs of autism. Thus, these children are thought to develop normally for several months or even years, after which time they may display self-stimulatory behavior and lose previously acquired skills, such as speech, social interest, play abilities, and bowel and bladder control.

Some children with higher functioning autism may not be diagnosed until they begin school. However, even without an official diagnosis, these children will likely have shown symptoms of the condition earlier in life.

? *How many children develop autism?*

At one time autism was considered a rare disorder, estimated to occur approximately 4 to 5 times per 10,000 births. However, more recent estimates suggest that autism is far more common. For instance, the Autism Society of America describes autism as occurring approximately 15 times per 10,000 births, which places the disorder as the third most common form of developmental disability. Other estimates of the prevalence of autism also suggest the condition to be more common than originally thought. Indeed, an ever-increasing number of children are identified as having autism and pervasive developmental disorders, with about 3 or 4 times more boys than girls being diagnosed with the disorder. Currently, as many as 67 per 1,000 individuals are being identified with autism-related disorders (Ehlers & Gillberg, 1993).

The reasons for this increase are not completely clear. However, it appears that the increase is, at least in part, associated with increased awareness of autism among parents and professionals and broadening in 1994 of the DSM–IV conceptualization of pervasive developmental disorders.

? *What causes autism?*

The exact cause or causes of autism have not been determined. Most experts, however, have concluded that autism occurs as a result of biological conditions. *Biological* (or biophysical) refers to physical factors (i.e., those within a person), including biochemical imbalances, neurological (brain) damage, genetic accidents, and so forth.

In contrast, *environmental causes* (i.e., a general term referring to anything external to a child, such as parental attitudes, home experiences, family relationships, school experiences, socioeconomic conditions, community attitudes, etc.) are believed to be unrelated to the development of autism. Although such factors may contribute to a child's educational and treatment program's success, experts agree that they do not cause autism.

Do parents cause their children to become autistic?

At one time some experts believed that parents were the cause of childhood autism. Specifically, it was thought that parents who were cold, aloof, and distant, or who otherwise had psychological or personality abnormalities, caused their children to become autistic. Thus, in past decades, terms such as "refrigerator mother" were common. Research has clearly shown, however, that children with autism do not all have parents with similar personalities. Clearly, *parents are not the cause of autism*. However, parents and families can determine, to a significant degree, the extent to which children with autism develop and acquire skills and abilities. Thus, children of parents who seek early intervention and who participate in treatment and educational programs tend to make the most significant progress.

Is it true that most children with autism have special talents and abilities?

A small percentage of persons with autism demonstrate unique skills and abilities. For instance, some children with autism have shown the ability to solve advanced mathematical problems without the assistance of a calculator; to reproduce on a musical instrument songs they have heard only one time; to memorize difficult and lengthy materials; and to otherwise show skills that are inconsistent with their overall abilities and functioning level.

Only a small percentage of children and youth with autism show special abilities, however. Moreover, the skills shown by these children and youth often have minimal functional value. For example, a child may be able to accurately calculate, mentally, the answer to difficult division problems, but be unable to make change for a dollar.

Is it true that children with autism have no obvious physical signs and experience no problems in addition to autism?

Unlike many children and youth with moderate and severe disabilities, children with autism may not show any physical signs of their disability, and some are considered to be exceptionally attractive. Consequently, casual observations of children with autism may reveal an absence of abnormalities. However, even individuals who know little about autism will be able to identify children with autism as exceptional if allowed to interact and observe their behavior.

Some children with autism have disabilities in addition to autism, including Down syndrome, deafness, and visual impairments. Moreover, the probability of children having autism and autistic-like characteristics increases when they have certain other conditions, including phenylketonuria (PKU) (an inherited condition that may result in brain damage and severe mental retardation), encephalitis (inflammation of the brain, which may cause brain damage and mental retardation), meningitis (inflammation of the brain and spinal cord), and tubular sclerosis (a genetic disease associated with convulsive seizures and mental retardation). Studies have also shown that seizures are common among individuals with autism, particularly among persons with IQs below 40.

Can children and youth with autism be educated?

Although curriculum and procedures will vary with individual needs, *all children and youth diagnosed as having autism will require and benefit from education and training*. Some children with autism are educated in regular classrooms. Others may require special education services designed for students with mild learning disabilities and social difficulties. Still other children and youth diagnosed as having autism may require a special education program designated specifically for students with autism or moderate to severe disabilities. These programs vary in structure, curriculum, and procedures; however, all have consistently been shown to make significant positive contributions to the lives of children and youth with autism.

What happens to autistic children and youth when they become adults? Are they easily cured?

There is no known cure for autism. Thus, children diagnosed as having autism will likely evidence at least some characteristics of the syndrome throughout their lives.

This does not mean that children and youth with autism cannot and do not make substantial gains and improvements; they do. However, even children who make substantial improvements will likely show some remnants of autism, such as social ineptitude, preference for solitude, and so on, even as adults.

It is difficult to say what will become of a child diagnosed as having autism due to the variety of symptoms associated with the syndrome and the variance in the degree of impairment. Children with relatively normal intelligence who have useful language tend to achieve the best outcomes (the best prognosis is for individuals who never were unresponsive to sounds, who gained useful speech by the age of 5, and who had no more than transient echolalia). Moreover, children who are treated by well-trained professionals representing multiple disciplines, including education, speech and language, medicine, psychology, parent and family support, occupational and physical therapy, and vocational and community living, tend to have the best success. Indeed, with increased opportunities for early intervention, improved educational and training programs, supportive employment programs for persons with disabilities, and community living programs (e.g., group homes), the long-term independent living outlook for persons with autism appears to be improving.

? *Is it true that children with autism have similar socioeconomic, cultural, and ethnic backgrounds?*

Autism does not occur primarily in persons from any one socioeconomic, racial, cultural, ethnic, or other group. Children who are wealthy, poor, black, white, Native American, Asian, Jewish, Baptist, or members of any other conceivable subgroup may develop autism. Moreover, autism has been observed to occur in every country and region of the world.

? *How are children diagnosed as autistic?*

Three primary areas of functioning are usually considered when determining whether a child has autism. First, children with autism fail to develop age-appropriate interpersonal relationships and tend to be unresponsive or abnormal in their responses and interactions with other people. As discussed earlier, this pattern of behavior may take a variety of forms (e.g., avoidance of eye contact, avoidance of people, difficulty mixing with other children).

A second consideration in making a diagnosis of autism is language. Virtually all children diagnosed as having autism have some level of speech and communication problems, and some fail to develop spoken language. As noted earlier, communication and speech problems take the form of language delays, echolalia, utterance of nonsense sounds, ineffective use of gestures, social clumsiness, and other communication abnormalities. These problems are discussed in a later section of the book.

Finally, children considered for a diagnosis of autism are evaluated on the basis of their behavior. Particular attention is given to the following: (a) insistence on sameness (e.g., a child insists on the window blinds at home being kept at precisely the same angle), (b) peculiar object attachment (e.g., a child insists on always having in her possession a particular piece of small string), (c) self-stimulatory and other unusual repetitive motor responses (e.g., body rocking, hand flapping), (d) odd play (e.g., spinning objects for long periods of time), and (e) inappropriate laughing or other emotional responses occurring independent of events typically associated with such responses (e.g., child laughs for extended periods of time for no apparent reason).

Three additional factors are considered when children are evaluated for autism: intensity, pattern, and duration of behavior. *Intensity* refers to the severity of a child's problem or problems. For example, does a child rock with such intensity that it makes him appear extremely odd, or is his self-stimulation a very subtle behavior, such as slightly moving a finger? Intensity also relates to the degree to which a response interferes with a child's ability to function. Obviously, a behavior that disrupts a child's ability to do other things is more significant than one that does not.

Pattern refers to the times when the problems occur. For example, does a child repeat nonsense words at home, but use functional language at school? Does a child interact in an age-appropriate fashion at home or in the neighborhood but have poor relationships at school? Does a child engage in self-stimulatory hand waving only when tired? Answers to these questions are basic to making an accurate diagnosis of autism.

Duration refers to the length of time a child's problems last. For example, the body rocking behavior of a child who rocks for a short time (e.g., a few weeks) subsequent to a family crisis (e.g., divorce, death of a parent) is viewed differently from that of a child who has been rocking since birth.

Children evaluated for autism should be assessed by a group of professionals (often referred to as *multidisciplinary evaluation teams*) representing several areas of expertise. These assessments are known as comprehensive evaluations. Autism is a complex disability that affects a number of areas of psychological development. Thus, diagnoses of autism should not be made by a single professional. Moreover, evaluations should consider a number of areas of development (e.g., motor, cognitive, behavior, speech and language, social). Multidisciplinary and comprehensive evaluations are able to most accurately and effectively identify children with autism.

? *Are there terms used to describe children with autism, in addition to autism and pervasive developmental disorder?*

One such term is *developmental disability*, a general term used to describe individuals with a variety of conditions, including mental retardation, cerebral palsy, and autism. Some professionals may use the term instead of more specific terms such as autism. The term refers to a disability of a person that (a) is attributable to a mental or physical impairment; (b) occurs prior to age 22; (c) is likely to continue indefinitely; (d) results in significant limitations in at least three of the following: self-care, language, learning, mobility, self-direction, independent living, or economic self-sufficiency; and (e) requires specialized care that is lifelong or of extended duration and that is individually planned and coordinated.

SUMMARY

The purpose of this chapter was to provide the reader with a general overview of autism. Thus, we have presented definitions and conceptualizations of autism, along with additional information on characteristics associated with these disorders. Each topic discussed (along with related topics) is dealt with in greater detail in later chapters of this book.

Causes of Autism

2

It is natural to want to identify a cause for human abnormalities, disabilities, and unusual behaviors. When a person encounters a child in a wheelchair or an individual with an obvious disability, an initial reaction is to wonder why and how such conditions developed. Thus, it is understandable that parents, family members, teachers, relatives, friends, and the general public want to know the cause or causes of autism.

Precise and definitive causes of autism are rarely known. However, more is being learned about the reasons for autism all the time. Meanwhile, myths and inaccurate notions about the causes of autism are being challenged and replaced with more valid and factual information.

MYTHS AND FALSE BELIEFS REGARDING CAUSES OF AUTISM

Dr. Leo Kanner observed several common family characteristics of the group of autistic children he described in 1943. Specifically, he noted that the parents were, for the most part, highly intelligent; many were professionals; they appeared to be preoccupied with artistic, literary, and scientific matters; and all were thought to be somewhat cold and aloof (e.g., Kanner noted that there were "few really warmhearted fathers and mothers" [p. 249]). As a result of Kanner's observations, a number of professionals incorrectly assumed that all parents of children with autism were cold and aloof and that such personality characteristics were primary causes of autism. Some psychiatrists, psychologists, and other professionals went so far as to recommend that children with autism be separated from their parents at an early age as a means of enhancing their chances of progress.

It is now known that *not* all parents and family members of children with autism are cold and aloof. The parents of children with autism display a range of personalities and dispositions (e.g., some parents are outgoing, some are reserved). Moreover, even in instances where parents may be somewhat aloof, such personality characteristics are not the cause of autism.

Autism also has been shown to exist in all cultures, races, societies, and subgroups. Thus, autism is not an exclusive condition of wealthy, professional people (or any other particular group), but rather a disability that may affect any family. It is also important to keep in mind that most families with a member with autism have other members who are normally developing.

UNDERSTANDING THE CAUSES OF AUTISM

A great deal has yet to be learned about the causes of autism; in fact, experts generally agree that understanding of the disorder is in the infancy stage. Nonetheless, a number of scientific theories are used to explain autism. In addition, observations and experiments have been used to gain information about the disorder.

Several reasons exist for a lack of clarity regarding the exact cause or causes of autism, including (a) disagreement over the nature and characteristics of autism and pervasive developmental disorders and (b) the manner in which scientific studies of the cause of human disorders are conducted. With regard to the nature of autism, children with autism share a number of characteristics with other groups of children with disabilities. For example, some experts may identify a child with intellectual limitations, poor adaptive and social skills, and self-stimulatory behavior as having mental retardation; others may identify the same child as having autism. Still other professionals may use more general terms, such as developmental disability or pervasive developmental disorder, to describe a child's condition. For youngsters with mild disabilities, professionals may debate whether a child's condition is the result of a learning disability, behavior disorder, or high-functioning autism disorder. This lack of agreement on precisely what constitutes autism makes it difficult to agree on a cause for the syndrome.

To compound matters, autism is a very complex disability that involves a number of elaborately interrelated and interconnected elements. Thus, children who are identified as having autism may demonstrate different characteristics and levels of functioning. Moreover, children, including those with autism, respond to their world in different ways. This normal complexity of human behavior, in combination with the different symptoms of the disorder, makes it difficult to precisely identify and understand the disability and its causes.

Finally, the manner in which scientific studies are conducted has adversely affected progress in understanding the causes of autism. Scientists who attempt to isolate the cause(s) of autism try to identify factors or conditions that may be associated with the disorder. However, for a number of reasons, it is impossible to fully control and understand these conditions. For example, evidence suggests that autism occurs more frequently among children who develop certain types of medical conditions, such as meningitis. However, every child who is diagnosed as having meningitis does not develop autism; further, scientists do not understand the exact relationship between meningitis and autism. Thus, they may conclude that there is a relationship (referred to as a *correlation*) between autism and certain factors, although this relationship may not be clearly understood to be a cause. This is a fundamental scientific principle and one that must be carefully considered when evaluating any cause–effect relationship. That is, since correlational research is a major means by which scientific knowledge of the causes of disabilities is accumulated, exact reasons for a particular condition are frequently unknown.

CAUSES OF AUTISM

Purported causes of autism are divided into two general categories: biological and environmental. Biological refers to inborn factors, including medical, physical, biochemical, and genetic conditions. Environmental causes (also known as *psychogenic* and *psychological*), on the other hand, refer to conditions and experiences that make up the day-to-day world. Parent, family, school, and community conditions are the environmental influences most frequently mentioned.

Biological Causes of Autism

Most current explanations of autism are of a biological nature. In this context, biological refers to inborn causal agents, as opposed to environmental factors. Frequently discussed biological factors include genetic influences, neurological abnormalities and impairments, and biochemical abnormalities.

? *Is autism a genetic disorder?*

Genetics refers to heredity. Each time an ovum and sperm unite, they merge into a single cell bearing hereditary characteristics from both parents. Evidence for the significance of genetic influences can be found by observing most families. Body shape, hair color, facial structure, and other physical characteristics link parents to their children and families to their ancestors. Nonphysical characteristics, including temperament and intelligence, may also be influenced by genetic factors.

Research indicates that autism may be associated with genetic factors. However, the exact nature of this genetic link is weak, in part because there does not appear to be a single gene mechanism responsible for autism. That is, although some evidence has shown that genetic influences may play a role in the development of autism, this influence is only a partial explanation. Autism appears to be associated with a variety of genetic mechanisms, thus making the role of heredity in the syndrome difficult to understand. Moreover, genetic influences often interact with environmental factors. That is, a child with autism can be expected to demonstrate certain behavioral patterns; however, family cohesiveness, health, interventions, and willingness to accommodate a child with autism significantly affect his or her behavior.

Evidence for a genetic link to autism is based, in part, on studies of brothers and sisters of children with autism (Folstein & Rutter, 1978). Findings of these studies reveal that siblings of children with autism are approximately 50 times more apt to be autistic than children in the general population. Studies of twin siblings of children with autism show that the chances of both children developing autism is even higher. Studies also reveal that brothers and sisters of autistic children demonstrate a higher incidence of cognitive and language developmental delays than do children without autistic siblings. Thus, even when brothers and sisters of children with autism are not autistic, they have a higher than average chance of developing cognitive and social problems.

? *Is autism the result of neurological impairment or abnormalities?*

Neurological impairment, neurological abnormalities, and brain damage are associated with a number of different factors, including oxygen deprivation (e.g., lack of oxygen at birth), disease (e.g., encephalitis), physical trauma (e.g., blow to the head), and congenital malformations (i.e., malformations present from birth). Damage to the brain or central nervous system caused by oxygen deprivation, disease, physical trauma, and congenital malformations ranges from severe destruction to malformation of tissue and structures. Problems associated with neurological impairments can range from death or serious disability, to tiny injuries and malformations that produce little or no behavior change.

Neither the meaning of neurological impairment nor its influence as a cause of autism has been agreed upon. Brain damage suggests dysfunction due to injury or malformation. The damage may be to brain cells (neurons), glia (non–brain cell materials), blood vessels, or central nervous system structures. If severe, neurological impairment may lead to loss or deterioration of certain functions (e.g., vision, coordination). Damage may occur as a result of lack of oxygen, physical injury, high fever, infection, toxins such as poison or drugs, or brain malformations.

Neurological impairment may be permanent or reversible. It is considered to be relatively common, and in most cases is inconsequential. Nearly every child falls and bangs into things, usually with no discernible long-term effect. In one often-quoted medical study of newborn children (Strauss & Lehtinen, 1947), examination of spinal fluid 1 week after birth revealed evidence of blood in half the infants. Blood in this context indicated that some degree of trauma had occurred to the brain or its wrappings in the birth process. However, because most of the infants in the study grew to become healthy children, it is relatively safe to assume that this problem was either minimal or reversible. This conclusion is not intended to minimize the importance of neurological impairment relative to individuals with autism. Rather, it underscores that the precise role of neurological impairment in causing autism is unknown. Indeed, it is incorrect to conclude that autism is solely the result of neurological impairment.

However, at least some individuals with the syndrome give evidence of having some degree of brain or central nervous system dysfunction. The exact nature of these dysfunctions is usually unknown, although brain lateralization dysfunction, malfunctions of brain systems that control arousal, and dysfunction of other brain mechanisms have been implicated.

Brain Lateralization Dysfunction. The human brain is composed of two hemispheres, each responsible for certain types of functioning, including specific activities. The dominant hemisphere is thought to be associated with language, whereas the other controls other functions, such as temporal (relating to time) and spatial (relating to space and perception) relationship activities. Increased specialization of the brain occurs with age; however, certain general functions appear to be lateralized in either the right or the left hemisphere of the brain from birth. With regard to autism, brain lateralization dysfunction refers to atypical operation of the two hemispheres of the brain. That is, activities and functions usually associated with a particular brain hemisphere occur through activity of the opposite hemisphere. Such "confusion" is thought by some to be at least partially responsible for autism.

Brain Systems that Control Arousal. Using sophisticated medical and behavioral diagnostic procedures, some researchers have concluded that autism may be associated with high levels of arousal. That is, as a result of abnormal brain development, persons with autism may be in a constant high state of stimulation and excitement. Such arousal is thought to interfere with the person's ability to take in and process information and to make appropriate responses.

Dysfunction of Other Brain Mechanisms. One explanation of autism that is based on theory and associated research maintains that components of the brain designed to process sensory information fail to function. As a result, the brain is unable to correctly and meaningfully process sensory information, thus explaining the cognitive, language, and social problems of persons with autism.

Biochemical Abnormalities. Human brains consist of masses of cells, called neurons. These nerve cells are designed to receive and transmit information through the use of chemical components called neurotransmitters. Some evidence suggests that failure of these neurotransmitters to function correctly is the basic reason why persons demonstrate characteristics of autism.

One group of neurotransmitters that has received particular notice in studies of autism is monoamines. Monoamines, consisting of serotonin, dopamine, and norepinephrine, are most commonly found in areas of the brain that control emotions and behavior. Studies have revealed that serotonin levels are elevated in children and youth with autism (Anderson & Hoshino, 1987). Although serotonin levels vary, some researchers report that the levels for some persons with autism are over 100% of what is considered normal. At present, the relationship between elevated serotonin levels and autistic behaviors and characteristics is unclear. In the absence of precise information, treatment is not clearly defined.

Another neurotransmitter that has been implicated in autism is dopamine, thought to be important in the regulation of motor activities and other functions. A few studies have suggested that stereotypic and other behaviors associated with autism can be reduced through use of dopamine reduction (Anderson & Hoshino, 1987; Tsai, 1998). However, the precise relationship between autism and dopamine levels is unclear.

Epinephrine and norepinephrine disturbances in persons with autism also have been reported. These neurotransmitters play an important role in regulating a number of physiological processes, including breathing, memory, attention, and arousal. However, because of minimal research and inconclusive results, the role of epinephrine and norepinephrine in explaining autism is unknown.

Other Biochemical Explanations. A number of other biochemical explanations have been proposed. One is that the brains of persons with autism produce too much of a natural form of opiates, called opioids. Over the past decade, various investigators (e.g., Cohen, Riddle, Laor, Young, & Shaywitz, 1983) have theorized that normally developing children, particularly infants, engage in a variety of social behaviors (e.g., seeking their mother's attention) because these activities trigger the brain to release opioids. The brains of children with autism are thought to produce too many opioids, thus explaining their lack of social interest and other abnormal behaviors. There is some research that indicates that administering children with autism medications designed to reduce opioid levels leads to more appropriate behavior, including reductions in self-abuse, self-stimulation, and social withdrawal (Tsai, 1998).

Conclusions About Biological Causes of Autism. There is no question that certain biological abnormalities are associated with autism. Although none has been delineated as *the* cause, genetic factors, neurological dysfunctions, and biochemical disturbances have all been implicated. The precise role these factors play in explaining autism await further study.

Environmental Causes of Autism

Environment is everything external to a person. Thus, environmental cause relates to the notion that a child's world, including home experiences, parent and family relationships, community and school experiences, influence his or her behavior and development. This view is not surprising because it is apparent that the values, attitudes, experiences, and expectations to which children are exposed affect their behavior. Thus, children who are exposed to unhealthy conditions are thought to be more susceptible to a variety of problems.

Leo Kanner, the psychiatrist who originally identified children with autism, concluded that the syndrome originated, at least in part, from a lack of parental affection. Others, especially between 1940 and 1969, agreed, supporting the notion that an autistic child's withdrawal and other abnormal responses occurred as a reaction to unfavorable parental personalities (e.g., emotional aloofness) or as a reaction to other adverse environmental conditions (e.g., family stress) (Rimland, 1994). Bruno Bettelheim (1967), a leading proponent of a psychogenic origin of autism, suggested that children with the syndrome perceived their environment as being so cold, threatening, and hostile that they attempted to reject it or shut it out.

From the beginning, skeptics doubted that such conditions, even if present, were the cause of autism (Rimland, 1964). Their resistance was based on several considerations. Because symptoms of autism were often present from birth, such extreme reactions as withdrawing from the world could not be explained as being the result of subtle personality characteristics such as emotional distance and aloofness. Likewise, extreme reactions such as total withdrawal from the world would likely occur only after a while rather than at birth. Also, it was noted that if psychogenic conditions were responsible for autism, a child's condition would deteriorate over time; however, such deterioration is not common.

Although parents are *not* the cause of their child's having autism, parents and families do have a significant influence on children with autism, as they do with any child. Thus, parents and families of children and youth with autism have the potential to facilitate development of skills (communication, social, self-help, etc.) as well as behaviors and attitudes. Consequently, parents and family members are extremely important to the development of children and youth with autism, even though they are not the original cause of the disability.

Effects of Family Experiences

Any of a number of factors or experiences may influence the behavior and emotional status of children, including those with autism. In particular, conditions that increase stress for a parent, family, or child are important, including financial problems, relocation, parent career changes, divorce, role changes (e.g., a mother who takes a job out of the home), and similar situations. Change is not necessarily negative, however. Just because a mother chooses to pursue a career does not mean that a child with autism will suffer. Yet, such changes often increase stress, at least temporarily, especially for children diagnosed as having autism. Because children with autism tend to resist change, shifts in routine, relocation, and similar factors may cause problems (e.g., increase in self-stimulatory behavior, tantrums, sleep disturbances).

An example involves a family, consisting of a mother, father, and three elementary-age children, one of whom has been diagnosed with autism. As a result of a job opportunity, the family moves from a small town to a large city several hundred miles away. In response to moving from a familiar community, house, neighborhood, baby-sitter, and grandparents, the child with autism displays a variety of behavior problems, including tantrums, resistance to going to school, and difficulty in completing home tasks he was able to perform prior to the move (e.g., dress himself, verbalize his needs). The child also experiences difficulty at his new school, including an inability to complete tasks he was able to do at his former school and resisting social interactions with his classmates. These problems further increase family stress, already high as a result of adjusting to the move. Thus, parents and siblings find that they must spend additional time doing things for the child with autism that he was formerly able to do himself (e.g., dress himself); the parents feel compelled to spend a substantial amount of time familiarizing their autistic child's teachers with his background and needs; and the two nonhandicapped siblings report feeling neglected as a result of the parents' increased time investment with the child with autism. These factors increase the family's stress level, which causes further problems in the child with autism. Fortunately, after a few months, the child with autism adapts to his new home and school and the family returns to a more normal existence.

This example illustrates the potential impact of family experiences on children with autism. Not every child or adolescent with autism will be adversely affected; however, awareness of and sensitivity to the potential of such conditions is important.

It also is important to remember that children and youth with autism, like all children and adolescents, are affected by the psychological conditions of the home. Thus, parents' personal problems, especially in combination with an unhealthy home environment, may contribute to children's difficulties. Accordingly, unstable and inconsistent parents often have children with behavior problems and skill deficits. This pattern applies to children both with and without disabilities. Thus, children with autism generally show the best behavior and social development when their home environments are characterized by structure and consistency. Again, this does not mean that parents *cause* autism; rather, parents have the potential to positively or negatively influence their children's behavior and development, regardless of whether those children have disabilities or are normally developing.

One way in which parents may influence children is through their expectations, rules, and management methods. For example, parents who are warm and loving and who clearly and consistently establish expectations, set rules, and follow through with consequences seem to get the best results. Although these conditions are extremely important for all children and adolescents, they are mandatory for individuals with autism. Under conditions of careful clarification and consistency, children with autism are often able to follow rules, understand expectations, and make the connection between their behavior and the consequences that follow.

? *Do children and youth with autism respond in the same way in different settings?*

Many autistic children and youth behave differently at home and school. Although they are autistic in both settings, their behavior may be quite different from one setting to another. Several explanations may be given for such differences. One is related to expectation: Children are expected to do different things at school and at home. For example, a child may be motivated and reasonably effective at talking at school, where she is expected to verbally communicate and is reinforced for doing so. However, at home she may be able to communicate and otherwise satisfy her needs without talking (e.g., by pointing or crying as a means of getting something).

Another explanation relates to structure. Some children and youth do well at home but not at school because of clearly stated rules and consequences. As noted previously, clarity, consistency, and clearly stated expectations are important for all children and youth; they are mandatory for individuals with autism.

Schools and Communities

As is true with parents, schools do not cause autism; however, they can facilitate the growth and development of children and youth with autism in a number of ways. One obvious way is by providing appropriate educational services. The vast majority of children and youth with autism can be appropriately served in public school settings, when appropriate educational options and support services are available. Not all school districts have specific programs for children and youth with autism; however, since the needs of these students vary significantly, they may be served effectively in a variety of educational settings. Thus, depending on their needs, students with autism may be appropriately assigned to classes for students with mental retardation, learning disabilities, or behavior disorders, as well as regular classrooms. Student success in these settings is usually a function of the school's commitment to students with disabilities and the availability of appropriate services and resources. Thus, schools not only must offer a variety of effective special education programs, but must have available specialists (e.g., language pathologists, occupational and physical therapists, psychologists, curriculum specialists) who are familiar with programs and methods for children and youth with autism.

School systems can significantly contribute to the growth and development of children and youth with autism by providing teachers who are well trained, committed to meeting the needs of every student, and familiar with methods and procedures for students with autism. Even if they do not have a separate program for students with autism, school districts should have educators available who are familiar with methods and procedures for meeting the needs of these students. Teachers of children and youth with autism must also be trained to communicate and cooperate with parents and families. Overwhelming evidence has proven that children and adolescents, including those with autism, make the best progress when parents and educators communicate and work cooperatively.

Communities also are not the cause of autism; however, they too can support individuals with autism and their families by providing adequate recreational facilities, supportive employment and workshops, vocational programs, independent community living programs, mental health and counseling services, appropriate medical programs, and other support services. Communities can also sponsor programs to increase the public's awareness of the needs of individuals with disabilities, including those with autism. Positive community attitudes toward individuals with disabilities result in a variety of benefits for persons both with and without disabilities.

SUMMARY

Autism was initially thought to be caused by parents' personalities, specifically aloofness, psychological coldness, or hostility toward their children. Such interpretations are incorrect. Parents and families are clearly not the cause of autism; however, they can significantly influence their children's growth and development. Most current theories of autism are of a biological or biophysical nature, but no single reason can be pinpointed as *the* cause.

Identification and Assessment of Children and Youth with Autism

3

For the reasons discussed earlier, autism is frequently difficult to diagnose. Many parents and families report that prior to a diagnosis of autism, their children were seen by a number of professionals, including psychiatrists, school psychologists, and clinical psychologists.

MAKING AN ACCURATE DIAGNOSIS OF AUTISM

Autism is a unique disability; nonetheless, children with autism share characteristics with children having a number of other types of disabilities. As noted in Chapter 1, four primary areas of functioning are considered in making a diagnosis of autism: (a) unresponsive and unusual interactions with people (e.g., withdrawal, lack of eye contact, unwillingness to acknowledge the presence of others); (b) speech and language problems (e.g., delayed speech, echoing others); (c) unusual behaviors (e.g., self-stimulatory responses, resistance to change); and (d) cognitive and learning characteristics (e.g., intellectual limitations, poor learning ability). Because these patterns also are shown by children having disabilities other than autism, it is often difficult for professionals to differentially identify and diagnose children with similar problems. For example, some children with mental retardation have language delays and engage in self-stimulatory behavior. Young children and those with milder forms of autism, such as Asperger syndrome, are particularly difficult to identify.

A second explanation for this identification difficulty derives from the scarcity of tests and procedures designed specifically to diagnose children with autism. Although several tests and diagnostic procedures can be used to assist in identifying children with autism, these scales and methods are not infallible. Indeed, many of these measures rely on verbal responding, an ability some children with autism lack. No test currently available provides conclusive autism results. Moreover, because of the complexity of autism and the many forms it may take, it is unlikely that such an instrument will be developed in the foreseeable future. As a result, professionals must make interpretations and draw conclusions based on various sources of information (e.g., interviews, observations), often leading to different diagnostic impressions. Differences of professional opinion are particularly evident for children and adolescents with mild symptoms and characteristics of autism.

A final reason that it is difficult to identify children with autism is that parents are often most interested in a diagnosis when their children are very young (i.e., between the ages of 12 and 48 months). Young children, in general, are more difficult to evaluate; besides, tests and procedures designed for children this age are less reliable than those for older children and adolescents.

PURPOSES AND REQUIREMENTS FOR AN APPROPRIATE EVALUATION

Evaluations should not be carried out for the sole purpose of determining whether a child or adolescent has autism. Rather, assessments should be designed to provide information about each child's or youth's educational, physical, social, and psychological strengths and weaknesses; unique ways of interacting with the world, including people in the home, school, and community; and possible problem-solving and treatment options. In fact, evaluations are conducted primarily to develop effective intervention, treatment, and educational programs. For this reason, professionals representing a variety of disciplines (e.g., psychologists, language pathologists, occupational therapists, physicians, educators) should be involved in the evaluation process. On the basis of each child's strengths, weaknesses, and needs, methods and strategies are individualized. Accordingly, an appropriate intervention and educational plan requires accurate and complete assessment information.

There is no way to assure a completely accurate evaluation of a child with autism, or any other child or adult for that matter. By their very nature, measures of human psychological and educational performance are less than perfect. Nonetheless, there are basic requirements relating to the assessment of children and youth with autism that will increase the validity and reliability of the information produced.

First, it is mandatory that the persons who administer tests and who use various diagnostic procedures are not only professionally trained and competent in using a particular instrument or procedure, but are also trained and experienced in using the tool with individuals with autism and other disabilities. That is, the examiner or diagnostician must know the content and characteristics of the test or procedure, and how to administer, score, and interpret it, including with children and youth with autism. Such skill and knowledge permit diagnostic personnel to correctly interpret patterns of behavior and children's responses that may be directly associated with their being in a novel testing environment or related to unexpected events (e.g., child resists responding to test stimuli because of difficulty making the transition from a previous preferred activity).

Second, when a child's test performance is evaluated relative to a normative sample (i.e., age or grade-level scores are statistically averaged to permit comparisons with a normative group), it is important that the test's normative sample permit evaluations of a child with autism. Because few tests include students with autism in their normative samples, however, diagnosticians must be able to make administration, scoring, and interpretation adjustments when conducting assessments of children and adolescents with autism.

A third basic requirement associated with conducting an accurate assessment of a child or youth with autism is that diagnosticians keep in mind that evaluations are based on samples of behavior that may or may not be representative of a child's ability. That is, in a testing room a child may be unwilling to perform a task that he or she routinely does at home. Thus, an important assessment principle is that performance and behaviors sampled during evaluations must be appropriately structured and be of sufficient quantity to permit diagnostic personnel to draw accurate inferences. Indeed, evaluations permit observations only of current behavior (i.e., what is observed during the testing or evaluation session). From these observations diagnosticians make inferences about the child's capabilities and future performance. These projections are merely inferences, and as such are *only predictions* of potential and future functioning.

EVALUATION PERSONNEL FOR CHILDREN AND YOUTH WITH AUTISM

Professionals representing a variety of disciplines (specific professions) are involved in an evaluation. These persons may be private practitioners or associated with schools or agencies. The following is a listing of some of these professionals, along with a description of their roles in the assessment process.

Psychologists: School and clinical psychologists collect and interpret information about intellectual ability, behavior and personality characteristics, social behaviors, academic achievement level, perceptual and neurological strengths and weaknesses, self-help skills, and language. To gather the necessary data, they use tests, parent and child interviews, and direct observations.

Psychiatrists: Although concerned with many of the same areas as psychologists, psychiatrists rely more on interviews and direct observations of behavior than on tests. In addition, because they hold medical degrees, they may prescribe medications for children, if necessary.

Educators: Educators test academic strengths and weaknesses and conditions under which learning is best achieved. They are also concerned with childrens' self-help skills, social interactions, communication abilities, and vocational and prevocational abilities.

Social workers: Both school and clinical social workers perform a variety of functions. However, their primary job is to serve as a link between evaluation personnel and families, schools, and community agencies. Social workers attempt not only to provide other diagnostic personnel with a complete history of a given child, but to obtain relevant information from such sources as physicians and mental health agencies.

Speech pathologists: Speech pathologists use a variety of tests and procedures to determine how children receive and process messages and how they communicate. Because children and youth with autism characteristically experience speech and language problems, information gathered by speech pathologists is particularly useful.

Audiologists: Audiologists participate in evaluations when a child's ability to hear is questioned. Where indicated, they use various methods and testing procedures to assess children's ability to hear.

Physical therapists: Physical therapists use tests and their own observational skills to assess physical ability and muscle control. Physical therapists are more likely to participate in evaluations involving neurological or perceptual problems.

Occupational therapists: Although occupational therapists appear to be dealing with the same areas as physical therapists, they are more concerned with assessing self-help, daily living, and similar skills. They use both observational and testing methods.

Medical personnel: When necessary, medical professionals—including nurses, pediatricians, neurologists, family practitioners, and optometrists—participate in evaluations. Their specialty skills add to a more thorough understanding of children and youth.

ELEMENTS OF AN EVALUATION OF A CHILD THOUGHT TO HAVE AUTISM

Children and youth thought to have autism typically demonstrate a number of problems and deficits, including cognitive, language, behavioral, social, medical, educational, self-help, and independent living. Each of these areas requires careful consideration. Accordingly, youngsters' strengths, weaknesses, and needs require complete and comprehensive evaluation and analysis. *Complete* in this context means that a variety of individuals representing several professional disciplines (e.g., psychologists, educators, language pathologists) are involved; *comprehensive* means that an array of procedures and techniques are used to gain a thorough understanding of a child.

Evaluations may be carried out by either school or clinical professionals. Even though school personnel tend to put more emphasis on educational matters than do mental health and other professionals, each group provides valuable evaluations, making it important for them to work together. Such cooperation usually results in more effective understanding and treatment of exceptional children and adolescents, including those with autism. The most important consideration is that all the individuals who conduct evaluations are familiar with assessment methods for children with autism.

AREAS CONSIDERED IN EVALUATIONS OF CHILDREN AND YOUTH WITH AUTISM

A variety of methods and procedures are generally used to obtain information in the following areas: cognitive development, environmental conditions, physical and medical factors, behavioral and social development, speech and language, academic and learning abilities and strategies, vocational skills, and self-help/independent living skills. Although a number of other areas are also suitable for assessment, these are considered the most significant and relevant.

Cognitive Development

The term *cognitive development* refers to a variety of mental processes, including reasoning, memory, comprehension, and judgment. The term *intelligence* is sometimes used interchangeably with cognitive ability.

A variety of tests are available for assessing cognitive ability of school-age children and youth. These tests can be divided into two general categories: group and individual scales. For the most part, group tests are pencil-and-paper scales, administered by written or oral directions of a trained examiner to a group of children or adolescents. Typically, these measures are used for large group assessment, as might be required for induction into the military or admission to a college or university. Although group tests may be used during screening, they are rarely suited for evaluation purposes. Moreover, many children and youth with autism are unable to take a group test independently.

Individualized tests, on the other hand, are designed for use with one person at a time. Administered by a professionally trained examiner, these tests are designed to evaluate cognitive abilities and developmental levels and to allow comparison between individual results and those of a group of persons of similar age and characteristics. As noted earlier, the comparison group is referred to as a normative sample, standardization sample, or standardization group. By means of such standardization groups, a child can be compared with other children of the same age on cognitive abilities, development, and related abilities.

For lower functioning children and youth, fewer options for cognitive assessment are available. Individually administered scales are generally used with children who have limited language or limited ability to attend and follow directions, and who may be considered otherwise untestable. These tests generally involve determining, by observation or interview, whether a child or youth has acquired skills typical of children at a certain age (e.g., abilities to build a three-block tower, identify body parts, assemble a form-board). Thus, these scales are used to estimate the developmental level of children and adolescents by comparing their performance with that of normally developing children.

Use of Standardization Groups

When placed on a graph, cognitive and developmental level test scores produce a bell-shaped curve (see Figure 3.1). Imagine, for example, that all students in a school system were given an intelligence test. If their scores were placed on a graph with a baseline ranging from the highest to the lowest IQ scores and another line representing the number of students with a particular score, a large hump would appear in the middle of the curve, tapering off at both ends. As shown, this bell-shaped curve simply means that the largest number of intelligence test scores would fall in the middle (average range) of the curve, with high and low scores at the ends. Over half the students would be expected to demonstrate average intellectual ability (IQs between 90 and 110), whereas only about 2% would score either in the superior range (130 and above) or in the mentally retarded range (70 and below).

Importance of Considering Cognitive Ability

Children and youth with autism characteristically experience reasoning, comprehension, and judgment deficits. Moreover, they often have difficulty acquiring useful information and skills and may experience developmental delays (e.g., show speech and language delays). Thus, it is important to identify overall cognitive abilities, as well as

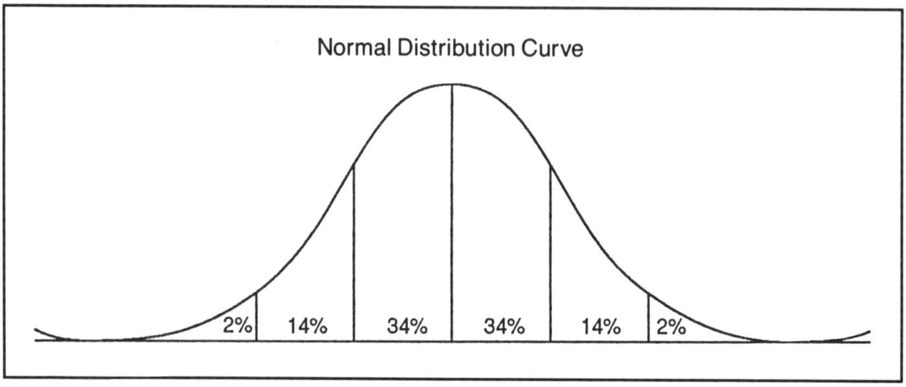

Figure 3.1. Bell-shaped curve showing percent of cases by portion of normal distribution.

specific strengths and weaknesses. Further, cognitive ability is considered one of the best predictors of a child's overall prognosis. The cognitive and intellectual abilities of many children and adolescents with autism fall in the mentally retarded range (or in the lower part of the curve shown in Figure 3.1), especially those with autistic disorder, childhood disintegrative disorder, and Rett's disorder, as diagnosed using characteristics described in the *Diagnostic and Statistical Manual of Mental Disorders–Fourth Edition* (American Psychiatric Association, 1994).

Tests of Cognitive Ability

Children's general abilities and skills determine the types of cognitive and intellectual tests they are given. For example, children and youth who possess spoken language, who have reasonably good understanding of other people's language, and who generally appear to be high functioning (i.e., are developmentally similar to their same-age peers) may be given one of three Wechsler intelligence tests.

The *Wechsler Preschool and Primary Scale of Intelligence–Revised* (WPPSI–R) (Wechsler, 1989) is designed for children ages 4 to 6 years, the *Wechsler Intelligence Scale for Children–Third Edition* (WISC–III) (Wechsler, 1991) for children and adolescents ages 6 to 17 years, and the *Wechsler Adult Intelligence Scale–Revised* (WAIS–R) (Wechsler, 1981) for individuals 17 years and older. Each of these tests yields three separate IQ scores: a Verbal IQ, a Performance IQ, and a Full Scale IQ (an IQ score based on combined Verbal and Performance IQs). The Verbal subtests focus on such areas as vocabulary, fund of general information, and ability to understand social situations; in contrast, the Performance subtests, which do not require verbal answers, target such skills as forming designs with blocks and putting together puzzle pieces.

Some children and youth with autism are relatively low functioning (i.e., have limited language, have difficulty following directions, comprehend poorly). Thus, the Wechsler series and similar intelligence tests designed for their chronological ages are not always appropriate. That is, it is useless (and professionally unacceptable) to ask a child questions he or she is unable to understand. Besides yielding little or no useful information, such practices frustrate both children and their families.

Scales that assess skills associated with particular developmental levels are often used with lower functioning children and youth instead of intelligence tests (e.g., the Wechsler scales). Often these tests use standardization samples that are younger than the children being assessed. For example, a nonverbal 8-year-old may be evaluated using a developmental scale designed for 2- to 4-year-olds. Although the 8-year-old cannot be precisely compared with a sample of 2- to 4-year-olds, a general impression of age equivalents may be obtained. That is, an attempt is made to determine the degree to which the 8-year-old has acquired skills typical of children between the ages of 24 and 48 months. In spite of benefits, most professionals acknowledge that use of tests and scales designed for much younger children also has limitations.

In addition to generic cognitive assessment scales, including the *Bayley Scales of Infant Development–Second Edition* (Bayley, 1993), the *Leiter International Performance Scale* (Leiter, 1948), and the *Merrill–Palmer Scale of Mental Tests* (Stutsman, 1948), there are a few developmental measures that have specific utility for children and youth with autism, in that they provide information that allows for the design of functional programs and interventions. The *Psychoeducational Profile–Revised* (PEP–R) (Schopler, Reichler, Bashford, Lansing, & Marcus, 1990) is particularly appropriate for students with autism who are under the age of 12 years and who function at or below the first-grade level. The PEP–R divides learning into seven academic areas (scored as passing, emerging, or failing): imitation, perception, fine motor, gross motor, eye–hand integration, cognitive performance, and cognitive verbal. Behavior, scored as appropriate, mild, or severe, based on the student's interactions with persons and objects in the test environment, is divided into four areas: relating and affect, play and interest in materials, sensory responses, and language. The PEP–R is especially useful in permitting evaluation personnel to develop effective and appropriate programs.

A similar measure to the PEP–R, designed for adolescents and adults with autism who function intellectually within the moderate to severe range of mental retardation, is the *Adolescent and Adult Psychoeducational Profile* (AAPEP) (Mesibov, Schopler, Schaffer, & Landrus, 1988). The AAPEP permits evaluation of vocational skills, independent functioning, leisure skills, vocational behavior, functional communication, and interpersonal behaviors. Data from this scale are particularly useful in permitting professionals and parents or families to develop life plans and transition goals.

The *Developmental Therapy Objectives Rating Form–Revised* (DTORF–R) (Wood, Davis, Swindle, & Quirk, 1996) attempts to combine a developmental approach with a consideration of a student's unique feelings, values, and self-concept. This test focuses specifically on identifying and strengthening underdeveloped skills that will assist independent functioning in a variety of settings. The DTORF–R, which addresses behavior, communication, socialization, and preacademics/academics, can be used with persons with autism ranging from preschool age through high school.

Environmental Assessments

Environmental assessments cover factors outside of the child that influence behavior. Attention is not on influences that are a part of the child (e.g., personality and genetic history), but rather on factors such as parents, family, and other environmental conditions. An analysis of these factors provides a better understanding of children and youth and allows professionals to more effectively plan intervention programs.

Environmental information is most frequently obtained through interview with a parent or legal custodian. Because parents have more intimate contact with and possess relevant history about their child, they are the logical source of such information. Further, parents tend to be more motivated and have more legal rights to be involved in the evaluation than anybody else. Finally, parents and legal custodians have authority to release to professionals significant records (e.g., medical, educational, psychological), if necessary.

Elements of a Parent Interview

Although each parent interview will have its own emphasis and objectives, certain elements are usually present. Parental impressions are usually sought before parents are given professionals' impressions of the child to avoid influencing their responses. That is, professionals often want parental descriptions of children's behavior before they relate information about the extent to which a child's behaviors are similar to those of individuals with autism.

Parents should also expect to be asked about their child's developmental history. Questions cover significant events, beginning with the parents' histories and continuing to the present. Of primary concern are genetic history; pregnancy or delivery problems; illnesses, accidents, and complications; and the age at which developmental milestones (e.g., walking, toilet training, speech) were achieved. Much of this information may be obtained prior to the interview from previous records and from asking parents to complete a developmental history form.

Another frequent subject of parent interviews is the parents' perception of their child's personality and his or her behavior and attitude toward friends, family, school, and so forth. Interviewers are also interested in parents' descriptions of their child's likes and dislikes, characteristics, and leisure activities. In addition, parents may be asked about their child's patterns of aggression, withdrawn behavior, and other similar behaviors.

For school-age children, a child's educational history according to the parents' perception constitutes a part of the interview. Parents are usually asked to describe their child's school-related history (e.g., schools attended), as well as previous professional measures taken to diagnose or remediate home or school difficulties.

Parents' expectations for their child will also be part of the interview. In particular, the interviewer is interested in goals that parents and family members have for youngsters, and whether these goals match their abilities and skills.

Finally, interviewers will attempt to obtain information to aid them in better understanding a child's environment. This includes the family membership and its cultural and ethnic makeup; the economic standing of the family, including the parents' occupations; the mental and physical health of family members; languages other than English spoken by the parents or others in the family; parental child-rearing practices; and the amount of supervision and contact children receive.

Again, the intent of the parent interview is to provide evaluators with a better understanding of a child's world and background. Such understanding facilitates understanding of and sensitivity to children and the development of effective intervention and training programs.

Evaluation of Physical and Medical Factors

The relationship between autism and medical and physical factors has been well documented. For example, conditions such as maternal rubella, meningitis, encephalitis, and tubular sclerosis have been associated with autism. Moreover, it is not unusual for parents of children with autism to have physical and medical concerns about their child (e.g., ability to hear, sleeping disturbances, eating problems). Thus, accurate diagnoses and subsequent treatment and intervention with children and youth with autism are enhanced by medical and physical information. In addition, many children with autism may be considered for drug treatment at some point, thus necessitating availability of relevant medical information.

Most physical and medical information is based on observations (e.g., examination by a physician), medical tests (e.g., seizure disorder evaluations), or tests designed to assess other areas of physical functioning (e.g., evidence of possible hearing impairment during cognitive testing). The specific examinations by a psychiatrist, neurologist, pediatrician, or other physician of children thought to have autism will vary in accordance with children's symptoms, abilities, and age. For instance, a child who has seizures will likely be examined specifically with reference to the neurological problems; children who are cooperative and verbal are dealt with differently than nonverbal, noncompliant children; finally, children's ages influence how examinations and evaluations are structured.

Most physicians who examine children thought to have autism are concerned about their pattern of growth and development. Specifically, they will focus on children's physical, language, mental, and emotional development, with reference to how they compare to normally developing children.

Most physicians, including psychiatrists and neurologists, are also interested in the child's and family's medical history, including parents' concerns about their child (including illnesses, complaints, and problems), as well as emotional, physical, environmental, and social histories and current conditions of the child and family. The following are typical questions: Was the child separated from his parents for an extended period of time at an early age? Did the child and mother receive prenatal care? Were there birth complications? What was the mother's physical and mental health while she was pregnant with the child? Did the child suffer an injury at an early age? What childhood diseases and illness did the child have? What is the emotional climate of the home?

Physicians also typically observe the child or youth with autism. They examine the child's manner and appearance; awareness of surroundings, people, places, and time; capacity to respond to directives; mood, affect, and emotional responses; activity level, response to external stimuli, and self-stimulatory behaviors; perceptual accuracy (i.e., whether the child sees and hears what others are seeing and hearing); memory and cognitive abilities; speech and language; judgment (i.e., capacity to behave appropriately and make decisions); and interactions with others.

Finally, physicians frequently conduct a physical examination of the child, similar to what any child goes through when visiting a physician (e.g., taking of temperature and blood pressure, investigation of physical abnormalities, systems review). Moreover, children suspected of having autism are often evaluated for neurological problems. Specifically, the following is frequently assessed: cranial nerve functioning (12 nerves that run from the brain stem and control various bodily functions), sight, smell, symmetry (balance of child across the sides of the body), balance, coordination, sensory sensitivity (e.g., response to light and deep touch), deep tendon reflexes (e.g., child's response to having his knee tapped), hand and foot dominance, and ability to engage in various motor activities (e.g., skip, catch a ball). If indications of abnormality are detected, specific tests are requested. For instance, if neurological abnormality is suspected, a doctor may request an electroencephalogram (EEG), an examination of electrical activity of the brain.

Physical and medical information is often of greatest value when interpreted along with other diagnostic information. This was found to be the case in the evaluation of a 3-year-old boy. During the assessment his mother reported that he frequently "would stare off into space," during which time he "went blank." Investigation of this pattern by a neurologist revealed that the child was having seizures. Although drug treatment of the seizure disorder did not "cure" the boy's autism, he was better able to benefit from educational and behavioral interventions subsequent to medical assistance.

Evaluation of Behavioral and Social Development

The nature of behavioral and social evaluations varies depending on the person conducting them as well as the child or adolescent under study. In general, however, psychologists, educators, psychiatrists, and other professionals (e.g., language pathologists, occupational therapists) use three basic methods: observations, tests and rating scales, and interviews.

Observations

Behavioral observation methods, the most direct form of behavioral and social evaluation, make no assumptions about the meaning of responses to artificial situations. Rather than attempting to determine if a child is socially withdrawn based on how she describes a picture or an inkblot (something many children with autism are unable to do), the child's interactions with others are directly observed. This approach is based on the assumption that the best way to understand children's social and behavioral strengths and weaknesses is to directly observe them. Children are observed not only in clinical settings (e.g., professionals' offices), but in other significant environments as well, including home and school.

An example of one direct observation data sheet, designed for children and youth undergoing evaluations for autism, is shown in Figure 3.2. Developed by Simpson and Regan (1986), the system allows for observations in six major areas: stereotypic/self-stimulatory behaviors, aggressive behavior, speech and language,

INFORMAL OBSERVATION DATA SHEET

Name:__________ Date:__________ Observer:__________

Time of observation: ________ to: ________

Description of observation environment: __________

Behavior	Specific description	Frequency of occurrence	Duration of occurrence	Site of occurrence	Comments
Example: Light filtering	Holds hands slightly higher than eye level; moves fingers back and forth. Fixed stare on finger movements.	𝍸 𝍸 I	30–50 sec.	Free time at desk	
I. Stereotypic/Self-Stimulatory Behaviors					
Light filtering					
Arm waving					
Object waving (paper, pencil)					
Object waving (twirling)					
Hand wringing					
Tapping (object or self)					
Smelling objects					
Body contortions/bizarre torso extensions					
Spinning self or objects					
Rocking					
Drooling/playing with saliva					

(continues)

Figure 3.2. Informal Observation Data Sheet. *Note*. From *Management of Autistic Behavior* (pp. 4:16–4:20), by R. L. Simpson and M. Regan, 1986, Austin: TX: PRO-ED. Copyright 1986 by PRO-ED, Inc. Reprinted by permission.

Behavior	Specific description	Frequency of occurrence	Duration of occurrence	Site of occurrence	Comments
Walking on toes					
Tooth flicking					
Grinding teeth					
Thumb-sucking					
Mouthing objects					
Ear plugging					
Covering eyes					
Banging hands together on a metal surface					
Other noisemaking					
Ruminating					

II. Aggressive Behaviors

Throwing					
Hitting self/others					
Grabbing objects or hitting with objects					
Biting self/others					
Hair pulling					
Tearing or shredding objects					

(continues)

Figure 3.2. *Continued.*

Behavior	Specific description	Frequency of occurrence	Duration of occurrence	Site of occurrence	Comments
Tantrumming (crying, screaming, hitting, biting)					
Head banging					

III. Speech/Language Behaviors

Echolalic speech					
Inappropriate vocalizations (nonsense words, jargon, phrases					
Self-stimulatory vocalizations					
Self-talking					
Inappropriate laughing/ giggling					
Unresponsiveness to speech of others					
Nonverbal responses to commands/ questions					

(continues)

Figure 3.2. *Continued.*

IV. Self-Care/Independent Living Skills

Behavior	Specific description	Frequency of occurrence	Duration of occurrence	Site of occurrence	Comments
Toilet training					
Self-feeding					
Self-grooming (brushing teeth, combing hair, washing face and hands)					
Self-dressing					

V. Social Skills

Behavior	Specific description	Frequency of occurrence	Duration of occurrence	Site of occurrence	Comments
Noncompliance					
Lack of response to adults/peers					
Fearful					
Lack of eye contact					
Negative response to touch of adults/peers					
Isolates self					
Lack of awareness of adults/peers					

(continues)

Figure 3.2. *Continued.*

VI. Independent Work Habits

Behavior	Specific description	Frequency of occurrence	Duration of occurrence	Site of occurrence	Comments
Stays on task					
Stays in seat					
Works independently without reinforcement					
Moves from activity to activity on request					
Follows 1-2-3-step directions					

Note preferences (toys, edibles, objects in room, etc.) which might serve as reinforcers:

Figure 3.2. *Continued.*

self-help/independent living skills, social skills, and independent work habits. Using the data sheet, trained observers record a definition of a behavioral target (e.g., self-stimulatory rocking); the frequency with which the behavior occurs (e.g., number of rocks within a 30-minute period); the duration of the target behavior (e.g., the length of time rocking occurs within a 30-minute period); the location of the target behavior (e.g., at home); and other descriptive information (e.g., child will stop rocking for short periods of time with a reminder).

The most efficient way of understanding children and adolescents is to watch what they do in those settings where they experience problems. Thus, a child who engages in self-stimulatory hand flapping at school is best understood through direct observation at school.

Rating Scales

Rating scales require that someone familiar with a child or adolescent (e.g., a parent or teacher) evaluate the individual's behavior using a structured form. Specifically, the person completing the form is asked to rate the child's behavior. Ratings may take the form of "yes" or "no" responses or evaluations using a range of dimensions (e.g., in answer to "Does child prefer to be alone?" the rater indicates *never*, *occasionally*, *often*, or *a great deal*).

An example of a behavioral rating scale, shown in Figure 3.3, is the Behavior Checklist developed by Simpson and Regan (1986). This rating scale allows information to be gathered in several significant areas (e.g., communication, social skills) from several sources, including teachers, parents, and family members.

Another example of a rating scale is shown in Figure 3.4. Part of the *Autism Screening Instrument for Educational Planning–Second Edition* (Krug, Arick, & Almond, 1993), this popular evaluation tool allows professionals to compare children and youth with autism with other groups of children with and without disabilities.

Behavioral ratings are used for evaluative purposes as well as treatment planning. That is, in addition to providing a method for evaluating a child's or youth's social and behavioral development, these measures can also direct interventions. For example, if a child is consistently perceived as having poor social interaction skills, this problem can be addressed in intervention plans.

Interviews

The nature and content of interviews vary depending on the person being interviewed (e.g., child, parent, teacher). Children or youth with good language and cognitive abilities may be interviewed. They may be asked to describe their problems along with the causes of the reported difficulties. Youngsters may also be encouraged to discuss their personality traits; attitude toward home, school, friends, family, and leisure-time activities; and likes and dislikes. Special attention will probably be paid to descriptions of their relationships with family and peers. Finally, youngsters may be encouraged to describe their home and family life.

Many children and youth being evaluated for autism are unable to respond to interview questions. Thus, other individuals, including parents, family members, and teachers, may be interviewed instead. In addition to questions asked of parents (see section in this chapter on parent interviews), teachers may be asked to provide information. For example, Figure 3.5 shows a teacher interview format developed by Simpson and Regan (1986).

Interview content also varies depending on the person conducting the interview and the age and problems of the child under study. For instance, psychiatrists are likely more interested in medically related information than are psychologists, whereas educators are probably most interested in childrens' school experiences and learning potential. Similarly, interviews of persons connected with school-age children focus, in part, on educational and school-related matters, whereas interviews of preschool children address home and community issues.

Tests of Adaptive Behavior

A significant element of behavioral and social assessment involves understanding individuals' adaptive social behavior. Several effective tests are available and often used for this purpose. One such instrument is the *Vineland Adaptive Behavior Scales*

BEHAVIOR CHECKLIST

Student: Teacher: Date:

Instructions: Circle a response in the left-hand column for each item that describes the student: N—Never, S—Sometimes, O—Often, NO—No opportunity to observe.

Communication

N S O NO 1. Indicates needs by gestures.
N S O NO 2. Makes inappropriate verbalizations. Specify:
N S O NO 3. Is echolalic; repeats sounds, words, or phrases.
N S O NO 4. Whispers instead of talking.
N S O NO 5. Speech appears uncommunicative.
N S O NO 6. Substitutes nouns and pronouns for "I" statements.
N S O NO 7. Substitutes words for other words.
N S O NO 8. Speech appears unrelated to actions.
N S O NO 9. Acts as if deaf.
N S O NO 10. Does not answer others' questions.
N S O NO 11. Uses little inflection or expression in voice.
N S O NO 12. Appears not to understand others' speech.
N S O NO 13. Uses questions or phrases for "no."
N S O NO 14. Avoids using pronouns in speech.
N S O NO 15. Repeats questions.
N S O NO 16. Reverses pronouns in speech.
N S O NO 17. Uses prepositions and pronouns as nouns.
N S O NO 18. Verbally fixates on specific objects, characters, or events. Specify:
N S O NO 19. Uses baby talk and/or paints instead of using appropriate language.
Clarification:

Learning

Patterns

N S O NO 20. Resists learning situations.
N S O NO 21. Appears oblivious to real dangers.
N S O NO 22. Demonstrates a good verbal memory for words repeated often.
N S O NO 23. Appears preoccupied with isolated sensory input; cannot ignore extraneous stimuli.
N S O NO 24. Demonstrates "splinter skills" (unusually high-level skills incongruous with functioning pattern).
N S O NO 25. Learns a simple task but "forgets" easily.
N S O NO 26. Has difficulty following teacher directions.
N S O NO 27. Uses poor visual discrimination when learning (tends to fixate on single characteristics).
Clarification:

Functional Skills

N S O NO 28. Has difficulty running simple errands.
Clarification:
N S O NO 29. Avoids asking for needed help.
Clarification:
N S O NO 30. Has difficulty feeding self.
Clarification:
N S O NO 31. Has difficulty dressing self.
Clarification:
N S O NO 32. Has difficulty taking care of personal grooming.
Clarification:
N S O NO 33. Fails to identify self by name.
Clarification:
N S O NO 34. Has difficulty taking care of toileting needs.
Clarification:

Social Relatedness

Personal Characteristics

N S O NO 35. Laughs inappropriately.
N S O NO 36. Demonstrates inappropriate attachments to objects.

(continues)

Figure 3.3. Behavior Checklist. *Note*. From *Management of Autistic Behavior* (pp. 4:4–4:5), by R. L. Simpson and M. Regan, 1986, Austin, TX: PRO-ED. Copyright 1986 by PRO-ED, Inc. Reprinted by permission.

N	S	O	NO	37. Spins objects.
N	S	O	NO	38. Demonstrates sustained odd play.
N	S	O	NO	39. Demonstrates marked physical overactivity.
N	S	O	NO	40. Engages in self-destructive behavior.
N	S	O	NO	41. Makes poor use of leisure time.
N	S	O	NO	42. Appears happiest when left alone.
N	S	O	NO	43. Smiles inappropriately.
N	S	O	NO	44. Grimaces or conceals eyes in natural light.
N	S	O	NO	45. Feels, smells, and/or tastes objects in the environment.
N	S	O	NO	46. Engages in ritualistic behavior, such as ordering objects.
N	S	O	NO	47. Shows difficulty caring for personal belongings.
N	S	O	NO	48. Has hypochondrical tendencies.
N	S	O	NO	49. Frustrates easily when challenged.
N	S	O	NO	50. Stares into space.
N	S	O	NO	51. Engages in rhythmical movements of the body (i.e., rocks).
N	S	O	NO	52. Repeats play patterns mechanically.
N	S	O	NO	53. Twists.
N	S	O	NO	54. Makes facial grimaces.
N	S	O	NO	55. Spins self.
N	S	O	NO	56. Jumps.
N	S	O	NO	57. Flaps hands, arms.
N	S	O	NO	58. Walks on toes.
N	S	O	NO	59. Bangs or twirls objects.
N	S	O	NO	60. Is destructive with own property.
N	S	O	NO	61. Appears sluggish and lethargic.
N	S	O	NO	62. Swears.
N	S	O	NO	63. Appears nervous and jittery; is easily startled.

Reaction to Others

N	S	O	NO	64. Cries easily.
N	S	O	NO	65. Has temper tantrums.
				Clarification:
N	S	O	NO	66. Fights with peers.
N	S	O	NO	67. Is easily led by others.
N	S	O	NO	68. Is destructive with others' property.
N	S	O	NO	69. Avoids activity with others.
N	S	O	NO	70. Fails to show consideration for others.
N	S	O	NO	71. Takes others' property without permission.
N	S	O	NO	72. Appears disinterested in strangers.
N	S	O	NO	73. "Looks or walks through" people.
N	S	O	NO	74. Is standoffish toward familiar people.
N	S	O	NO	75. Establishes little eye contact.
N	S	O	NO	76. Resists physical affection.
N	S	O	NO	77. Has difficulty mixing with other children.
N	S	O	NO	78. Behaves passively toward others.
				Clarification:

Reaction to Authority

N	S	O	NO	79. Resists change in routine.
N	S	O	NO	80. Attends poorly in group situations.
N	S	O	NO	81. Reacts poorly to criticism.
N	S	O	NO	82 Demonstrates disruptive or resistive behavior.
N	S	O	NO	83. Talks back.
N	S	O	NO	84. Displays negativism; tends to do the opposite of what is requested.
N	S	O	NO	85. Is easily embarrassed.
N	S	O	NO	86. Attends poorly in 1-to-1 situations.
				Clarification:

Figure 3.3. *Continued.*

(VABS) (Sparrow, Balla, & Cicchetti, 1984). Three independent forms of the VABS are available, including two administered by interviewing the child's primary caregiver and a third by interviewing the child's teacher. All three forms assess communication, daily living, socialization, and motor skills, and the two caretaker surveys contain a maladaptive behavior domain. Because the VABS is a norm-referenced test, students' scores can be compared against a standardization group.

AUTISM BEHAVIOR CHECKLIST

Autism Behavior Checklist Record Form

Student's Name ______________________________

Date ______________________________

Examiner ______________________________

INSTRUCTIONS: Circle the number to indicate the items that most accurately describe the child.

	Sensory 1	Relating 2	Body and Object Use 3	Language 4	Social and Self Help 5
Whirls self for long periods of time			4		
Learns a simple task but "forgets" quickly					2
Frequently does not attend to social/environmental stimuli		4			
Does not follow simple commands given once (sit down, come here, stand up)				1	
Does not use toys appropriately (spins tires, etc.)			2		
Poor use of visual discrimination when learning (fixates on one characteristic such as size, color, or position)	2				
Has no social smile		2			
Has pronoun reversal (you for I, etc.)				3	
Insists on keeping certain objects with him/her			3		
Seems not to hear, so that a hearing loss is suspected	3				
Speech is atonal and arhythmic				4	
Rocks self for long periods of time			4		
Does not (or did not as a baby) reach out when reached for		2			
Strong reactions to changes in routine/environment					3
Does not respond to own name when called out among two others (Joe, **Bill**, Mary)				2	
Does a lot of lunging and darting about, interrupting with spinning, toe walking, flapping, etc.			4		
Not responsive to other people's facial expressions/feelings		3			
Seldom uses "yes" or "I"				2	
Has "special abilities" in one area of development, which seems to rule out mental retardation					4
Does not follow simple commands involving prepositions ("put the ball on the box" or "put the ball in the box")				1	
Sometimes shows no "startle response" to a loud noise (may have thought child was deaf)	3				
Flaps hands			4		
Severe temper tantrums and/or frequent minor tantrums					3
Actively avoids eye contact		4			
Resists being touched or held		4			
Sometimes painful stimuli such as bruises, cuts, and injections evoke no reaction	3				
Is (or was as a baby) stiff and hard to hold		3			
Is flaccid (doesn't cling) when held in arms		2			
Gets desired objects by gesturing				2	
Walks on toes			2		
Hurts others by biting, hitting, kicking, etc.					2
Repeats phrases over and over				3	
Does not imitate other children at play		3			
Often will not blink when a bright light is directed toward eyes	1				
Hurts self by banging head, biting hand, etc.			2		
Does not wait for needs to be met (wants things immediately)					2
Cannot point to more than five named objects				1	
Has not developed any friendships		4			
Covers ears at many sounds	4				
Twirls, spins, and bangs objects a lot			4		
Difficulties with toilet training					1
Uses 0–5 spontaneous words per day to communicate wants and needs				2	
Often frightened or very anxious		3			
Squints, frowns, or covers eyes when in the presence of natural light	3				
Does not dress self without frequent help					1
Repeats sounds or words over and over				3	
"Looks through" people		4			
Echoes questions or statements made by others				4	
Frequently unaware of surroundings, and may be oblivious to dangerous situations					2
Prefers to manipulate and be occupied with inanimate things					4
Will feel, smell, and/or taste objects in the environment			3		
Frequently has no visual reaction to a "new" person	3				
Gets involved in complicated "rituals" such as lining things up, etc.			4		
Is very destructive (toys and household items are soon broken)			2		
A developmental delay was identified at or before 30 months of age					1
Uses at least 15 but less than 30 spontaneous phrases daily to communicate				3	
Stares into space for long periods of time	4				
TOTALS					

1 + 2 + 3 + 4 + 5 = Total

Figure 3.4. Autism Behavior Checklist. *Note*. From *Autism Screening Instrument for Educational Planning–Second Edition*, by D. A. Krug, J. R. Arick, and P. J. Almond, 1993, Austin, TX: PRO-ED. Copyright 1993 by PRO-ED, Inc. Reprinted by permission.

TEACHER INTERVIEW FORM

Interviewer: ______________________ Date: ______________________

Informant: ______________________

Student: ______________________ Sex: M F Race: ______________________

Date of birth: ____________ Grade: ____________

Home address/phone: ______________________

Teacher statement of student problem: ______________________

____

____

EDUCATIONAL SETTING

1. No. of students in class: boys: ________ girls: ________
2. No. of full-time teachers: ________ aides: ________
3. Description of class (regular vs. special, traditional vs. open concept): ______________________
4. Description of teaching style (structured vs. unstructured): ______________________
5. Description of class seating arrangement(s) (including rows, clusters, isolation booths): ______________________
6. Special seating for student (including proximity to board or teacher; isolation; other): ______________________
7. Important physical features of the class: ______________________
8. Additional information: ______________________

PARENT COMMUNICATION

1. No. of parent conferences this year: ________ attending parent(s): ________
2. Special parent communication systems in operation (including a description of type of frequency): ______________________

   parent role/followthrough in communication systems: ______________________
3. Other specialists/agencies involved: ______________________
4. Description of teacher relationship with parents (including parent attitude toward school/cooperation): ______________________
5. Additional information: ______________________

HEALTH/PHYSICAL CONSIDERATIONS

1. Current medications: ______________________
2. Allergies: ______________________
3. Seizures or convulsions: ______________________
4. Vision: ______________________
5. Hearing: ______________________
6. Speech problems: ______________________
7. Motor skills: fine: ____________ gross: ____________
8. Other health/physical problems: ______________________
9. Classroom or teaching modifications as a result of health/physical considerations (including special PE, motor programming, limited recess, modified behavior programs): ______________________
10. Additional information: ______________________

ACADEMIC FUNCTIONING

1. Academic strengths: ______________________

   weaknesses: ______________________
2. Academic likes: ______________________

   dislikes: ______________________

(continues)

Figure 3.5. Teacher Interview Form. *Note*. From *Management of Autistic Behavior* (pp. 4:7–4:8), by R. L. Simpson and M. Regan, 1986, Austin, TX: PRO-ED. Copyright 1986 by PRO-ED, Inc. Reprinted by permission.

3. Test data:
   IQ ______ Source(s) ______
   Reading ______ Source(s) ______
   Math ______ Source(s) ______
   Spelling ______ Source(s) ______
   Language arts ______ Source(s) ______
   Speech ______ Source(s) ______
   Other ______ Source(s) ______
4. Performance levels:
   Reading ______
   Math ______
   Spelling ______
   Language arts ______
   Speech ______
   Other ______
5. Spec. ed. services received: ______
6. Rate of learning (including progress on academic goals): ______
7. Impression(s) of school attitude: ______
8. Additional information: ______

PERSONAL AND SOCIAL ADJUSTMENT

1. Behavior Checklist: complete form (Exhibit 4-2).
2. Management techniques: ______
3. Reinforcers/likes (identify spontaneous vs. elicited) (refer to Checklist of School Reinforcers): ______
4. Punishers/dislikes (identify spontaneous vs. elicited) (refer to Checklist of School Reinforcers): ______
5. Leisure-time activities: ______
6. Other special problems or situations (including reactions to lunch, field trips, specials, substitutes): ______
7. Additional information: ______

IMPRESSIONS

(Include a statement of teacher and student needs and goals, responses or comments from other school personnel concerning the student, overall teacher impressions of the student, special parent considerations or areas to probe.)

Figure 3.5. *Continued.*

Another adaptive behavior test frequently used with students with autism is the *AAMR Adaptive Behavior Scales–School: Second Edition* (ABS–S:2) (Lambert, Nihira, & Leland, 1993). This test is administered to another person (e.g., parent, caregiver), who rates a student's behavior. Because the ABS–S:2 is a standardized instrument, it permits comparison of scores with those of other students with disabilities.

Evaluation of Speech and Language

As noted, virtually all children and adolescents with autism have speech and language problems. As mentioned in Chapter 1, *speech* refers to forming and using the sounds of oral language, whereas *language* is a broader term referring to use of a communication system. Speech problems may take the form of making and using incorrect speech sounds, whereas a language problem is the inability to effectively communicate with others.

Children's speech and language development is so integral to other areas of development (e.g., cognitive development, social interactions) that professionals give it particular attention during evaluations. An important goal is to help each child and youth with autism to develop an effective communication system.

A variety of techniques exist for evaluating children's communication systems, including tests, interviews, observations, and clinical methods (specific procedures used by speech pathologists and other communication specialists). More and more, experts rely on procedures that allow them to understand communication systems within the context of children's individual worlds—how children communicate their needs at home and in other natural settings, how they relate their feelings and concerns, and how they interact with people. For instance, does a child lead his mother to the sink to let her know he wants a drink of water? Does he run around when he needs to use a toilet? Does he cry in response to a disruption in household routine? Information of this type is useful in the development of intervention programs.

Speech and language assessment typically is not designed to compare children's nonfunctional communication abilities (i.e., those infrequently used in day-to-day interactions) with those of their same-age peers, but to discover a child's communication strengths and weaknesses along with strategies for improving communication. For example, it may be of little value to confirm through test results that a child knows the meaning of fewer words than her same-age peers. Instead, professionals involved in speech and language evaluations will be most interested in knowing about the communication methods used by children and youth in their day-to-day interactions as well as methods for improving these skills.

Speech and language assessment may take a variety of forms. Parents, family members, and teachers may be interviewed; children and youth may be observed in a variety of natural settings (e.g., classroom, home, baby-sitter's house); and children may be engaged in functional tasks designed to uncover their communication strengths, weaknesses, and strategies. Each of these approaches yields unique information; thus, each is needed to understand children's communication. Furthermore, a multifaceted approach almost always yields information needed to identify strategies for improving children's speech and language systems.

Evaluation of Academic and Learning Abilities and Strategies

Although virtually all children and youth with autism demonstrate academic achievement problems, not all of them will be working in an academic curriculum. For instance, it is unlikely that a 17-year-old with poor communication skills, mental retardation, and severe behavior problems is able to read and do high school level mathematics. At the same time, it is unlikely that advanced reading and writing are emphasized in his curriculum, given his other needs and his limited potential for academic success. For this student, therefore, it would be more typical that a curriculum emphasizing social skill development, communication, vocational training, independent living, and other basic skills would take precedence over academic training.

Many children and youth with autism will have the potential to pursue an academic curriculum, at least in part. Thus, knowledge of these children's academic strengths and weaknesses must be identified and understood so that suitable programs can be planned. Assessment of academic skills and abilities, therefore, must be part of the overall evaluation.

Evaluation of academic and learning abilities and strategies of children and youth with autism is often undertaken via informal means. In this context, *informal* refers to use of nonstandardized measures and procedures. That is, observations and trial teaching methods, as opposed to standardized tests, are used to understand students' unique needs, abilities, and learning styles. Diagnosticians present various tasks as a means of better understanding unique issues of students with autism, including stimulus overselectivity (focusing on a limited number of environmental cues; e.g., when presented color-coded cards with the accompanying verbal instruction, "Point to blue," a student with stimulus overselectivity continually selects the card on the left side of the table); poor motivation (discriminating between a student's inability to complete a task and a lack of interest in the task); self-stimulatory behavior as related to learning (determining the extent to which self-stimulatory behavior such as light filtering occurs in response to various tasks and the extent to which it interferes with performance); and echolalia (determining whether echolalia serves a communication purpose or as a learning strategy).

Informal assessment is often designed to understand *how* a student learns rather than *what* a student knows. Such information has obvious implications for instructional planning. Thus, one specific element of an informal educational assessment involves understanding *student learning traits*. Student learning trait assessment involves identifying factors that facilitate or hinder learning, including external variables such as the environmental conditions of a classroom (e.g., where a student's desk is located in a classroom) and internal factors such as how a student receives, processes, and stores information (e.g., a student observes other students rather than listening to directions given by the teacher). Knowing that a student learns best in a relatively quiet setting, that she tends to respond best when tasks are presented in a part-to-whole fashion, that she has an excellent short-term memory for meaningful information, and that she does best when permitted to self-talk should be extremely important information for educators when planning her program.

Informal assessment involves diagnostic teaching. That is, diagnosticians systematically present students with tasks that permit observations of their problem-solving strategies and related behaviors. For example, a child might be presented with unfamiliar word cards, instructionally presented in different ways. Some words are presented such that the child is required to phonetically sound them out, some are presented in a "sight-word" fashion, and some are presented in the context of a story that the child dictates to an examiner. By assessing the student's performance and behavior under the various instructional conditions, the diagnostician is often in a position to better understand a child's unique learning style and to offer the teachers useful teaching strategies.

Other Evaluation Considerations

In addition to cognitive development, environment, physical and medical status, behavior and social development, speech and language, and educational strengths and weaknesses, assessment of children and youth with autism and pervasive developmental disorders may include consideration of vocational skills and aptitude for independent living. These areas are particularly significant for youth and young adults, but may also be evaluated in children.

Vocational Evaluations

Unless youth are being considered for placement in a workshop setting or other job role, evaluations may not routinely provide in-depth analysis of children's and adolescents' vocational skills. However, an attempt is often made to provide a general impression of an individual's readiness for a work or vocational setting. For example, task compliance, ability to work without direct supervision, social interaction skills, and other factors and behaviors deemed significant in successfully placing persons with autism in work and vocational settings may be considered. The vocational area is considered significant because many individuals with autism will be placed in workshops, supported employment, and similar settings as adults. Although demands for workshop and other types of vocational programs for adults with autism outweigh the availability of such services, educational programs must nonetheless provide appropriate diagnostic and training programs so that children and youth may compete for available workshop positions.

Independent Living Evaluations

The final assessment area we discuss is determining the extent to which an individual is able to live independently or semi-independently, and what types of training he or she will need to become more independent. For instance, can an individual handle his own self-care needs (e.g., grooming, shaving)? select and prepare food? use public transportation? use money? engage in appropriate leisure time activities? This component is particularly significant when an adolescent or young adult is being assessed. However, independent living skills are so important that they are also considered in evaluations of children.

Few tests adequately evaluate independent living skills. As a result, information in this area is usually obtained through interviews with parents and family members and direct observations. While useful in making diagnoses of autism, independent living information is most helpful in selecting training goals. Thus, for example, a child who is unable to brush her teeth would likely be scheduled to learn this skill.

HOW TO GET A CHILD EVALUATED

Evaluations can be obtained from professionals in private clinical settings; city, county, state, and other public facilities; and school districts. Individuals seeking an evaluation of a child manifesting characteristics of autism should contact their private physician or local, county, or state medical society (or a university medical center); local, county, or state mental health association; director of special education of their local school district; or the local, state, or national Autism Society of America for referral information. Early intervention is a key to effective intervention with children with autism. Therefore, parents suspecting a problem should not wait for the situation to improve on its own—it usually will not happen.

SUMMARY

Assessment represents a significant part of meeting the needs of children and youth with autism and pervasive developmental disorders. Although autism is often difficult to diagnose, special procedures are available for this purpose. With skillful application of these methods, children and youth requiring professional attention can be identified and receive appropriate training, education, and treatment.

Major Problems and Needs of Children and Youth with Autism

4

In this chapter we take a closer look at the problem behaviors exhibited by children and youth with autism and pervasive developmental disorders. Behaviors of individuals with autism and similar developmental disorders are not subtle. That is, it is obvious to most observers that the behaviors of those persons, whether extremely disturbing to others or extremely withdrawn, are atypical. Except for persons with higher functioning autism disorders, these behaviors may be so severe as to interfere with these individual's living totally independent lives. It is important to understand that, although many interventions can be used to help individuals with all levels of severity of autism, two important facts remain: individuals with mild autism do not develop severe autism, and individuals with autism will not be "cured" of this disorder.

Autism is a difficult disability to diagnose and label. Children with severe autism are usually identified within the first 3 years of life. Moreover, some undiagnosed children who demonstrate characteristics of autism may have their diagnosis changed to autism later in childhood, after professionals have had additional opportunities to study their behavior and development.

Autism has been described as a spectrum disorder. This means that any individual may or may not have one or more of the behaviors associated with autism, which we listed in Chapter 1 of this book, to various degrees. Additionally, understanding autism requires that professionals consider behaviors related to the disorder in terms of severity (how intense the particular behavior is, or whether the problem is due to an absence of a typical behavior such as social interaction), duration (how long the behavior lasts), and pattern (when and where the behavior occurs). Indeed, it is critical to consider both the behaviors and the conditions associated with these behaviors when considering a possible diagnosis of autism.

As mentioned, much time and effort have been devoted to identifying and assessing children and youth with autism. The purpose of evaluating and classifying these individuals is to gain a better understanding of their needs, and ultimately to provide optimally effective treatment. However, many of the characteristics associated with autism are also found in persons with other disabilities, such as mental retardation.

Accordingly, as mentioned in previous chapters, it is often difficult to obtain a definitive diagnosis of autism, especially for children who are very young and those with severe disabilities. The nature of autism (e.g., poor communication skills) makes it very difficult to obtain accurate and meaningful assessment information in such areas as intelligence. For example, according to one study, about 80% of persons with classical autism may have intelligence quotients (IQs) in the retarded range, similar to individuals who have been diagnosed with mental retardation. Yet, children and youth with autism can be expected to have unique characteristics, such as exceptional memories, good motor skills, and so forth.

In this chapter, we divide the problems and characteristics associated with autism into broad categories: (a) developmental, (b) sensory, (c) social, (d) speech and language, and (e) unique abilities. Problems and characteristics within one of these categories may interact with those of another. For example, a child with speech and language problems may also experience social problems because of the inability to communicate verbally.

> ▶ **CAUTION:** The behaviors identified in this chapter may be indicative of autism only when their intensity, pattern, and duration fit the characteristics of the disorder (see Chapter 1). Most human beings, with or without autism, exhibit these behaviors in less exaggerated instances from time to time. Thus, their occasional presence may be independent of a diagnosis of autism.

DEVELOPMENTAL RATE AND SEQUENCE PROBLEMS

In this context, *development* refers to such aspects of human growth as self-concept, interactions with others (e.g., in play), physical skills, intellectual skills, understanding and communicating feelings, values, social skills, communication, and self-discipline. With regard to these behaviors, society identifies certain skills and patterns of behavior needed for a so-called normal existence. Thus, developmental delays are said to be present when children's and youths' behaviors are significantly behind those of their age group. Virtually all children and youth identified as having autism demonstrate developmental delays.

As mentioned in Chapter 1, many children and youth with autism demonstrate developmental delays in three general areas: cognition, social adaptation, and motor skills. Before we can discuss the delay notion, however, we need to clarify what is considered "normal" cognitive, social adaptive, and motor development.

Statistically speaking, defining normality is not an easy task. "Normal" behaviors are usually those that can be measured and identified within certain age groups. Thus, normal 4- and 5-year-olds exhibit certain behaviors that have not yet developed in normal 2- or 3-year-olds. Accordingly, if an 8-year-old child cannot perform tasks normally mastered by a 3- or 4-year-old, there is cause for concern.

Often cognition is the easiest developmental delay to identify. A significant cognitive developmental delay is commonly labeled as mental retardation. For example, 8-year-old children with autism may have the intellectual capability of those who are 4 years old. However, unlike children with mental retardation, they occasionally have age-appropriate development during their first 2 years and then regress. Thus, it is important to note that there is little direct evidence to suggest that a cognitive developmental delay of an individual with autism is the same as that for mental retardation. For example, for some children with autism, skills (e.g., toileting, talking) may be delayed, appear, and then disappear, or they may never appear at all. The physical appearances of those with moderate and severe retardation are also markedly different from those of children and youth with autism (whose appearances are often indistinguishable from the majority of children). Further, some individuals with autism possess normal development in some areas (motor or language) and have significant delays in others. Some may do well with traditional schoolwork, whereas others may be bewildered by what is expected from them.

Much controversy surrounds the meaning of these apparent delays in persons with autism. Some professionals believe that the seemingly delayed behaviors are not due to a lower IQ (see the earlier discussion about the difficulties of obtaining an accurate IQ score) but to other factors, such as perception, communication, social interaction, and so forth. Moreover, the experiences of children with autism with such delays and the reactions by those in their environment may further or mitigate these delayed behaviors. Indeed, families and professionals have enormous influence on children's developmental delays.

? *If my child has developmental delays, what kinds of behaviors might I expect?*

It is very difficult as well as unrealistic to generalize specific behaviors to all children and youth. Nonetheless, certain behavior patterns are common among many children and youth with autism. Delayed behavior patterns can be seen in a variety of ways. For example, individuals with autism may be significantly behind others in their age group with regard to self-care, emotions, language, and learning. Self-care problems may include delays and regression in the ability to maintain bladder control (called enuresis), bowel control (called encopresis), or both.

Some age-related inappropriate feelings or behaviors, including severe withdrawal from people, unrealistic fears, or temper tantrums, may also be indicative of a developmental delay (they may also be indicative of other factors, such as sensory deficits). With regard to these feelings and behaviors, a developmental delay is inferred because excessive displays of these behaviors are rare in normally developing children.

Will my child be able to live independently as an adult?

Many individuals diagnosed with autism can lead normal adult lives. These individuals typically have milder forms of autism, such as Asperger syndrome. Individuals with more severe forms of autism are less likely to lead independent lives. However, even adults with severe forms of autism can live semi-independent lives (residing in assisted living environments); that is, they are able to live outside of institutions and their parents' homes when provided appropriate supervision and structure.

It is important to recognize that more persons with moderate and severe forms of autism than ever in our history are able to acquire skills needed for independent living. For example, they become toilet trained; learn to use public transportation; and acquire other self-help skills needed for independent living, including the following:

- Communication: receiving and giving information in a meaningful fashion
- Orientation and mobility: understanding where they are in reference to their environment and moving around in that environment
- Hygiene: washing, tidiness, dressing and undressing, developing normal sleep habits
- Independence: being aware of dangers, getting things that are necessary for daily living, eating in restaurants, using a telephone, utilizing public services

Why doesn't my baby like to be cuddled? Instead, she seems to be preoccupied with herself, rocking in her crib, looking at her fingers.

One of the first signs of autism is a lack of normal responsiveness to one's environment. For example, one would typically expect young children to enjoy parents' physical nurturing, such as cuddling. However, different parents interpret the same behavior in many ways. Interestingly, the behavior pattern of your baby may have been interpreted by some parents as an indication of being a "good" baby (the baby is not bothering anybody). Certainly, another parental interpretation of a child who is not cuddly or who fails to enjoy being picked up by a parent is one of concern. Although children who are preoccupied with themselves do not automatically have autism, a lack of responsiveness is a major concern and should be evaluated by a professional.

? *Why isn't Christopher identified as mentally retarded? He fits the adaptive and cognitive criteria that were mentioned during the team meeting.*

Intelligence is commonly measured by standardized intelligence tests, whereby performance on certain tasks and behaviors is assessed and compared with that of other individuals who are of the same age. Not only might the scores of children and youth with autism fall in the mentally retarded range, but the abilities of these individuals to perform adaptive tasks are often similar to those of individuals labeled as mentally retarded.

However, there are major differences between the two groups. For example, individuals with mental retardation tend to score uniformly low in all areas, whereas people with autism often demonstrate variability in skill and ability areas. Many individuals with moderate and severe mental retardation also demonstrate physical evidence of their disability (e.g., short stature), whereas persons with autism rarely appear different (except by their behaviors).

? *What can I do to enhance the development of my child with developmental delays?*

In general, the chances of eliminating a developmental delay are not very good. However, by using techniques such as those described in Chapter 6, skills can be developed and improved. The likelihood of normal functioning for children with severe developmental delays is not high. The goal with all children, including those with autism, is to help them reach their potential.

? *My child is able to do some schoolwork. Will she be able to improve in this area?*

Depending on their ability and factors such as motivation and length of attention span, children with autism can accomplish schoolwork at various levels. However, the school work must be within their ability range and should apply to their personal needs. For instance, few professionals would argue the importance of enhancing communication skills. Other appropriate academics might include money use, time identification, knowledge of the days of the week, development of prereading skills, and art. Particularly with students with higher functioning autism, more abstract school subjects are appropriate. Indeed, large numbers of children and youth with milder forms of autism, such as Asperger syndrome, are able to successfully follow the same curriculum as their peers without disabilities.

SENSORY PROBLEMS

Sensory capabilities enable people to interact with their environment. For example, sensory responses (i.e., reactions) are made to sounds, visual stimuli, temperature changes, internal body sensations, touch, taste, and smell. According to some experts (Berkell, 1992; Freeman & Duke, 1996), it is distortions in understanding these sensory signals that prevent individuals with autism from effectively relating to their environment. However, there is some controversy regarding the possible causes of these problems. Whereas some experts believe they are due to sensory problems, others believe that they are caused by cognitive or neurological problems (Hobson, 1993; Mitchell, 1997).

? *Tommy gets very upset with certain sounds. For example, when the telephone or doorbell rings, he actually seems to get depressed. Why does this happen?*

Over- or underreaction to sounds is not unusual in children and youth with autism. Such reactions may take the form of sadness, anger, or fascination. Whereas some children withdraw upon hearing sounds that they interpret as unpleasant, others repeatedly create sounds, such as scratching and vocal noises, and seem to derive pleasure from listening to them.

Interestingly, there are documented cases of individuals with autism who overreact to the sounds of another person's voice. Most often, this is related to people who have high-pitched voices.

? *Sara seems to be fascinated and overly attentive to different objects. Is that unusual?*

These behaviors are not unusual among individuals with autism. Some of these children and youth focus poorly on objects and generally seem unable to notice anything except outlines and forms. Others focus with exceptional ability and attention on details and small objects. Some individuals seem to be distracted by lights or shiny objects. Still others engage in behaviors such as flicking their hands or moving their fingers near their eyes, watching things spin, or concentrating on one particular aspect of an object, such as a screw on an electrical outlet or the knob on a television set.

? *Why is it that John can look at an object for hours while ignoring extremely chaotic surroundings?*

Some children with autism tend to focus on only certain things (e.g., the color blue), using only one of their senses (in this case visual). That is, they virtually ignore other environmental variables because they do not simultaneously use, for instance, their hearing. This is called stimulus overselectivity. You may want to try to redirect John into another task so that his focused attention can be broken.

? *The other day, Tina was outside in freezing weather without her coat. Can't she feel the cold?*

It is not unusual for children and youth with autism to seem to ignore extreme ranges of temperature or pain. We deliberately use "seem" here because it is often unclear if these individuals are unable to express pain or if they have different sensitivity thresholds.

Another interpretation of these reactions is that some children enjoy temperature extremes. For the same reason, some experts believe that some individuals with autism inflict pain upon themselves (i.e., to experience the feeling of pain).

At the other extreme, some children and youth with autism show great sensitivity to even slight degrees of heat, cold, or pain. As a result, a minor bump may result in an exaggerated response (i.e., what one typically would expect following a major accident).

? *Evan approaches everything in an almost ritualistic manner. Everything has to be exactly the same way, each time. If his routine is disrupted, he gets very upset. Is this normal?*

As with other behavioral patterns discussed in this chapter, ritualistic behavior is common among children and youth with autism. This desire for sameness has been interpreted as a way to gain security. Whereas many individuals without disabilities share this feeling, some individuals with autism become extremely agitated if changes occur, for example, in morning routines, types of food ingested, utensils used, or even shapes, colors, and food smells. Many individuals with autism appear to experience high levels of anxiety when change occurs and behave in a manner that seems to shut out the world around them; others become aggressive.

? I have seen autistic children and youth engage in odd body movements, such as rocking. Why do they do that?

Nobody understands exactly why individuals with autism engage in repetitive behaviors, referred to as self-stimulation and stereotypical behaviors. Some believe that autistic individuals find comfort in such behaviors as rocking (after all, that is why many people like rocking chairs), jumping, or hand and arm flapping. Also, these behaviors may reduce the anxiety that was discussed previously. Common self-stimulatory behaviors include the following:

- Saliva swishing (i.e., in mouth)
- Knocking knees against each other
- Rubbing eyes, ears, mouth, clothes, and/or objects
- Teeth clicking
- Tapping fingers against objects
- Pressing or twisting ears or nose
- Flexing muscles
- Grimacing
- Tapping feet on floor
- Manipulating objects
- Head weaving
- Light filtering
- Object spinning
- Hand moving (flapping, finger movements)
- Rocking
- Humming
- Squinting

? Laura gets very upset when I make her change her favorite clothes. This is getting to be a very big battle in our home.

Most everyone has comfortable clothes they prefer to wear. Temple Grandin (1988), a woman with autism, recounts how she would throw tantrums when forced to wear petticoats, because to her the garment felt like sandpaper. She also talks about how long it would take her to get accustomed to pants and shirts after she spent time wearing shorts. Individuals with autism may also be overly sensitive to both visual and auditory sensations or stimuli.

Lighting in a room, noisy appliances, or even everyday sights and sounds may set off reactions for a child. Due to being puzzled or even frightened by the child's reactions, adults may not look at what may be causing the response. In some cases, the events that are bothering the child can easily be altered so that the child can react in a calmer manner (e.g., by replacing a door chime with a manual knocker).

? *Are there other strange behaviors that children and youth with autism display?*

Absolutely! This population demonstrates a wide variety of behaviors. For example, some children like walking on their toes; others have clumsy or unusual finger movements; and still others demonstrate odd postures such as thrusting chests forward or inward. Some children with autism, while apparently unable to clap their hands, can thread a needle. Other children with autism confuse directions such as up and down, back and front, or left and right. These behaviors may reflect their ability to follow verbal directions as well as to imitate other people's behavior.

? *Jack's way of approaching objects is similar to that of an animal. Isn't this weird, even for an autistic child?*

Touching, smelling, and attempting to taste unfamiliar objects are not unusual behaviors for children and youth diagnosed as having autism. Some experts (e.g., Happe, 1995) believe that their ability to receive auditory and visual information is impaired so they rely on their other senses (taste, smell, etc.) to experience their world.

It is important to remember that these behaviors often look "worse" than they really seem. In fact, all individuals may use the same behaviors, though not to the same extent. For example, you may briefly sniff food before you eat it, whereas your son may take the piece of food to his nose and sniff it for several minutes.

? *I know of an autistic boy who repeatedly bangs his head against a wall. Is this something I can expect my daughter to do?*

Self-injurious behavior (SIB) is not common among persons with autism; however, it does occur, particularly in individuals who have abilities falling in the severe mental retardation range. Again, it is important to remember that the frequency and intensity of this behavior is a crucial consideration. For example, many very young children occasionally bang their heads during a temper tantrum. The self-injurious behavior to which we are referring, however, is not occasional; it is frequent and potentially very damaging. It includes head banging, self-biting, hand chewing, self-scratching, hair pulling, inflicting self-injury with objects, and ingesting inedible objects.

There are many possible explanations for these behaviors. Some professionals believe that individuals exhibit SIBs because they are very frustrated. Others feel that their sensory system is very dull and they hurt themselves so they can experience "any kind" of feeling (no matter what it looks like to an outside observer).

Results of untreated SIB range from minor injuries to permanent injury or even death. Various interventions, including those described in Chapter 6, are used with individuals who exhibit self-injurious behaviors.

? *What causes the frustration that you are talking about?*

Frustration is often caused by an inability to do or communicate something. Typically any person who wants to succeed at or communicate something, and cannot do it, becomes frustrated. It may be something at work or play. People with autism may feel frustrated with not being able to communicate, play, or even get things done. When that happens, they may behave in a variety of ways. They may act out or withdraw.

? *It's not simply the inability to recognize others. The child seems to be so cold, even to members of his family. Why is that?*

As mentioned, failure to respond to touching or cuddling is not uncommon. Moreover, many children and youth who have autism fail to demonstrate "spontaneous" affection. Although this lack of response may be shown toward all people, some individuals with autism behave like that only with children of their own age or only with adults.

It is critical to note that many people with autism do feel comfortable with physical and emotional contact. Remember, we must look at these children as unique individuals. Each child may or may not possess many of the behaviors mentioned in this chapter.

? *I don't know how to describe it, but Mei Ling acts weird. On occasion, she laughs or cries uncontrollably or gets very angry for no apparent reason. What causes such behavior?*

Many children and youth with autism display emotional and social responses that are inconsistent, erratic, or maybe nonexistent. It is often impossible to judge what is going on in their minds; however, some experts speculate that the responses are related to an inability to accurately perceive their environment.

? *What about hallucinations and delusions? I heard that these occur frequently among individuals with autism.*

Hallucinations (seeing or hearing things that do not exist in reality) and delusions (believing that fantasy conditions exist) are not symptomatic of autism. Instead, these conditions are more likely to be associated with schizophrenia and other severe emotional disturbances.

SOCIAL PROBLEMS

? *My daughter has attended a special school for 3 years. Her social behaviors have always been minimal, but lately have taken a turn for the worse. She became very attached to her teacher who temporarily left the school to have a baby. When the teacher left, Janey refused to interact with others except in our living room. After awhile, she stopped speaking at all (her teacher has subsequently returned with no change in Janey's behavior).*

Virtually all children and youth with autism experience major problems with social behaviors. Some experts believe that problems in the social arena are due to an inability to accurately perceive the environment because of sensory problems, others attribute these problems to developmental delays, and still others associate the inability to initiate and maintain satisfactory relationships as an element of communication (speech and language) problems.

Children and youth with autism demonstrate a variety of social problems. Some children do not show affection; many have no friends of their own age; some appear unable to initiate intimacy; and many isolate themselves from others. In some cases, a careful assessment of the environmental conditions surrounding Janey's life may illuminate the reasons why her behaviors have changed (see Chapter 3). In other cases, there may not be an explanation and "new" appropriate behaviors may have to be taught to her. As one parent said, "Sometimes I feel like it is one step forward and two steps backward."

Avoidant Behaviors

Individuals with autism are frequently described as aloof, standoffish, or shy. They are described this way because they do not interact with other people on any level, whether through words, body language, or facial expressions. For example, they may scream, have tantrums, resist physical touch, or even run away from others. This description infers a psychological purpose on behalf of these individuals; that is, they purposefully avoid others because of their desire to be alone or because of their fear or dislike of others. Without trying to sound too confusing, we need to stress that this (psychological) explanation is only one possible reason for these social problems. There may be other (biophysical) reasons for these behaviors.

It is impossible to provide an explanation that covers all individuals who exhibit this behavior because of the different possibilities that exist. For example, some people may not be able to relate to other people because of their disability, and others may not find satisfaction from social interactions.

? Tyrone simply ignores whatever I try to do with him. No matter how exciting or reinforcing our time together, he simply refuses to respond. What can I do?

It is highly unlikely that Tyrone is truly ignoring everybody around him, or that he is "choosing" not to respond. Appearing to exist in a world of his own—that is, being aloof or withdrawn from the surrounding world—is one of the most common characteristics of children and youth with autism.

It is important to keep in mind certain ramifications related to one's perception of Tyrone's behavior. For example, if someone believes that Tyrone is choosing to behave in the manner described above, then that person might react in a negative manner (see Chapter 8). If, however his un- or underresponsiveness is believed to be caused by a sensory problem, then the behavior takes on new meaning, allowing the person to be more accepting and positive.

? But it is not only me whom he ignores. He doesn't respond to other students, his brothers, or sisters. Why is that?

If, in fact, Tyrone has a biophysical problem, he may have difficulty differentiating among people. Consequently, he may have limited ability to recognize and differentially respond to the people he encounters. Or, like some individuals with autism, he may treat all people as if they were total strangers.

? Yet, I know that Tyrone can communicate because he comes to me, albeit in an awkward manner, whenever he wants something.

Telling somebody that you want something is one form of communication. It can be termed egocentric; it is from the perspective of the individual doing the communication without taking into account the feelings and behaviors of the other person. Consequently, it is not an indication of two-way communication. One-sided communications are important to satisfying one's needs, yet they are not fully developed forms of social behavior.

Indifferent Behaviors

Some individuals with autism rarely interact with others, and some, such as those with Asperger syndrome, may respond in a socially awkward fashion. Many individuals with autism do not seem to mind being alone. Indicative of this behavior is what seems to be a lack of empathy toward people. Empathy is the ability to understand and relate to other individuals. It is crucial that people have a sense of reality and an awareness of others for this to occur; however, many children and youth with autism do not seem to connect with the world around them. Some researchers believe that the reason for this is that these individuals only perceive their environment as it physically appears. For example, in one study (Baron-Cohen, 1991) children with autism and children without disabilities were asked to look at a sponge that was painted to resemble a rock and label what they thought it was. Both groups said "rock." When they were allowed to touch the object, however, the children without disabilities correctly said "sponge," whereas the children with autism continued to say "rock." It appears that they were unable to accommodate the new information regarding the sponge.

? *Tyrone does seem to know if one of us is happy or sad.*

Results of some studies suggest that many individuals with autism can correctly identify the feelings of others based on physical evidence. For example, children with autism could identify someone who smiled as being happy. However, they could not correctly infer feelings from a story. For example, if something sad happened to the main character and she smiled, the individual would say she was happy.

? *What happens when Emily encounters real dangers?*

We have attempted to establish that it is extremely difficult for many children and youth with autism to understand and adjust to their environment. They apparently do not display fear, even in the most dangerous situations. Hence, to avoid injury, many individuals with autism require close supervision and structure.

It is difficult to teach some children with autism safety issues, especially if circumstances surrounding the issue vary. For example, a youth with autism may be taught never to open the door to strangers. Parents and teachers may even practice this behavior with the child using several role-play scenarios. However, the child's ability to generalize that behavior to the numerous possible situations that may arise may be limited. The same can be said for other safety issues, such as not touching a hot stove or an electrical outlet.

Play Behaviors

Many children and youth with autism may engage in ritual-like behaviors with toys, but rarely engage in meaningful play. For example, they may spin objects, stack blocks, or arrange toys for hours. The nature or purpose of these toys may have little relationship to how they are used. It has been hypothesized that these behaviors may be a means of maintaining self-control, although a variety of other explanations have been advanced.

Further, as mentioned above, these individuals often have difficulty developing friendships, and in fact may have little interest in making friends. It is not that they avoid other children; it is that other children do not seem to have meaning or value to them.

? *Sam never seems to play with his toys. Don't children with autism have imaginations?*

Children and youth with autism tend to interact with the world in a very concrete manner. If they have a ball, they may spend their time staring at it, or perhaps licking or smelling it. It is less common for them to think of the various possibilities of play that a ball may bring.

When Sam reacts to a ball only as something to smell or touch, he severely limits opportunities for extending it to other activities such as playing catch. Yet (there always seem to be exceptions to the common rule), the vast majority of children like Sam can be taught to engage in structured play with peers or adults.

? *Sometimes, Hannah doesn't seem to recognize acquaintances, especially if we are in an unfamiliar environment. Is this common?*

An inability to identify and respond to familiar people is a common characteristic of individuals with autism. The added confusion of being in a strange environment often compounds the problem. Even children who are responsive to certain people may seem unaware of their presence if they are outside the environment in which they are normally seen. For example, a teacher may be recognized at school but not in the grocery store.

It is important to determine the manner in which a child gives evidence of recognizing others. Eye contact, blank stares, brief flashes of recognition, or contact for brief periods of time may be incorrectly interpreted as an indication of recognition.

? *Joshua continually plays the same record over and over and assembles and takes apart the same model over and over. Why does he do that?*

We cannot be sure of the exact motivation behind such behavior: However, doing the same acts in the same way seems to provide a certain degree of comfort for many people. Whether in play or in the daily routine, these repetitive behaviors are common for children and youth with autism. Again, it is important to recognize that many people enjoy this sameness—the difference is the degree and duration of these behaviors.

? *Are there other unusual behaviors that I may expect?*

Because of their difficulty or inability to communicate and interact with the outside world, many individuals diagnosed as having autism display a wide range of behaviors. These behaviors may include, but are not limited to, aggressiveness, screaming, grabbing at things, running away, being destructive, and withdrawing from everything. However, it is important to remember that, although youth with autism may show these behaviors, they can usually be taught more appropriate responses (see Chapter 6).

SPEECH AND LANGUAGE PROBLEMS

The terms *speech* and *language* are often used interchangeably. Both relate to the manner in which human beings communicate; however, they have different meanings. Communication involves the ability to deliver and receive understandable messages. Speech involves the physical, conceptual, and technical processes or oral expression. Speech is the process by which people orally communicate, that is, by talking. Factors considered by speech professionals include articulation (the actual production of meaningful sounds), fluency (the flow of speech), and voice (the quality of our sounds).

Language refers to the broader act of using rules and symbols to communicate meaning. Thus, language disorders relate to difficulties in delivering or understanding thoughts based on the rules and symbols of language. Each language system has rules that help people to communicate (e.g., verb tenses that indicate past, present, and future). Language symbols may take the form of words, or they can be concrete, such as in sign language. In other words, language does not have to be orally communicated.

Virtually all children and youth with autism demonstrate significant speech and language problems. These problems affect not only their ability to express their needs, but also their ability to relate to others, their ability to learn, and so on.

? *Is it unusual for Maria to be mute? Is she voluntarily choosing to shut us off, or can't she talk?*

As noted earlier, almost every child diagnosed with autism has speech and language problems. In fact, it is believed that approximately 50% of individuals with classical autism fail to develop speech. Some speak only a few words or phrases; others are able to learn meaningless phrases, such as those from radio or television commercials. Still other children learn to communicate quite well.

There is little evidence to suggest that autistic children and youth choose to be mute. Indeed, elective mutism is very rare among children and youth with autism.

? *Bob is 9 years old and still does not talk. Will he ever be able to learn to communicate effectively?*

This question has two parts. First, it is unlikely that Bob, a 9-year-old, will totally overcome his language problem. Research suggests that children who fail to acquire language by age 5 to 7 usually continue to show communication deficits. However, as discussed in Chapter 6, alternatives to spoken language may allow Bob and other nonverbal children to communicate.

? *When Dana speaks, which is rare, she seems to be on the level of an infant. Will her language improve?*

Many parents of children with autism first notice a problem in their child's development at the age of 2 or 3 when speech and language skills normally develop. In fact, speech and language professionals are often the first to make professional contact with children and youth with autism.

A variety of speech and language problems are demonstrated by children with autism. Some children speak in long, disjointed, and meaningless sentences; others utter occasional words; and still others repeat previously seen or heard passages. The common link among these cases is that words are being used for purposes other than meaningful communication. Many speech and language interventions are currently being used that offer much hope for improved communications (see Chapter 7).

? *Could my child have a language disorder rather than autism? Isn't there something called aphasia?*

Autism is far more inclusive than specific language disorders, including aphasia. Children with aphasia, which is a language disorder, may have an inability or difficulty in sending or receiving meaningful information. Although many people with aphasia demonstrate secondary social problems, most of them attempt to communicate with others via a behavior that is not apparent in many persons with autism.

Further, people with aphasia may exhibit many of the same speech and language problems as children and youth with autism. However, the difference is in the typical intent by persons with aphasia to communicate with others by means other than speech (e.g., gestures). Also, children with aphasia are more likely to play appropriately with peers and symbolic objects, to use their imaginations, and to understand more abstract concepts.

? *The way Patrick repeats whatever I say is extremely annoying. Sometimes he says the whole sentence; at other times, he might repeat part of what I say. What's the purpose?*

Patrick's behavior is called echolalia, which may be immediate or delayed. Immediate echolalia refers to individuals repeating a word or phrase immediately after it is said by another person, whereas delayed echolalia describes repetition of something that was heard earlier.

There is currently debate regarding whether Patrick, and other children with echolalic behavior, use speech to communicate. That is, Patrick may not be trying to express his needs or to understand the needs of others. For instance, his parrot-like behavior may be a reaction to a seemingly unrelated environmental stimulus. For many children and adolescents, echolalia seems to be most prevalent when they are in unfamiliar surroundings or are otherwise anxious.

One technique that has been found useful with some children and youth is pairing concrete objects to their words. For example, you may say ball, your son repeats the word, and then you hand him a ball.

? *I notice that sometimes Katherine substitutes the word "I" for "you." Instead of saying "I want to eat," she says, "You want to eat." Why does she do this?*

Katherine is demonstrating what is referred to as pronoun reversal or pronoun substitution. The origin of this behavior is unclear. Some experts think it is a learned behavior, that is, that Katherine is repeating what is said to her. Others believe this behavior relates to an inability to personalize communication. Although pronoun reversal may occur in all individuals with autism, it is most frequent among younger children.

? *I don't understand why Amir can't use better language. His memory is actually very good. So what is causing it?*

Many aspects of language supersede the simple memorization of words. Knowing the meanings of individual words and how they relate to other words, and understanding the social implications of verbal and nonverbal communication seem to be beyond the capabilities of many children and youth with autism. Thus, they do not grasp the ideas behind the words. An example of this deficiency is their inability to comprehend simple jokes.

Amir's language deficit might be similar to that of a computer. He can recall many words, but cannot meaningfully use the words on his own.

? *What other forms of communication problems are common among those with autism?*

As mentioned earlier, a prime indicator of autism is a deficiency in communication. Accordingly, understanding and expressing language, by definition, are major problems for children and youth with autism. For example, their vocabulary may be limited; their comments may be inconsistent with an ongoing conversation; their speech may be too loud; they may reveal various levels of pitch; or their speech may seem flat, atonal, and arrhythmic. Further, they may be unable to use social and communication gestures effectively.

Children and youth with autism may also have unusual voice inflections. For example, they may end sentences with an inflection that suggests a question when in fact no question is intended. Finally, individuals diagnosed with autism may be deficient in the ability to understand abstract language concepts.

? *Kayla doesn't use language, but she also doesn't use gestures, facial expressions, yes or no nods, or anything else to get what she needs. Is this common?*

Gestures, head nods, and similar behaviors are all forms of nonverbal (nonspeech) communication. Kayla lacks not only speech but also other methods by which she can interact with the world. Perhaps the severity of her condition limits her ability to communicate verbally or nonverbally. Or maybe she has not been trained to communicate. Chapter 7 presents techniques that are useful for teaching a child to develop communication skills.

UNIQUE ABILITIES

Some children and youth with autism possess unique skills that appear to be inconsistent with their disability. In the past, individuals with these skills were called "idiots savant" (meaning "wise idiots"). In most cases, these skills are not functional.

? *Aaron has an incredible memory. It seems that even the most minute piece of information stays forever in his mind. However, he doesn't seem to make any use of this skill. He will bring up the information at the most unusual times.*

Aaron appears to possess extraordinary memory. It is understandable, therefore, that his parents and teachers become frustrated that he seems to have a useful skill yet is unable to effectively use it. Children and youth with this characteristic may remember things such as poems, songs, and television commercials, yet be unable to attach any significance to what they remember.

Other unique skills shown by children and youth with autism include the ability to memorize maps and carry out complex numerical calculations. Finally, some students with autism can "read" extremely difficult words, but have no comprehension of the words they read.

? *Joy has the most incredible singing voice. Is this due to autism?*

Pitch is the perceived high or low quality of one's voice. The highest quality of voice is called absolute pitch, which may be a characteristic among some individuals who have autism. Others may have different outstanding musical abilities. For example, some individuals with autism have been known to have the ability to play a song on a musical instrument from memory after hearing it only once.

? *Alex can take apart and put together a radio. Does that mean he might be able to get a job repairing radios?*

Perhaps, but these special skills are usually unique to particular situations. Often, special abilities shown by persons with autism do not generalize to different radios, or to the ability to diagnose and repair specific problems within radios.

? *Pamela seems to be losing her special skill as she gets older. Should I be concerned?*

Losing special skills is not unusual. There seems to be a relationship between the attainment of social skills and the loss of unique abilities. Therefore, Pamela may be behaving in other ways that may be more useful to her.

SUMMARY

In this chapter we discussed many of the problems and characteristics that individuals with autism may encounter. Some of these problems may be minor, such as reactions to lighting (minor because the reactions can be altered by changing the environment). Others are more significant and may never change. The characteristics discussed in this chapter, which are common among persons with autism, fall someplace in between.

It is incorrect to assume that all the problems identified in this chapter are present in all children and youth with autism or that these are the only problems. Rather, we have tried to compile a listing of relatively common characteristics. Further, just because a child demonstrates a certain behavior does not mean that he or she has autism. As mentioned in Chapter 1, the severity, pattern, and frequency of the characteristics must be considered as crucial to such a diagnosis.

Sources of Assistance for Children and Youth with Autism

5

A wide range of services are available to individuals with autism. In fact, because of the increased advocacy for these students and the passage of special education laws, there are now more options for services than ever before. Educators refer to these options as the *continuum of services*. The continuum ranges from services for students living at home with their parents and attending general education classrooms with no supportive help to placement in residential settings. (We describe these options later in this chapter.) Any placement should be determined by carefully evaluating the needs of the children and youth. Consequently, the chances of most children with classic autism being placed in a general classroom, without supportive services, are slight. However, such placements commonly occur with higher functioning individuals, such as those diagnosed with Asperger syndrome.

The purpose of this chapter is to review the roles of the people who may be working with children and youth with autism and to examine the placement and treatment alternatives that may be considered. In considering these two matters, it is important to keep in mind that only limited numbers of professionals may be trained to meet the educational, affective, and vocational needs of individuals with autism. Therefore, treatment and educational programs for persons with autism may serve other groups of exceptional persons as well. Nonetheless, the staff must make the adjustments necessary to accommodate individuals with autism.

? *What happens to the child who has been diagnosed as having autism?*

Chapter 3 discussed identification and assessment. In spite of its great importance, assessment means little unless it tells professionals how to proceed with treatment, remediation, and educational programs. In this regard, placement decisions directly determine the dynamics of intervention and training programs.

Parents need to be an important part of the entire process, including assessment and educational decisions. They need to be able to give the important information that only they know about their children. Further, they need to be able to receive the information that the school personnel know so that they can give informed input. Because communication is two way, schools must present information in a clear and easy-to-understand manner. Parents need to remind school personnel to clarify anything that may be confusing. Remember that language that school personnel use to better communicate with each other may be confusing to parents.

For many individuals with autism who are high functioning, general classroom placements are a reality and pull-out services are rarely required. However, these students may require monitoring to ensure that their needs are being met. Others who have significant behavioral and academic needs may be found among the many placements discussed later in this chapter.

? *What factors need to be considered prior to the placement of my child?*

The most appropriate placement and treatment options are determined by a number of factors. In particular, parent and family considerations are vital. Hence, in addition to professionals' input, parent and family needs and recommendations must be taken into account. The following are typical parent and family member questions and concerns:

- Will our son live at home forever?
- Will I be able to control my child as he grows?
- What community resources are available to him?
- If he goes to a community program, does that mean I am giving up my responsibility as a parent?
- What will his brothers and sisters think?

Because a family's influence plays an important role in the child's ability to function in a given school environment, placement and treatment decisions should be based on joint family and professional recommendations and input. These may also change over time, depending upon a number of factors (e.g., child's needs, family changes). The intention of this chapter (and book) is to help answer these questions.

? *How is the most appropriate environment determined?*

The most appropriate educational placement, as stated in the federal law—the Individuals with Disabilities Education Act of 1990 (IDEA)—is called the "least restrictive environment." The least restrictive environment for students with disabilities is determined through careful examination of each student's needs and subsequent selection of the program(s) that most effectively meet these needs.

Conflicts between parents and school professionals occasionally develop due to different interpretations of how to most effectively meet a child's educational needs. A practical way to operationalize the least restrictive environment dictum is to determine if the individual's disability is preventing him or her from learning in a particular setting (despite all attempts).

Parents obviously want the very best program for their child. This goal is desirable for all students; however, under the least restrictive environment interpretation of IDEA, public schools are required to place students in settings that are appropriate and as close to those of nondisabled students as possible. This is not always the same as the best possible setting.

When considering the least restrictive environment, you should ascertain how your child is being taught. For example, a concept that has recently come into prominence is that of the natural environment. Research suggests that students can use the skills they are taught when they learn in a setting that is similar to the "real world." Consequently, you may want to ask how instruction is presented. We know that students learn best when their environment is closely monitored. This allows the students to receive the feedback necessary to learn. Placements should not be superficial settings that merely reflect those settings. In other words, we believe that the best placement option is one from which the education can generalize to the real-world requirements of the students' home and community. Although we prefer that all students be integrated, as discussed later, that may not be a realistic option. What needs to be considered is that placements reflect the environs of the real world.

One question that will help determine whether the proposed placement option is a natural environment would be to ask if family members (or caretakers) are part (when possible) of the student's program. Also, are there opportunities for interactions with nondisabled peers (in both the student's educational placement and the general education settings)? Finally, are ample skills being taught in the setting and then practiced in the community?

? *But doesn't the law state that all students must be part of inclusion?*

Inclusion is not a law. Rather, it is an important social movement that will hopefully pave the way for increased acceptance of all students in general education settings. Also, people who speak of inclusion may in fact have different ideas about its meaning. Some people believe that it means that students need to spend all of their time in the general education setting. Others believe that students in general education settings may also require part-time pull-out services so that their unique needs can be addressed.

A decision regarding inclusion must take into consideration many factors. The most important factor to consider is what is good for each child. We believe that a good inclusion setting will meet all the student's social and academic needs. People who believe in the full inclusion model believe that students with disabilities will have more friendships or, minimally, be more accepted by others if they are exposed to them. They also believe that more appropriate peer modeling takes place in the general education setting. That is, when students with different behaviors are grouped together, they may model each other's different behaviors. Others believe, however, that students may experience frustration and perhaps ridicule regarding schoolwork because they are unable to meet the demands of their classroom, and thus need an environment that will allow them to learn new behaviors.

Another possible benefit of inclusion is that students with disabilities who are in general settings may learn more academics from their teachers and peers because of typically higher expectations. Opponents of inclusion believe, however, that it would be very difficult for students with autism to have their academic needs met in the general setting because of the variance between their individual needs and the needs of those without disabilities. The everyday demands that are placed upon general education teachers are very high. Most general education teachers have not been taught to work with students with disabilities, especially with a disability as demanding as autism. This lack of training is most apparent in the higher grades where academic demands are more difficult.

Finally, some people believe that special education costs too much money and that it would be more efficient to have only one program. However, others believe that, in order to be successful, inclusion may in fact cost more money than traditional special education programs (because decentralization of students requires more personnel support).

It is tempting for us to write about the glories of inclusion, and to recommend the general education classroom as being good for all students. We agree that in a perfect world, all students with disabilities should be educated in such a setting. Unfortunately, such a world does not exist for all students. Also, the current demands of teaching in a general education setting are extraordinary. It would seem highly unlikely that students with extraordinary needs can be adequately placed in a general setting without support. The question that needs to be considered prior to placement is "What are the social and functional needs of the student, and is there a probability of meeting those needs and those of the other students in the classroom?" It is crucial to understand that not all teachers, paraprofessionals, administrators, students, and community members have the ability or the desire to make the accommodations necessary for inclusion.

? *What should parents consider when choosing educational and treatment placements?*

Living with a person with autism can be extremely stressful. Hence, it is important to identify options that will serve both persons with autism and their families. First and foremost, it is important to read as much as possible about the various options (this can be cumbersome, because some of the literature can be quite technical). For example, by reading the literature we have learned that early intervention seems to enable many students with disabilities to be better prepared when they enter school. Consequently, we recommend that, whenever possible, students with disabilities enter early intervention programs. Another important factor to assess is the knowledge base of the non–special education personnel who may be involved in caring for a child with autism. Finally, if schools are available that employ special programs, such as the TEACCH program (Schopler & Mesibov, 1992; Schopler, Van Bourgondien, & Bristol, 1993) or one that was designed by Ivar Lovaas (1996), it is crucial to get all the information possible about the program. The school should be able to provide data (numbers) that indicate the areas in which the school is particularly successful. (Early interventions are discussed in detail in Chapter 6.)

In trying to make the right choice, parents should attempt to answer the following questions:

- Is the family member with autism violent to self or others?
- How restrictive an environment is needed to guarantee safety for the individual with autism?
- What community and family resources are available for the child when he or she becomes an adult?
- How prepared is the family to deal with sexual issues?
- How effectively does the family deal with a member who has poor communication and human relations skills?
- How available and effective is child care for the family member with autism?
- How effectively do the normally developing children in the family relate to a brother or sister with autism?
- Are siblings given responsibility (too much?) for the care of the individual with autism?
- Has the individual with autism hampered or significantly altered family recreational, church, or community activities?
- Is the parents' age and physical health an issue?
- Is the emotional health of the parents and family members such that they are able to care for a family member with autism?
- Does the family's economic condition hinder their ability to care for a family member with autism?

? What does the parents' age have to do with educational and treatment decisions for a family member with autism?

Parenting normally developing children and adolescents is difficult. However, as the vast majority of children grow, the responsibility of being a parent lessens. That is, as children become older, they are able to play with other children, take part in activities, join groups, and eventually live on their own. This typical developmental rearing process is not a reality for many families with an autistic child, however. In some cases, persons with autism need full-time care throughout their lives. Therefore, parents' age and health must be considered when planning for the children.

? What educational and treatment placements are available, and how are they similar and different?

Although the placements discussed in this chapter differ in many ways, they also share certain characteristics. For example, the types of professionals who work across settings tend to be the same and generally include diagnosticians, teachers, principals and directors, vocational educators, social workers, psychologists and psychiatrists, speech and language specialists, paraprofessionals, and adaptive physical education teachers. In addition, residential programs also employ child care workers and other support staff. A brief discussion of the roles of these individuals follows.

Diagnosticians. The job of the diagnostician is to coordinate and participate in evaluating persons with autism. The diagnostician may be a psychologist or another individual, such as a classroom teacher. Whatever the background and training of this person, he or she is responsible for collecting and evaluating information from other agencies and service personnel, as well as from the staff of the program conducting the diagnostic assessment.

Information gained from the various evaluations should be communicated to parents and other professionals in a clear, understandable manner. Children's specific strengths and weaknesses should be discussed in terms that translate into effective programming. Diagnosticians must be able to do more than simply identify students with autism. To be effective, they must be able to direct intervention and treatment efforts as well as ensure that ongoing evaluations will occur throughout the time a child is in a program. That is, diagnosticians are involved in assessing the effectiveness of various interventions and students' overall progress.

Classroom Teachers. Whether the teacher of a child with autism is a general or a special educator, he or she needs special training. Besides learning how to teach, the educator needs to learn how to be a careful observer and recorder of the children's social and academic behaviors. This individual must be able to communicate to the parent and other team members regarding each student's progress in very specific terms. Previously, many special education teachers responsible for educating students with autism received intense training in methods and techniques. Currently, they have the added responsibility of communicating with general educators, when necessary, regarding the needs of these students. When thinking about placements, parents should consider the following specific competencies these teachers should have in order to be successful:

- Behavior management and social interaction enhancement techniques for students with autism
- Speech and language development techniques for students with autism
- Nonverbal communication techniques for students with autism
- Ability to develop curricula for students with autism
- Evaluation and assessment techniques for students with autism
- Expressive therapy (e.g., art, music) programming for students with autism
- Daily living-skill programming for students with autism
- Self-care skill programming for students with autism
- Working with parents and families of students with autism
- Directing and supervising classroom paraprofessionals
- Vocational programming for students with autism
- Community and independent living programming for students with autism

This list is not exhaustive. The competencies that teachers need to demonstrate are many, because the needs of individuals with autism are many. Unfortunately, not enough teacher training programs are preparing teachers to work specifically with students with autism. Consequently, few teachers are properly trained, so many must receive their training on the job.

Team Teachers. Team teachers are general and special educators working together, most often for a part of the school day. There are many configurations of team teaching, ranging from a partnership of instruction for the entire group, to the special education teacher's working solely with the students who have disabilities within the particular classroom. The latter model seems to minimize the benefits of integration into the general education classroom because the students are separated from the main group.

Principals and Directors of Programs for Individuals with Autism. Principals and directors of programs for individuals with autism play a major role in the education and treatment process. They are responsible for monitoring the provisions of the students' Individualized Education Programs (IEPs). They coordinate what is taught, how it is taught, and who teaches. They also are involved in staff development, legal compliance, communicating with parents, and acting as liaisons among the various agencies serving students with autism.

If a student with autism attends a school that also serves students without disabilities, the building principal is responsible for all students in the building. Principals need to be aware of the behavioral and academic differences of the students with disabilities so that appropriate plans can be developed (e.g., a current controversy involves the behavioral management of students with disabilities in the general setting—whether they should be treated as if they did not have a disability). If the school or program serves exclusively students with disabilities, the principal will likely be a specialist in special education. If a child or adolescent is in a hospital or residential treatment setting, the school's principal will work with a general administrator, who oversees all facets of the program, including education.

Vocational Educators. According to IDEA, all youth with autism over the age of 14 will have transition programming. This programming may be provided by the special education teacher, the general classroom teacher, or a designated specialist called a vocational educator. This teacher generally integrates community resources, teaches appropriate work behaviors and habits, and provides a variety of job experiences.

Vocational educators have expertise in preparing students for postschool activities, including work. They teach such skills as responsibility, dependability, work-related social skills, and hygiene, all of which are necessary competencies for students' vocational success. Specific technical skills may also be taught to prepare students to work in a sheltered workshop or for competitive employment. Vocational educators may also be responsible for communicating with potential employers and workshop personnel regarding autism and some of the specific characteristics of the disorder.

Social Workers. Clinical and school social workers perform a variety of functions, but their primary job is to serve as a link (sometimes called liaison) between professionals, families, and community agencies. In addition, they may counsel family members and, on occasion, students with higher functioning autism disorder.

Psychologists and Psychiatrists. Psychiatrists and school and clinical psychologists are usually actively involved as diagnosticians, and may also perform family or individual counseling. Such counseling might involve helping families or individuals recognize feelings and emotions that might be impairing their family relationships. Further, it is the psychiatrist's responsibility to diagnose and prescribe and evaluate the effects of any necessary medications. Psychologists have recently begun to give traditional psychological tests (with modifications) to individuals with autism.

With regard to their roles in schools, psychologists are often responsible for initial evaluations and 3-year reevaluations. Ideally they also are involved periodically throughout the year with these students to provide teachers and parents with suggestions regarding behaviors and academics. They may also teach others how to enhance their observational skills.

Speech and Language Specialists. As noted in earlier chapters, speech and language problems are clearly among the most frequent and debilitating among individuals with autism. The development of functional and language skills must be a priority among the clinicians who work with a child. Traditional therapies may not be appropriate for each child. Ideally, much of the clinician's work will be conducted and practiced among normally developing peers.

Teaching communication is the major task of speech and language specialists. Thus, they work with the individual with autism and may teach family members to help increase communication at home (see Chapter 4 for an explanation of the speech and language problems that individuals with autism may exhibit).

Paraprofessionals. Paraprofessionals play an important part in most educational settings. They may serve in a variety of roles, including classroom managers, classroom assistants, observers of behavior, and teachers of specific skills. Also, they assist children in practicing previously taught skills. They can be extremely useful to the classroom teacher and, more important, to your child. Nevertheless, you need to be careful to monitor the classroom situation so that the paraprofessional is not solely responsible for the education of your child. The classroom teacher should be primarily responsible for these duties.

Paraprofessionals' duties may range from providing custodial care to being instructors. Their role is often integral to the functioning of many programs for students with disabilities because they work with teachers in order to help observe and record data (daily information regarding both academic and social behaviors) and to teach new behavioral and functional skills. In an ideal situation, they will communicate with both teachers and families regarding the progress of the students.

Adaptive Physical Education Teachers. Leisure activities are an important part of everyone's life, including individuals with autism. Adaptive physical educators are trained specifically to develop and implement programs and to teach coordination and play skills to individuals with autism. As for students without disabilities, physical education activities are critical for students with autism. Beginning social skills that revolve around game playing can be nurtured by these teachers. In addition, adaptive physical educators help students with their gross motor skills and movement therapies.

Occupational Therapists. Occupational therapists may be found in any of the placement options listed later; however, they are generally not involved as often in general education settings. Their primary function is to teach individuals with autism such life skills as self-care (e.g., feeding, hygiene, grooming, housekeeping) and the activities that enhance their free time. They may also teach skills needed by persons with autism to be successful in the workplace.

Physical Therapists. Physical therapists develop individualized programs designed to help individuals with autism enhance their strength and coordination. They teach flexibility and movement, which may overlap with social and language skills, and they may provide mobility training, exercise programs, and other physical activities.

? *What placement options exist for individuals with autism?*

Placement for children and youth with autism is based on many factors. For students who are able to attend public school, the size of the school system, its location, its relative wealth, and its commitment to education all affect the quality and quantity of educational services for students with disabilities, including those with autism. With the popularity of inclusion, increasing numbers of individuals with autism are being placed in general education settings. Because students with autism are frequently placed in different classrooms throughout the school, they are receiving fewer services. It is crucial to ensure that, whatever the placement, each student's needs as stated on the IEP are met. Many issues must be considered when looking at the best fit. For example, rural areas typically will not have many of the services described in this chapter.

It is particularly important that school districts have available professionals who are certified (i.e., licensed by a given state) or experienced in working with students with autism. School-related placement options fall along a continuum, as described in the following text. Again, remember that not all of these options are available in every school district.

General Education Classrooms. The general education classroom is often perceived as the least restrictive placement. We define the *least restrictive environment* as the placement that, with accommodations, will not be handicapping to the student's disability. Consequently, for many students with autism, the general classroom is not the most appropriate option and, in fact, is restrictive. Such placements are staffed by general education teachers, who usually lack knowledge and experience regarding students with autism. Yet, they will assume major responsibility for these pupils, perhaps with *some* supportive help. Therefore, students placed in a general education classroom may be required to function with little or no special assistance. Because general education teachers are responsible for teaching 20 to 35 students, it is unrealistic to expect them to be able to meet the needs of children and youth with autism for the entire day unless the students are higher functioning.

Before placing a student with autism in a general education classroom, a careful assessment should be made of the student's academic and emotional needs, and whether these needs can be adequately served in a general education program. Decisions related to inclusion must be carefully made and well planned with an emphasis on social integration activities. Most professionals would agree that, for students with disabilities to be successful in preschools, the setting needs to be sensitive to all children and have a well-trained staff. Parents should ask for some concrete evidence of the training of teachers and other staff members. Many preschools are licensed by such organizations as the National Association of the Education of Young Children. These organizations have standards that the schools must meet before receiving licensure.

In elementary schools, peer interactions should be structured because they do not always happen spontaneously. Public schools can be confusing to all children, and careful attention must be paid to the interactions that enhance success. Contrary to popular press, students who have disabilities are often avoided by other students.

Further, one must be wary of "window dressing inclusion." An example of window dressing inclusion, or bad inclusion, would be the assignment of a full-time one-to-one paraprofessional who has little or no training specific to a student's disability. In reality, these paraprofessionals serve more as behavior managers than as instructional aides to the teacher or the student.

Middle and high school inclusion is more problematic for many students with moderate or more significant autism as the academic demands for these classrooms are often too high for them. In other words, the gap between students with and without autism may be too great to expect a teacher to bridge. Although the social rewards of inclusion may still be present, these students may not be developing the skills that they will personally need to succeed simply by sitting in the general education setting. Consequently, although many parents and professionals may have aspirations of normal functioning for individuals with autism, they may discover that the general education classroom is not appropriate for some of these individuals. Thus, this placement should be chosen based only on strong evidence that it is the most appropriate alternative for a student. Interestingly, general education placements were initially perceived to be the least expensive for school districts. However, when done correctly, with the appropriate supports, they may cost more than the more traditional special education classrooms.

For every "rule," however, there are exceptions. Some children and adolescents with autism do learn best in general classrooms. In addition, some school districts may assign an appropriate aide to students with autism, making general placement even more feasible.

Consultant Services. Educational or behavioral consultants are often used in general education classrooms, resource rooms, part-time special classes, and self-contained classrooms. Because many teachers in these settings have neither the training nor the experience to work independently with students with autism, consultants serve to advise these teachers.

Consultants observe teachers and students, identify areas of need and action with which teachers may be unfamiliar, and offer teaching and management suggestions. Consultants can also provide training (inservice or staff development training) to staff and sometimes parents. Consultants also work with teachers as students are moved to general education classrooms and resource rooms.

Resource Room and Part-Time Special Class Placements. Resource rooms and part-time special class placements are designed for students who are able to function in general education settings for at least part of each day. Resource rooms typically provide educational services for up to 3 hours per day to (mostly) students with mild disabilities of different ages (e.g., 8- to 10-year-olds), grades (e.g., Grades 3 to 6), and abilities (e.g., learning disabilities, higher functioning autism).

Students in part-time special class settings attend special education classrooms for most of the day, but are integrated into general education settings for a few class periods. Often the general education classes include industrial education, art, music, and physical education, along with more traditional academics in areas of students' strengths. Many times, resource room teachers also serve students in the general education setting as team teachers or have a "corner" in the general setting where they work with students with special needs.

Full-Time or Self-Contained Special Class Placements. Students in full-time or self-contained special class placements attend special classes for the entire day, with the possible exception of lunch, recess, and physical education. With regard to public school options, this is the most restrictive setting discussed thus far. These classes may contain only students with autism or combine them with other students who have significant special needs. Only students with significant disabilities are given special education services for the majority of the school day. Ideally, this classroom is staffed with a full-time teacher trained to work with students who have autism.

Some authorities suggest that only students under 12 years of age should be assigned to full-time or self-contained special education, and that there should be no more than five or six students in a class. These grouping recommendations are based on the developmental similarities of preadolescent students, which make instructional grouping easier.

Day Treatment Programs. Day treatment programs usually follow a typical school schedule, although some have extended days. They are often in a public day school, although they are in segregated settings for students with disabilities. Most often these settings have students with moderate to severe disabilities, who often exhibit behaviors that are dangerous to themselves or others or who have such significant needs that they cannot be served in other settings. These programs tend to be traditional, in the sense that they serve school-age children and youth from kindergarten through Grade 12. (In some states, special education services are provided to students up to 26 years old.)

In addition to their physical location, the difference between a self-contained classroom and a day treatment program involves the additional support services available in day programs. For example, paraprofessionals (classroom aides), psychologists, behavioral consultants, and speech and language specialists are usually consistently available to day treatment students and staff. In contrast, such resources may not be so evident in self-contained classrooms, which are usually staffed by a teacher and an aide who share support staff with other programs in the building or district.

When day treatment programs are housed in or adjacent to public schools, nominal integration may take place, such as shared use of lunchrooms, recess facilities, and so on. Although this might seem attractive, there is a difference between *real* integration (i.e., social interaction between students with and without disabilities) and settings in which contact between children and youth with autism and their normally developing peers is restricted. Meaningful and well-planned interaction and integration can be extremely beneficial and is often needed for success.

The primary benefit of day treatment programs lies in their ability to provide specialized and individualized programs for students with autism, including curricula in life skills, vocational training, and counseling. However, because day treatment programs for students with autism are not available in every community, this option may not exist for many students and families.

Private Day Treatment. Except for being independent of public school settings, private day treatment is virtually identical to day treatment programs discussed previously. Private day treatment occurs in segregated settings that provide services that are not given by the public sector. Consequently, the costs incurred for services are paid by the public schools or insurance.

Homebound Instruction. Homebound instruction is intended primarily for students whose illness or disabling condition prevents them from attending school. An instructor, who may or may not be a certified teacher, travels to a student's home usually from 1 to 3 days per week for 1 to 3 hours per day to tutor the student on the academics that are being taught in school. Occasionally, homebound programs are utilized with students who have intense behavior problems that prevent them from learning in a general setting. We believe that, except for very short periods of time, this option is inappropriate for individuals with autism because of the brevity of time that services are delivered.

Community Agencies. In recent years, there has been an increase in the involvement of community services in the support of education of persons with autism. More important, these agencies are beginning to work together so that the services may be better coordinated, both preventing overlap and filling in gaps.

In some locations, community agencies may be very active in the education of children with disabilities. In some areas, community agencies may provide many of the services that one would expect the school to furnish. They may become involved in children's assessment and assignment to community resources, such as Head Start, day care providers, mental health agencies, vocational opportunities, and medical facilities. Minimally, these agencies can offer a wide variety of information regarding potential resources.

Supported Employment. Many efforts have been made to increase the opportunities for individuals with disabilities to be employed. Many higher functioning students have been gainfully employed in traditional service industries (e.g., restaurants, hotels) and a variety of other businesses. Chances of success are greatly enhanced when there is on-the-job support.

There are various types of on-the-job support. The concept of natural support suggests that support becomes part of the culture of the employment site, as opposed to a specialized program to aid only individuals with disabilities. Any individuals at the job site may help, or sometimes family, friends, or volunteers from within the community can also offer support. A more formalized approach may include job coaches who "shadow" the employee and give assistance when necessary. A job developer may actually create meaningful work that the individual can learn to achieve.

? *Is our son's age a consideration regarding a placement outside our home?*

This is a very difficult question to answer. If a child requires placement outside the home, we recommend that the action be taken promptly, and that the child be returned to a less restrictive setting as soon as possible. For example, many younger children find it easier to adjust to settings outside the home. However, this varies from individual to individual. Also, younger children tend to have younger parents, who may have the energy and time required to monitor a placement and communicate with a school or treatment program.

? *Professionals have recommended that our child be placed in a residential treatment program. The nearest placement under consideration seems to be of a lesser quality than others we have seen, whereas the best programs are some distance from our home and would lessen our contacts with our child. What can we do?*

Placement decisions such as this one are particularly difficult for parents. If one program is only slightly better than another that is closer to home, the decision may be different than if the two programs differ significantly in quality. In addition, children adjust to different programs in different ways. Accordingly, a decision on the best program for a given child can best be made after a child is given an opportunity to be involved in a particular program for several months. Remember that it often takes time for the child to feel comfortable and for the staff to learn how to best support each child as a unique person.

? *What out-of-home placement options exist for children and youth with autism?*

Out-of-home placement options are residential facilities that furnish educational and custodial care for individuals with moderate to severe disabilities whose needs cannot be met in a home or homelike environment. In recent years, the trend has been to reduce the number of persons living in institutions, resulting in increased placements in foster and group homes. These placement options provide 24-hour care for individuals with autism, while being more "normalized" than institutions. Services vary, but may include counseling, medication, and management techniques (e.g., physical restraint) that might be difficult to implement at home.

Some individuals with autism need to be supervised, as they can be destructive to self, others, or property. Although more moderate placements for these individuals may be possible, it is critical that their placements include close supervision and monitoring. An unfortunate consequence occurs when the placement is designed solely to provide supervision without remediation. People hired merely to baby-sit often have limited or no ability or skills necessary to work with individuals with autism. The most normalized setting possible will allow even the most severely affected person with autism to learn important skills.

Foster Home Placements. Foster homes offer individuals with autism a family-like atmosphere. They are normally state-licensed settings. In some cases, respite care and other services for the foster parents are provided. Ideally, this placement will be a therapeutic situation, with foster parents who have been trained or who have access to the specialized training that is needed.

Residents who live in a foster family setting receive special services (e.g., education, vocational training) as needed. Foster home personnel should be trained to serve as "parents" of persons with disabilities, including those with autism.

Group Homes. Group homes are designed to serve small numbers of persons with disabilities. According to some professionals, the optimal number of residents in a group home is one or two. Although these numbers may be realistic in some cases, they vary depending on the size of the home, the number of available staff, and the needs of the residents. In some instances, such programs serve homogeneous populations; that is, they specialize in serving persons of similar age, ability, or diagnosis. Because these homes are located in communities, as opposed to institutions, they afford clients access to real world as much as possible and allow for a more personal and individualized approach than the institutional setting.

Group homes rely on community resources, including public schools, for educational services. Because of the varied and sometimes intense needs of persons with autism, effective community resources are essential for the proper functioning of group homes. Further, group home personnel administer services (e.g., behavior or medication therapies) that allow the residents to function better.

Some group homes have financial problems, which severely limit travel and activities of persons they serve. These placements have been criticized in the past for their inhumane treatment to persons with disabilities. Most environments have responded to those criticisms and now provide appropriate care. Families considering group home placement for a person with autism should investigate this option closely.

Psychiatric Programs and Hospitals. Psychiatric programs or hospitals are full-treatment placements, and are generally used on a short-term basis. A stay in such a setting might range from a few days to several months, sometimes longer. Decisions to use this type of program are often the result of out-of-control behavior of an individual with autism. Psychiatric hospital treatment is usually comprehensive, although the primary therapy is medical (medications and other therapies are often emphasized).

Respite Care Alternatives. Respite care provides a variety of services for individuals who are responsible for the care of a person with autism. Services include occasionally taking care of the individual with autism to allow the primary caregiver some relief time. These services may be reached by contacting the local mental health community agency.

Institutions. Although placement of individuals with disabilities in large institutions has fallen into disfavor, the reputation and quality of any particular program should not automatically be assumed to be poor. Decisions to place persons with autism in residential or institutional settings are complex and should include consideration of the following questions:

- Are sufficient staff (often called client-to-staff ratio) available to serve the needs of individuals?
- Does the program provide appropriate services and training, including living skills, recreation, and education?
- Is the institution integrated or isolated from the community?
- Is the institution able to provide appropriate levels of attention to individuals?
- Does the institution house clients in smaller units or cottages as opposed to large barracks-type living quarters?

? *Why might our child need to live someplace besides our home?*

It may not be necessary to consider an out-of-home placement. Some students with higher functioning autism can live independently with little or no help. Adequate social skills and the ability to communicate are necessary prerequisites for this to occur. Residential placement is usually recommended as a last resort, and is often due to inadequate placement options (a problem that is not unusual in small communities) and the severity of a child's condition. According to the least restrictive environment concept discussed earlier, children and youth should live someplace other than in their own home only if they are unable to learn and live safely in a less restrictive environment.

Some students may have problems that are so severe that they are simply unable to live at home and attend a public school. Also, some family situations may contribute to a child's problems so that at least a temporary change becomes necessary. Thus, an out-of-home placement can sometimes provide a time-out from a very difficult situation, allowing those involved to examine critical issues that may be causing problems in the care and accommodation of a family member with autism.

? *Doesn't placement outside the home mean that I've failed as a parent?*

One of the least productive reactions to dealing with a family member who has autism is to place blame (see Chapter 8). It is very easy to blame children for their behaviors and emotions. It is also easy for parents to blame themselves for the way their children develop. Quite simply what has happened, has happened. To examine and cross-examine the whys and wherefores only takes attention away from the main issue: how to resolve the problems at hand.

Regardless, there may be some shame ("What will others think of *me* if Joe is sent away from home?") or guilt ("Maybe this wouldn't have happened if . . .") associated with the decision to send a family member to a residential program. If these feelings are very strong, we recommend counseling. Many families share the same feelings and problems. Support groups or family counseling might be helpful. Finally, most residential programs recognize the need to include families in their programming. Consequently, they generally welcome family input and provide special services to parents and family members.

? *But these feelings are very real. They are not so easily explained away. So what do I do?*

We are not trying to "explain away" feelings associated with making difficult decisions regarding a family member with autism. Placing a child in a residential program after considering all the relevant factors is usually a sign of genuine concern for the child and the family. It is an indication that the parents have the child's best welfare in mind.

? *How do you know how it feels to be in this situation?*

We only know what we have been told by others. But the point is well taken. Talk to people who are in similar situations. Ask the administrators of the program(s) under consideration for references (i.e., from other parents whose children are in the setting).

We also recommend taking the kinds of actions needed to make any important decision: visiting programs, asking questions of the staff, and talking candidly with administrators. Questions relative to the educational and treatment program may include these: Is the atmosphere institutional or homey? Are the other residents similar to your son or daughter with respect to characteristics, strengths, and weaknesses? Does the staff show evidence of training and knowledge about autism? Do they appear to be caring and sincere in their interactions with their clients?

? *Is there anywhere else we can go to find out about these feelings and about the types of placements available in my area?*

The Autism Society of America (see Chapter 10 for contact information) and its local and state chapters is one source that we strongly recommend. You may also want to contact the state departments of education, social services, mental health, or mental retardation for the names of other organizations and programs that focus on autism.

? *What should my family say when asked about Tammy?*

The answer to this question will probably vary depending upon the person to whom you are talking. For instance, you might decide to give more detailed information to close friends or relatives than to strangers. There is nothing shameful about somebody's having problems, especially a disability. Thus, your response can be that "Tammy is going to a school that can be more responsive to her needs."

An important message underlies your question. Tammy has a condition that requires care. Her problems may be due to a variety of factors, most of which are described in this book. Avoiding this reality may create more problems. Fabricating stories and lying about Tammy's condition rarely helps and sends mixed messages to any siblings. Are you ashamed of her?

A common misconception about placing individuals in residential schools is that the process involves locking someone away in a medieval institution. Most residential facilities are caring places that provide more than adequate educational, social, vocational, and living facilities. Selecting an appropriate (and least restrictive) placement for an individual with autism is not an easy task. In particular, it is important that the needs of both the persons with autism and the family be matched with available program options and support resources.

Treatment and Interventions for Children and Youth with Autism

6

Autism is a lifelong disability for which there is no known cure. Children and youth who are identified as having autism will most likely carry at least remnants of the disorder throughout life. Thus, even high functioning adults diagnosed with autism are often socially withdrawn, prone to use of monotonous intonation in their speech, and perceived as "different."

The absence of a cure should not be interpreted to mean that children and adolescents with autism cannot make progress. The vast majority of children and adolescents with autism can and do make significant gains. However, such progress does not occur by accident, and autism is not a disorder that children outgrow. Rather, improvements result from carefully formulated training programs and intervention strategies. Temple Grandin (1988), who was diagnosed as having autism as a child but who nonetheless managed to become a successful professional, gives credit to teachers and therapists for her gains: "I am deeply grateful to the dedicated teachers and therapists who worked with me. They were responsible for my [improvement], and their importance cannot be overemphasized" (p. 1).

This chapter presents several major treatment and intervention methods used with children and youth with autism, including education, behavioral interventions, social skills training, and medical treatments. The role of psychotherapy and the use of controversial treatments with children and youth with autism are also discussed.

EDUCATION

Most experts who work with children and adolescents with autism acknowledge that education is the key to improvement. Because of the nature and severity of the condition, many individuals with autism are poor candidates for psychotherapy. That is, they are often unable to discuss personal issues and concerns, including feelings and perceptions, with a therapist. Such activities require cognitive and language skills far beyond those of many individuals with autism.

Education and training have proven to be effective tools in working with persons with autism because they require that children have few prerequisite skills and they provide direct intervention in areas of greatest need. For example, a child who lacks speech and language, has cognitive problems, and demonstrates a number of stereotypes (e.g., self-stimulatory behaviors), although unable to discuss his problems with a psychotherapist, would be very appropriate for an educational program. Because his problems involve failing to do certain things (e.g., communicating, interacting with others) and excessively engaging in inappropriate activities (e.g., flapping his hands for extended periods of time, thus prohibiting involvement with others), "treatment" would logically involve instructing the child in more productive and adaptive behaviors.

In the context of programming for children and youth with autism, education and training sometimes differ greatly from what is typically thought of as education. Thus, successful methods may involve little in the way of traditional schoolwork (i.e., reading, writing, arithmetic). Instead, students may receive instruction in more basic areas, such as self-help skills (e.g., toileting, grooming), independent living (e.g., money use, use of public transportation), social and behavioral skills (e.g., greeting, responding and interacting with others), communication (e.g., verbally expressing needs), and vocational training (e.g., collating, packaging). Children and youth may also receive academic instruction, particularly to enable them to be more independent. Typically, their academic curriculum will involve more basic goals and objectives than their normally achieving peers. For example, reading instruction may focus on teaching survival words, such as *men*, *women*, *exit*, and *danger*. Higher functioning students with autism will frequently receive their education in a regular classroom, and follow the same curriculum as their nondisabled peers.

Structuring for Students with Autism

Educational programs for children and youth with autism are usually very structured to enable children and adolescents to behave in more productive and adaptive ways. *Structure* in this context means that the program is consistent and predictable, organized, and designed so that students understand the relationship between their behavior and the consequences of such behavior. Thus, parents and professionals attempt to follow the same programs and procedures, relying on predictable and organized strategies. As a result, students learn that every time they engage in a desirable or undesirable behavior, predictable consequences will follow (e.g., after successfully putting together a puzzle, a child is allowed to play with a desired toy for several minutes).

Several components of structure are common to programs for children and youth with autism. First, structure involves clearly identifying *individualized goals and objectives*. That is, unique expectations and methods are designed to fit each child or adolescent's needs. Accordingly, only materials, methods, and activities appropriate for a given child are used.

Second, structure involves using task analysis and shaping. *Task analysis* refers to breaking down desired behaviors into small units, and then teaching these individual segments (e.g., the steps in a vocational assembly task are divided into small increments and sequentially taught). *Shaping*, on the other hand, means that a desired behavior is taught by instructing students in successive approximations of that behavior (i.e., teaching tasks step by step until a goal is achieved). For instance, if the goal is to teach a child to independently travel to and from her classroom and school bus, she is successively taught to travel greater and greater distances between her classroom and bus without assistance until she is able, independently, to make the trip. To be successful, task analysis and shaping require that positive consequences be used such that children understand what they are being asked to do, and that activities and materials are appropriate and within the children's range of abilities and needs.

A third feature of structured programs is *use of routines*. Used to reduce uncertainty for children and to help them understand what to expect, this element of structure is particularly effective in enabling children and youth with autism to understand and predict the happenings of their world. One of the most effective means of clarifying routines for children and youth with autism is to use visual schedules. An example of one such schedule is shown in Figure 6.1.

A fourth element of structure involves *arranging a classroom's physical environment* to accomplish desired goals and objectives. For instance, a child may be seated away from a distracting classroom noise, or floors may be carpeted to reduce certain types of self-stimulation (e.g., the noise associated with a child's self-stimulatory toe tapping). Moreover, classrooms may be designed so that certain areas are associated with certain activities. A child may learn that group work is done in certain areas of the class; individual assignments are completed at a study carrel (i.e., a small work area designed for use by one student at a time); vocational activities occur at a work table in one corner of the classroom; and free time takes place in still another. Assignment of activities to certain areas helps students understand teacher expectations, thereby reducing confusion about what they should be doing.

As students progress, educators often attempt to reduce this basic assignment of specific activities to certain areas of a classroom. Thus, teachers assist students to recognize that peer interactions can occur in places other than at a group area in the classroom and that individual assignments can be worked on in a variety of areas. Nonetheless, at least initially, many students with autism benefit from the structure associated with careful planning of physical space and arrangement.

Skills Training

As noted earlier, education and training programs are individualized according to each student's needs. Thus, it is unlikely that even students in the same classroom are assigned exactly the same activities and curricula. In spite of individualization, programs for children and youth with autism generally emphasize development of six

8:00 a.m.	bus routine (put up coat and backpack, bathroom, review schedule with teacher or paraeducator)	
8:15 a.m.	breakfast	
8:30 a.m.	morning group	
9:00 a.m.	math activities	
10:00 a.m.	reading activities	
11:00 a.m.	adaptive physical education	
11:30 a.m.	lunch time	
12:00 p.m.	recess	
12:30 p.m.	work time (prevocational activity)	
1:30 p.m.	leisure time	
2:00 p.m.	language group	
2:30 p.m.	recess	
3:00 p.m.	music time	
3:15 p.m.	closing time	

Figure 6.1. Sample visual schedule. From *Asperger Syndrome: A Guide for Educators and Parents* (p. 55), by B. S. Myles and R. L. Simpson, 1998, Austin, TX: PRO-ED. Copyright 1998 by PRO-ED, Inc. Reprinted with permission.

basic skill areas: behavior and social skills, communication and language skills, self-help and independent living skills, prevocational and vocational skills, academic skills, and motor skills.

Educational programs for children and youth who are severely affected by autism emphasize *functionality*. That is, students learn skills and behaviors that they can use in their everyday lives, such as toileting, eating, grooming, social interaction, language, and community living. Programs for higher functioning students tend to emphasize social and social-language skills, along with pursuit of many of the same academic goals as their peers without disabilities.

Behavior and Social Skills

Parents and teachers of children with autism and pervasive developmental disorders are particularly concerned about reducing unacceptable and deviant behaviors (e.g., self-injurious behaviors, self-stimulation), while increasing desirable behaviors that occur too infrequently (e.g., appropriate peer social interactions). Accordingly, education and training often include a great deal of behavior and social skills development. Again, individual programs vary in this regard, depending on students' needs. However, because this area is so important and so basic to autism intervention, it constitutes a significant part of most curricula. A primary method of instruction for accomplishing this goal involves use of behavior modification, which is discussed later in this chapter.

Communication and Language Skills

As with behavior and social skills, almost all children and youth with autism demonstrate speech and language problems. As defined earlier, *speech* refers to forming and using oral sounds (i.e., making and using correct speech sounds in communication), whereas *language* is a general term that relates to using communication systems. Children with language deficits may lack spoken language; parrot what others say; fail to use appropriate nonverbal communication skills, such as eye contact and facial expression; or generally have difficulty communicating with others.

Like other curriculum areas, communication and language programs are individualized based on students' needs. Thus, a student who has difficulty using pronouns (e.g., refers to himself as "you") would have a different program from that of a nonverbal student.

For lower functioning and nonverbal students, speech and language programs often start by training students to sit in a chair, attend to their teacher (i.e., make eye contact), model a trainer (e.g., touch their head when the trainer touches his or her head), follow simple commands (e.g., "Sit down," "Come here"), and avoid engaging in deviant behaviors. Many experts agree that, without these basic skills, children and youth are unable to profit from training.

Language training for nonverbal and lower functioning children may include object use training. In this type of training, students are shown objects (e.g., a ball) and a demonstration of each object's function, followed by cues to perform (e.g., "roll ball"). Such training expands children's language, preparing them for advanced programs.

Nonverbal and lower functioning children may also receive motor and vocal imitation training. Students are trained to imitate the trainer's motor movements (e.g., child touches trainer's shoulders in response to trainer touching his) and the trainer's sounds. Imitations of basic sounds may then be shaped into words. For example, once a child is able to say "ba" upon command, that sound may be shaped into "ball" and other meaningful words. These students may also be taught a variety of *receptive language skills*, such as following directions and instructions and identifying objects and pictures. *Expressive language skills* are often taught by teaching children to point at specified items, imitate sounds and words, label objects and pictures, and verbally request desired items.

For students who have been unable to acquire spoken language, nonverbal communication programs may be used. Such programs may involve instructing students to use signs as well as communication boards, which include picture and object boards. These programs teach children and youth to communicate their needs by pointing to pictures or objects. For instance, a nonverbal adolescent might point to a photograph of a drinking fountain to express that she is thirsty, or a child may learn to exchange an icon representing "toilet" to indicate his need to use the restroom. Augmentative communication systems, involving use of typewriters or computers, are commonly used with some children and youth to allow them to interact with others. Although communication boards and other augmentative communication systems are often viewed as alternatives to teaching children to talk, they may actually stimulate verbalizations. That is, some children and youth begin talking after being trained to sign, use a communication board, or communicate via a typewriter or word processor.

Children and youth who are verbal also receive speech and language training. Programs include training children to identify and label objects and pictures, and to use their language to meet their needs (e.g., obtain desired objects) and engage in social interaction with peers. Thus, these speech and language programs emphasize instruction in the use of communication skills to deal with the world. By using language to express their needs and to communicate with others, students make language a functional tool that improves with practice.

Speech and language training is carried out by a variety of individuals in a variety of settings. That is, speech and language training does not occur only when a speech pathologist takes a student to therapy (pathologists often conduct their training in the classroom or home). Communication training is so important and so integral to autistic students' development that teachers, therapists, and others provide speech and language training whenever they are with students. To ensure such a generalized approach, speech pathologists often serve as consultants to teachers, parents, and family members by suggesting procedures they may use to stimulate speech and language. (Additional information related to speech and language training is provided in Chapter 7.)

Self-Help and Independent Living Skills

Instructing children and youth with autism in self-help skills (i.e., skills needed to meet their own needs, such as bathing, grooming, toothbrushing, hygiene, dressing, eating, toileting) and to perform activities that will allow them to live more independently (e.g., using public transportation) assists them in positively responding to their disability and, ultimately, in leading more productive and normal lives. Often children and youth with autism fail to acquire skills that normally developing children master (e.g., dressing themselves), thus making them dependent on others and, therefore, more "handicapped" than they might otherwise be. Indeed, although a child with autism may have a disability, the role of education is, in large measure, designed to assure that he or she is not handicapped more than absolutely necessary. Consequently, education and training programs should be designed to train children and youth in those skills that most directly help them and their families live more normal lives. Parents and families should expect that at least a part of their children's education and training will involve independent living and self-help instruction. Not every student will require such training; however, for those who do, it is an extremely important program component.

Prevocational and Vocational Skills

As adults, many individuals with autism can be expected to work in sheltered workshops for citizens with disabilities, assume noncompetitive employment positions, or seek supported types of competitive jobs (i.e., supportive employment). Supportive employment offers the services of a job coach or other assistance to aid individuals with autism in understanding and completing their work assignments. Not every child diagnosed as having autism will need to be in a sheltered workshop or other type of supportive employment. Indeed, many high functioning persons with autism will lead relatively normal lives, including in the area of employment. However, some will be unable to work in "regular" jobs and, therefore, need vocational training to acquire the skills required for post-school life, including employment.

Vocational training for students with autism is highly individualized. Thus, some students may be involved in technical fields (e.g., computer training), whereas others require more basic training (e.g., learning to do simple packaging). Nonetheless, a core of common elements underlies vocational training: attending to a task without engaging in disruptive behavior; following directions; imitating motor movements (e.g., assembling an object in the same manner as a trainer); successfully completing match-to-sample activities (e.g., setting a table according to a place-setting model); successfully completing discrimination tasks (e.g., sorting various items according to their function); and accurately and independently repeating specified tasks for set periods of time.

As school-age youth with autism become older, they may be placed in vocational education settings and otherwise assisted with transition planning and training. That is, their programs may concentrate on enhancing their vocational skills, making them better able to enter work and vocational programs, and to live maximally productive and independent lives subsequent to leaving school.

It must be emphasized again that, although not every child and adolescent with autism needs a vocational curriculum, so many do that curriculum in this area is a basic element of most students' programs. Similarly, most individuals with autism require transition planning and support when they complete school.

Academic Skills

To the extent that they are able, students with autism pursue a curriculum similar to that of their peers without disabilities. Thus, at the elementary level they may study reading, writing, arithmetic, English, spelling, social studies, and so on. At the secondary level, they pursue a course of study consistent with their abilities and interests. For students whose disability necessitates deviation from a standard academic curriculum, special academic goals and objectives may be developed. For instance, academics may focus on recognizing functional words (e.g., *exit, poison, men, women, bus stop*), writing one's name, and learning money skills. Finally, programs for students with severe impairments may put little emphasis on academics. That is, rather than focusing on English, history, and math, these students may be involved in learning to communicate and interact appropriately with others, in addition to developing vocational, self-care, and other skills.

Motor Skills

Motor relates to coordination, muscle strength, and control and direction of muscles of the body. Although every child and youth diagnosed as having autism will not experience motor problems, such deficits are not uncommon. Accordingly, many children and youth need programs to improve their muscle strength, physical coordination, and motor dexterity. The content of such programs is frequently developed by specialists, such as physical therapists, occupational therapists, and physicians; however, the programs themselves may be carried out by others, including teachers, parents, and family members.

In addition to programs designed to improve motor problems, students with autism, like all children, benefit from physical education, leisure skill training, and opportunities to interact with peers in game and play situations. Such opportunities provide them a chance to develop new skills and interests, as well as to apply previously developed skills to new situations (e.g., social interaction skills in a group play setting). Motor and physical activities, including sports activities, board games, and various leisure activities, should be included as a part of each youngster's education and training program, regardless of age or severity of disability.

BEHAVIORAL INTERVENTIONS

Basic Attending and Learning Skills

Parents and teachers frequently report that children and youth with autism lack basic attending and learning skills, such as motivation to learn new behaviors, attention, and other behaviors that are compatible with adaptive learning. It is sometimes difficult to determine whether a student's deficits are a result of an inability to understand and complete tasks (e.g., a student is unable to identify objects) or stem from resistance to following instructions (e.g., the student is capable of identifying objects, but avoids doing so). Indeed, compliance is a major issue in planning for and instructing students with autism. Thus, it is frequently part of students' programs.

Development of basic attending and compliance involves using the following general method. First, a student is told to attend, in the form of a verbal or nonverbal cue. The trainer (e.g., therapist, parent, teacher) gives a command and waits for the child to attend (e.g., eyes on adult, hands on lap). At this stage, behavior may need to be shaped for some. A typical instructional sequence for attending follows:

ADULT: "Tony, get ready." [Adult models attending behavior by placing hands on own lap and making eye contact with child.]

CHILD: No response.

ADULT: "Tony, get ready." [Adult prompts attention by touching child's hands.]

CHILD: No response.

ADULT: "Tony, get ready." [Adult moves student's hands to child's lap, holding hands there until they remain in the desired location for 2 seconds.]

In the example, the adult initially used a verbal request to get the student's attention. Only after the child was unable or unwilling to pay attention did the adult use a prompt and, ultimately, physical assistance. This process is repeated as needed (i.e., as an initial training step, children must demonstrate attention each time).

Subsequent to gaining the child's attention, the trainer gives instructions to perform. At first, commands are simple and straightforward (e.g., "Give me blue"). Although usually verbal, instructions may be nonverbal (e.g., signs) if required to assure the child's understanding.

Basic attending and learning skill training commands are always presented in a hierarchical manner, starting at a level that allows children and youth to perform independently. Hence, children are given the opportunity to perform tasks without prompts. If children are unable or unwilling to perform correctly, increasing levels of assistance are provided. For example, if a child does not perform successfully on her own, a trainer provides a prompt or cue. If a prompt does not result in correct performance, the adult helps the child complete the task, a procedure known as *put through*. Thus, put through means that a child is physically assisted in doing a task (e.g., a teacher takes a child by the hand and assists him in pointing to the correct answer).

An adult often gives a child a single command until independent performance is obtained. For example, a teacher might work with a student on "Give me blue" until the student is able to give the teacher a blue block on command independently. When this is achieved, the teacher may move to another task (e.g., "Give me red").

The obvious goal of basic attending and learning skill training is to have students follow directions and participate in desired educational activities. These skills are so basic to learning that little occurs without them.

The essential elements of the aforementioned strategy for developing attending and learning skills with children and youth with autism are widely used as an instructional procedure for children and adults, both with and without disabilities. Coaches, for example, frequently use such procedures with normally developing children and youth. Specifically, they provide cues for attention (e.g., whistle for attention), model a correct response (e.g., show the players how to shoot a free throw in basketball), and provide physical prompts (e.g., physically assist players in properly holding the ball).

Also, the procedures used by professionals to develop basic attending and learning skills can, and frequently are, used by parents and families. Indeed, parents and families often seek professional guidance in hopes of making their children more compliant and amenable to instruction. Accordingly, parents and family members may be instructed in the aforementioned training procedures, thereby assisting their offspring in becoming better able to live successfully in a normalized environment.

Of course, not every parent or family member of a child or youth with autism can appropriately or effectively carry out basic attending, training, tutoring, and other treatment programs. Due to such factors as interest, time, resources, temperament, motivation, and a host of others, some parents and family members will not, or should not, serve as trainers. However, given the requisite interest and aptitude, parents and family members may use compliance training to facilitate the growth and development of autistic children.

Behavior Modification

Behavior modification, also known as *behaviorism*, *applied behavior analysis*, and *operant conditioning*, describes a set of principles and procedures for understanding and systematically changing behavior. Most educational and training programs and intervention procedures for children and youth with autism are based on behavioral principles. Similarly, most therapists (e.g., speech pathologists, occupational therapists) use behavioral procedures when working with individuals with autism. For instance, proponents of applied behavior analysis will systematically teach incremental segments of a desired behavior using a set sequence of instructions, methods, and reinforcement, and regularly assess students' progress through data inspection.

Unlike traditional therapeutic approaches, which consider maladaptive behaviors and learning problems as symptoms of underlying psychological and emotional problems, users of behaviorally based methods view problems as targets for change. That is, users of behavioral techniques do not support the notion that learning difficulties and other problem behaviors, including those associated with autism, are signs of deep-seated emotional conflict, but rather consider them learned patterns of maladaptive behavior. According to this model, therefore, developing maladaptive behaviors is no different from learning adaptive responses. For instance, children with autism may learn that they are able to manipulate their parents through tantrums or that kicking peers is an effective way to control others. Behavior modification principles are used to decrease maladaptive behaviors and increase learning and other adaptive responses that occur infrequently. In the preceding examples, tantrums, kicking, and learning difficulties are viewed not as signs of underlying psychological problems, but as *the problems*, and procedures are subsequently developed to modify these behaviors.

Applied Behavior Analysis

Effective instructional procedures and curricula are keys to success for children and youth with autism. One important tool for individualizing for students' educational and other needs is applied behavior analysis. The term refers to pinpointing and thoroughly analyzing a behavior to be learned, including identifying subcomponents of a skill (i.e., task analysis); teaching the subcomponents of the skill to a set criterion, using clear and systematic presentation of tasks and cues, modeling, prompting, shaping, reinforcing, and so forth; continuously evaluating a student's performance; and making instructional decisions based on data.

Applied behavior analysis is not used exclusively to educate and train students with autism. Rather, applied behavior analysis is a method that has been used with any number of individuals of varying abilities and needs. Nonetheless, use of this method bodes well for students with autism, and there is overwhelming evidence that applied behavior analysis is an effective tool for these students.

In spite of its positive record and potential, however, applied behavior analysis has been the subject of much recent controversy. Debate over the use of this tool is associated with the outcomes related to use of applied behavior analysis, and the extent to which applied behavior analysis should be used with students with autism.

The debate over outcomes associated with the use of applied behavior analysis with children with autism was accelerated with the publication of a 1987 study by Lovaas. Lovaas reported that preschool children who were exposed to intensive and systematic home-based applied behavior analysis training programs had a significant chance of "recovering" from autism (i.e., being cured of the disorder). Lovaas's highly optimistic outcome claims remain unvalidated, and there is general agreement that the study on which the claim was made was limited and flawed. Thus, although applied behavior analysis is clearly an extremely useful tool, there is much skepticism over this tool's actually being a cure for autism.

The extent to which applied behavior analysis should be used with students with autism, the second controversy, is also connected to the work of Lovaas and other strong proponents of applied behavior analysis. Based on the contention that applied behavior analysis is the key to successful outcomes with students with autism, including a cure for the disorder, some advocates (e.g., Maurice, 1996) have positioned that all students with autism should exclusively be instructed via use of applied behavior analysis. Indeed, some have advocated for one-to-one adult support personnel to work with students with autism to exclusively implement applied behavior analysis programs. The controversy, then, relates to exclusive use of applied behavior analysis, including abandonment of all other methods, and assigning each student with autism to a separate teacher.

The debate over the appropriate use of applied behavior analysis is likely to continue. Although we believe that applied behavior analysis is an important tool, we think it is unlikely a cure for autism. Moreover, we think professionals and parents would be prudent not to overly rely on this tool. A number of other methods can successfully be used with students with autism, and they all deserve consideration. Indeed, applied behavior analysis works well with *some* students and *some* behaviors, but not all (e.g., teaching social skills can often be best undertaken using procedures other than applied behavior analysis). Finally, we think it is counterproductive and ineffective to arbitrarily assign an adult to work one-to-one with all students with autism, since such a procedure may increase prompt dependency and impede skill generalization and transfer. Indeed, we think that identifying the appropriate role for use of applied behavior analysis is among the most significant challenges that will face parents and professionals in the 21st century.

Basic Principles of Behavior Modification

As mentioned, a basic rule of behavior modification is that maladaptive behaviors are learned and maintained in the same way as adaptive behaviors. Further, users of behavior modification do not accept the theory that problem behaviors are caused by unobservable psychological factors (e.g., a child's anger at a parent results in a permanent loss of language). Accordingly, maladaptive behaviors of children and youth with autism can be unlearned and replaced with more adaptive and functional behaviors. Similarly, children can be taught to engage in desired school-related behaviors through systematic manipulation of instructional methods and curricula.

As a result of this fundamental principle, behavior modification deals with specific, observable behaviors. Behaviors identified for change, therefore, must be overt (e.g., failure to complete assignments, kicking another child) and measurable. *Measurable* refers to behaviors that can be counted or measured. Thus, instead of targeting self-stimulation for change (self-stimulation means different things to different people, making it difficult to measure), the target for change might be body rocking at home. Body rocking at home is a behavior that can be seen, agreed upon, and counted.

According to another principle of behavior modification, it is not necessary to assign a diagnostic label (e.g., autism, pervasive developmental disorder) to children or youth in order to teach or develop intervention programs for them. Therefore, behavior modification practitioners attempt to improve behaviors that interfere with a child's adjustment without becoming overly concerned with how the child is diagnosed. For example, a child who avoids interacting with peers would be exposed to procedures designed to increase appropriate peer interactions. Whether the child had previously been identified as autistic would probably not affect the manner in which the program is applied.

According to behaviorally based principles, the effectiveness of an intervention method is not known until it has been tried. Thus, a procedure that has proven effective with one child cannot automatically be assumed to work equally well with another. Only by systematically applying and evaluating a behavior management procedure can its effectiveness be determined.

A final assumption of behavior modification is that most behaviors are controlled by events and experiences that happen before and after them. A child's tantrums, for example, might be the result of parental attention to crying and screaming. The significance of this principle for successfully modifying behavior is great: By isolating and changing the events that support a behavior identified for change (e.g., attention), behavior problems may be replaced with more adaptive behavior.

A variety of persons use behavior modification, including teachers, parents, therapists, and vocational trainers. Although successful use of these methods requires training and guidance, one need not be a professional to use them. In fact, children often show the greatest gains when a variety of persons, including parents and family members, make consistent use of behaviorally based methods.

Procedure for Using Behaviorally Based Methods

Four primary steps underlie successful use of behaviorally based procedures: (a) identify, define, and measure a behavior to be increased or decreased; (b) determine where, when, and with whom a target behavior occurs; (c) identify factors that may be promoting or maintaining a target behavior; and (d) apply appropriate intervention procedures. As noted earlier, these steps may be applied by a number of persons, including parents and professionals.

Identifying, Defining, and Measuring a Behavior

In accordance with the notion that problem behaviors are not symptoms of underlying difficulties, individuals who use behavior modifiers attempt to change (i.e., increase or decrease) the behaviors that interfere with a child's or adolescent's adjustment and to facilitate learning. Thus, *specific, precisely defined behaviors* are targeted for change. Examples of such behaviors include failure to follow parents' or teachers' commands, self-stimulatory hand flapping, hitting another person, or a host of self-help, language, vocational, and preacademic or academic skills (e.g., matching items to a sample, discrimination). All these behaviors may be measured; that is, a teacher, therapist, or parent can count the number of times they occur and can share with others their observations and interventions without the interference of subjective interpretation and misunderstanding.

Clark-Hall et al. (1976) recommended that behavioral targets include four basic parts: (1) identification of the person for whom the program is being developed; (2) description of the target behavior; (3) specification of when the target behavior will be observed; and (4) determination of where the target behavior will be observed. The following are examples of target responses containing the aforementioned elements.

- *Self-stimulation:* Use of matching-task materials by Leon in a manner other than that modeled by the teacher during daily classroom vocational activities from 1:10 to 2:05 p.m. Self-stimulation includes placing task materials in his mouth or waving materials in front of his face.
- *Noise making:* This behavior is defined as Lana's making an audible noise by bringing her foot or leg in contact with her desk during all classroom activities (8:15 to 2:45 p.m).

After a target behavior has been identified, observation and measurement strategies are planned. Typically, observations are made by means of frequency counts (the times a target behavior occurs), duration recordings (the length of time a target behavior occurs), or the occurrence of target responses within segments of a specified time frame (interval and time sampling).

Social validity is an important consideration in selecting target behaviors. Students with autism have myriad needs in a variety of cognitive, social, language, and other areas. Social validity refers to selecting for change those responses that have the greatest potential for significant changes in children's and families' lives.

Identifying Environmental and Situational Contexts of Targeted Behaviors

As part of thoroughly understanding a target behavior, the person attempting to bring about a change must be familiar with the setting in which the behavior occurs and the circumstances surrounding it. For example, a child who is noncompliant only in the presence of a baby-sitter would probably undergo a different intervention program than a child who displays such behavior around a number of people. Similarly, an adolescent who has behavior problems only during the dinner hour or in school would be dealt with differently than somebody who exhibits problem behaviors across different times and settings.

Related to children and youth with autism, this step involves determining whether a target behavior occurs primarily at certain times of the day (e.g., after lunch); in certain settings (e.g., unstructured group time in regular education classrooms); in certain classes or subjects (e.g., math); in the presence of particular people (e.g., paraprofessionals); under certain conditions (e.g., transitions from one classroom activity to another); or variably or consistently across settings, people, and situations.

Conducting a Functional Analysis of a Target Behavior

As noted earlier, behavior modification is based on the assumption that individuals learn from experience to do particular things in particular ways. Thus, a toddler may learn that banging his head against a wall is an excellent way to gain his parents' attention (i.e., whenever he bangs his head, someone attends to him) or that hitting allows him to control or escape from an undesired situation. Not all behaviors are so simply analyzed; however, identifying factors associated with the occurrence of a problem behavior is important. Accordingly, behavior modification involves attempting to uncover those factors that may be controlling a child's behavior and, subsequently, establishing the most effective and efficient intervention program that relates to these factors.

Common functions of behaviors of concern to educators and parents associated with children and youth with autism include attention seeking (e.g., a child engages in an unacceptable behavior to gain the teacher's attention); escape or avoidance (e.g., a child engages in an aggressive behavior in an attempt to avoid a disliked training activity); control (an adolescent engages his mother in an argument for the purpose of frustrating her); and self-expression (e.g., a nonverbal child is self-aggressive during schedule disruptions at school because he lacks more appropriate ways of communicating his frustration related to changes in regular classroom activities). The complexity of human behavior, including that of individuals with autism, makes it unlikely that professionals and parents will definitively understand the functions of a behavior. However, identifying major factors that influence a person's behavior and gaining an understanding of the outcomes that occur subsequent to a particular child's response patterns are important determinants of successful program development and implementation.

Based on observations and other diagnostic methods, hypotheses are formed regarding the functions of target behaviors. For instance, professionals and parents may hypothesize that a student's self-stimulatory verbal behavior during independent work times at school may be related to her desire for one-to-one adult attention. To test this hypothesis, the student's teacher first confirms the conditions under which these responses occur (i.e., when she is assigned to do independent classroom work). The teacher then systematically provides intermittent social reinforcement for independent work. Based on the student's response to this trial program, an intervention program is implemented and evaluated.

Selecting and Applying Interventions

The responses of children and youth with autism may be changed by systematic use of consequences and antecedent modifications (see Table 6.1). *Consequences* refer to positive or negative events that happen *after* a child has engaged in a behavior that someone wants to increase or decrease. For example, a child may receive a hug for correctly modeling the motor response of a trainer (e.g., raising arms above the head, as shown by a trainer). In a classroom a student may receive additional free time after she successfully finishes her daily math assignments. Similarly, a student may lose his recess time whenever he engages in self-injurious behavior. Successful use of consequences requires that an agreed-upon intervention plan be followed each time a specified behavior occurs. As shown in Table 6.1, consequences can be of three types: reinforcers, planned ignoring (extinction), and behavior reduction methods (negative consequences).

Interventions may also take the form of *antecedent modifications*. Antecedents are environmental conditions and other factors that are used to obtain desired responses through manipulation of environmental factors. That is, unlike consequences, which follow target behaviors, antecedents precede responses. For example, a teacher might

TABLE 6.1
Summary of Behavioral Intervention Options

Consequences
Reinforcers
Social
Tangible
Contingent activities
Token systems
Differential reinforcement
Planned Ignoring (Extinction)
Behavior Reduction
Response cost
Time-out
Overcorrection
Antecedent Modifications
Environmental changes (e.g., seating, curriculum, schedules)

move a child who is easily distracted by noises in the hallway of his school to a less distracting area of the room, instead of attempting to shape his attention through the use of consequences.

Reinforcers. Reinforcers are consequences that increase the likelihood of future occurrences of a behavior. That is, children and youth are rewarded for specified behaviors to increase the chances that the desired behavior recurs. For example, a teacher may praise a child each time she verbalizes, or a youngster may be allowed to play a computer game at school if he completes an assignment within a specified time. In the preceding examples, teacher praise for verbalizations and playing with a computer for successfully completing an assignment function as reinforcers if they increase the specified target behavior.

Reinforcers for children and adolescents usually fall into the following categories: (a) social rewards (e.g., hugs and verbal praise for desired behavior); (b) tangible rewards (e.g., edibles and toys for displaying specified behavior); (c) contingent activities (e.g., recess and free time for compliance); (d) token systems (e.g., child receives tokens or similar items for desired behavior, which may be exchanged for various reinforcers); and (e) differential reinforcement. Differential reinforcement is a frequently preferred reinforcement method. This procedure involves reinforcing behaviors that are incompatible or appropriate alternatives to unacceptable responses. Thus, maladaptive or inappropriate behaviors are weakened by having parents and professionals attend to and reinforce suitable alternative behaviors. Differential reinforcement takes several forms: reinforcing individuals for engaging less often in undesired behaviors; reinforcing individuals for engaging in behaviors that are incompatible with an unacceptable response (e.g., a child prone to self-stimulatory hand waving while waiting in line at school is reinforced for placing her hands in her pockets); and reinforcing individuals for engaging in behavior that is more acceptable than the undesired one (e.g., a child who is prone to self-stimulatory spinning and jumping at recess is reinforced for participating in a group jumping game).

Planned Ignoring. Children and youth with autism sometimes seek attention by displaying unacceptable behavior. For example, a student may get out of his assigned seat without permission to gain teacher attention or throw a tantrum to control his parents' actions. Planned ignoring (extinction) involves systematic withdrawal of attention for unacceptable behavior followed by replacement of attention for desired behavior. Using this approach, a child may be ignored when she has tantrums but attended to when she engages in acceptable social behavior. Extinction may not work with every child. However, for children who are motivated by attention, it is usually an effective consequence.

Behavior Reduction. Behavior reduction (punishment) means different things to different people (e.g., a trip to the woodshed, withdrawal of privileges). Related to behavior modification, behavior reduction (or negative consequences) refers to any event that decreases a behavior it follows. For example, a child who reduces noncompliance as a result of losing TV privileges is said to have his behavior modified through negative consequences. Behavior reduction programs for children and adolescents with autism often involve response cost, time-out, and overcorrection. Spanking and other forms of corporal punishment are rarely considered appropriate forms of behavior modification punishment, and aversive procedures may be appropriate only in the most extreme situations, if at all.

RESPONSE COST. Response cost refers to systematic removal of rewards when specified unacceptable behaviors occur. For example, children may lose TV or other privileges for failing to abide by established rules at home.

TIME-OUT. Time-out involves removing children and youth from reinforcing situations whenever they display specified maladaptive behaviors. Time-out may require children and youth to sit quietly in a corner for short periods of time following unacceptable behaviors or otherwise restrict them from participating in reinforcing activities or being in reinforcing environments. For example, a child may be required to quietly lay her head on her desk for 3 minutes whenever she throws an object in class. Time-out has been used successfully by both professionals and parents. However, in spite of its popularity, time-out may not be effective with all children and adolescents with autism. Unless a child with autism is removed from a reinforcing setting for specified behavior, time-out will be ineffective. For example, if a student with autism enjoys sitting in a time-out room while engaging in self-stimulation, it is highly unlikely that such a time-out program can be used to reduce unwanted behavior.

OVERCORRECTION. As a behavioral intervention procedure, overcorrection consists of two main parts, *restitution* and *positive practice*. The first, restitution, requires that individuals who disturb or destroy things clean up or otherwise restore a situation to its original state. For example, an adolescent who purposely throws food on the floor may be made to clean the soiled area. The second, positive practice, requires that a child or youth practice an appropriate behavior related to a maladaptive response. Thus, the adolescent who throws food may be required to transfer blocks from one container to another for several minutes. In this case, transferring blocks is an alternative behavior to throwing. Overcorrection is often a time-consuming and complex process; however, it sometimes offers an effective management procedure for children and youth with behavior problems that are severe or that have been unresponsive to other intervention methods.

AVERSIVE CONDITIONING. Aversive conditioning refers to use of noxious or painful stimuli to reduce negative behaviors. That is, each time an individual engages in a previously specified, unwanted behavior (e.g., head banging), he or she receives a supposedly harmless, yet uncomfortable stimulus. Aversives include electric shock; foul-tasting substances, such as lemon juice; and other uncomfortable stimuli, such as water sprayed in the face.

Use of aversive procedures is highly controversial. Some professionals, parents, and advocacy groups strongly resist use of any aversive procedure, under any conditions. Others recommend use of aversives only in the most severe situations, such as in cases of self-injury or self-abuse. For instance, when an individual is apt to severely hurt himself by attempting to strike his eyes, aversive procedures might be recommended. If aversives are to be used with a child or adolescent with autism, this conditioning usually takes place in a restricted setting, such as a hospital or residential facility, and only with the permission of parents or a legal custodian and subject to close professional monitoring.

Antecedent Modifications. As opposed to using consequences, antecedent interventions operate by means of changing environmental conditions. Structuring or modifying environmental conditions is thus used to shape appropriate responses. For example, a teacher who determines that a student is less likely to be on task when seated next to a window might move the student's desk to another part of the room. Establishing and maintaining routines and schedules, establishing and following home and classroom performance expectations and rules, and consistent use of effective instructional curricula and methods are only a few of the antecedent strategies applied with children and youth with autism.

SOCIAL SKILLS TRAINING

Professionals agree that children and youth with autism experience social deficits, including developing and maintaining appropriate interpersonal relationships and responding to others. A number of experts, in fact, contend that social deficits are the most significant handicap experienced by persons with autism. For instance, parents of autistic children regularly report that their offspring are indifferent to attention and are generally oblivious to others, and teachers of these children often express concern over their avoidance of eye contact and social isolation. Even high functioning persons with autism are perceived to be socially peculiar. Hence, it is not surprising that parents and professionals agree that social skill enhancement efforts are an important part of these childrens' programs. That social interaction skill development of autistic children correlates positively with long-term success in living and working in normalized environments further emphasizes the need for attention in this domain. *Social interaction* refers to developing and maintaining positive and appropriate social relations with others, including making suitable social initiations and appropriately responding to social initiations of others.

There are two primary ways in which social skills are taught to children and youth with autism: *adult-mediated programs* and *peer-mediated interventions*. Adult-mediated procedures rely on an adult to train or prompt appropriate social behavior, whereas peer-mediated social interaction programs involve teaching peers of children with autism to initiate and prompt social behaviors, such as sharing, playing, and verbally interacting. Social interaction instruction can also be structured around instructional activities, especially peer tutoring.

Regardless of whether a program is adult or peer initiated, it should include several basic elements. First, the program should be designed to facilitate cooperation and interactions. That is, it should be engineered to facilitate contact and interactions between at least two people. Such a principle might appear to be so basic that it need not be stated; however, one need only consider that a number of so-called social interaction programs involve primarily passive observation skill development (e.g., sitting and watching others) or observing tapes of social interactions without ever making contact with another person. A second basic principle of social interaction programming is that programs should rely on age-appropriate activities and materials. Of course, consideration also must be made of individuals' interests and ability levels. Third, programs should be designed to generalize social interactions across settings and persons. Only through such efforts can skills learned in one setting be transferred to other situations and to interactions with different individuals. Finally, the social validity of any program must be considered. That is, the outcomes of the social skills training should be determined to be important and beneficial to the person with autism, nondisabled peers, family, and community. To this end, Simpson, Myles, Sasso, and Kamps (1997) suggested that persons who design social interaction programs pose the following question: Does the social interaction program increase friendships or relationships between persons with autism and the important people in their world?

Adult-Mediated Programs

Adult-mediated social interaction training programs primarily take one of two forms: direct skill instruction and antecedent prompting procedures. *Direct skill instruction* involves identifying important social skills needed for enhanced functioning; breaking down the skill into small units suitable for instruction; sequentially teaching each of the task-analyzed steps to criterion using modeling, repeated trials, prompts, and reinforcement with peers in the natural environment; and planning for skill generalization. For example, an adolescent might be taught to shoot baskets in the school gymnasium via modeling, shaping, prompting, and reinforcing her ball playing until she meets a specified criterion. Following this instruction, the student might be taught to initiate interactions with peers to engage in basket shooting. Such training might make use of socially responsive peers, an instructional script, role playing, practice, and playing ball with multiple peers in order to transfer the skills across persons.

Advantages of direct social interaction training are that this method assists children and youth with autism to learn a skill that they enjoy and that gives them control over when and where they participate in social interactions. Second, instruction that is based on task analysis, multiple practice sessions, prompts, shaping, and reinforcement strategies has been shown to be an effective social interaction intervention strategy. The primary disadvantage of a direct instruction approach to social interaction training relates to skill transfer and generalization. That is, learning a particular social skill with an adult in an instructional setting is no guarantee that that skill will be used in a natural setting.

Adult-mediated social interaction training programs can also be in the form of *antecedent prompts*. In accordance with this strategy, a teacher, parent, or other adult prompts a child to engage in some specified social behavior. The child is provided positive reinforcement upon occurrence of the desired response.

Adult-mediated social interaction training tends to yield best results when basic steps are followed. First, the individual with autism is paired with a peer in a play setting. The nondisabled peer is instructed to remain in proximity to the child with autism and, contingent upon the child's signaling a desire to engage in a specified game or social activity, to interact with the person. Most important, the adult involved in the program stays in the play area and provides periodic verbal prompts to the child with autism to engage in various interaction behaviors, such as initiating, sharing, and so forth. Subsequent to giving a verbal prompt, the adult provides praise, encouragement, and reinforcement. If the child fails to show the desired social response, the adult may repeat the prompt or physically assist the child. A popular example of this strategy involves having children with autism and nondisabled peers exchange various forms of physical affection (e.g., hugs, pats on the back) in response to songs, such as "If you're happy and you know it, shake your friend's hand."

Adult-mediated programs have been found to increase social interactions of children and youth with autism, especially when they include use of willing and socially competent peers in normalized environments. These programs also facilitate generalization of desired social responses to other settings and with other peers.

A weakness of adult-mediated programs is that adult prompts can disrupt ongoing and more naturally occurring social interactions and exchanges. Children who are exposed to adult-mediated social interaction training may also become prompt dependent; that is, they will initiate and respond only when instructed to do so by an adult.

Peer-Initiated Strategies

Peer-initiated social interaction training programs rely on socially competent peers, who are taught to initiate and encourage social interactions with children and youth with autism in natural settings, such as schools and communities. Following social interaction training, peers without disabilities are placed in natural settings for social activities with children and youth with autism.

Peer-directed programs have been shown to be extremely effective in producing desired social outcomes and peer acceptance of students with autism, especially when high-status peers are involved in interaction programs. The primary advantage of peer-initiated programs is that they rely on natural social environments and contexts. That is, rather than using contrived and artificial training conditions, these programs bring together individuals with autism and their peers in real life natural settings, thus ensuring realistic training and generalization conditions. The major weakness of peer-initiation programs is that generalization and maintenance evidence is limited.

Peer-Tutoring Programs

Peer-tutoring programs offer a means of both developing the academic and other cognitive skills of students with autism and providing opportunities for social interactions between general education peers and students with autism. Prior to the initiation of tutoring activities, general education peers are given an opportunity to become familiar with the characteristics of individuals with autism; and students with autism and their peers are given informal interaction opportunities. Following this orientation, peers are provided tutoring instructions, and structured, supervised, regularly occurring tutoring sessions are held.

Peer tutoring is an efficient means of increasing interactions between general education students and children with autism. On the other hand, a potential weakness of peer tutoring is that it creates inequitable relationships between students with disabilities and their nondisabled peers. That is, nonreciprocal tutoring arrangements, by their very nature, create environments in which one student is in control of another. Thus, while peer tutoring creates opportunities for social interaction, it also presents situations that may potentially produce social interaction challenges.

MEDICAL TREATMENTS FOR AUTISM

As noted previously, there are no cures for autism. Thus, physicians are unable to write prescriptions for medications that will cure the disorder. Nonetheless, medications are sometimes used with children and youth with disabilities, including those with autism. Although not cures, such medications sometimes assist children and youth in dealing with their disabilities. They are most effective when used in conjunction with other treatments, such as education and behavior modification.

Because children and youth diagnosed with autism may experience seizure disorders, antiseizure drugs are among the most common medications prescribed. Drugs may also be prescribed to alleviate symptoms associated with autism. However, the utility of drug treatment in reducing symptoms varies from individual to individual, and the utility of a number of drugs with individuals with autism is unclear.

Anticonvulsant Medications

As noted previously, individuals diagnosed with autism may experience seizures. It is not uncommon for complete control of seizures to never be achieved; for multiple anticonvulsants to be needed to achieve satisfactory control; or for physicians to accept occasional seizures over prolonged use of anticonvulsants, which tend to cause behavioral and cognitive side effects.

The most commonly prescribed antiseizure medications include phenobarbital, Tegretal, Dilantin, Depakene, Depakote, Clonopin, Mysoline, Zarontine, Felbatol, and Neurontin. As noted above, these medications are often associated with significant side effects.

Tranquilizer Medications

Major tranquilizers, or neuroleptics, are sometimes prescribed for children and youth with autism to reduce hyperactivity, self-stimulatory behavior, tics, emotional outbursts, and bizarre and aggressive behavior. Specific forms of these medications include Thorazine, Mellaril, Trilafon, Stelazine, and Prolixin. A butyrophenone (a neuroleptic drug), Haldol, has also been successfully used. Although debate continues over the use of these medications with children with autism, a number of physicians contend that they may reduce disorganized thinking and generally help manage individuals with severe behavior problems. These drugs are often associated with severe side effects, in particular, marked drowsiness, blurred vision, impaired motor performance, anemia, and tremors.

Stimulant Medications

Central nervous system stimulant medications are a popular intervention for children with attention deficits and hyperactivity. These drugs are thought to stimulate concentration and attention, thereby reducing unnecessary activity, overactivity, and behavioral problems. Although experts are unable to explain precisely how the drugs work, they do seem to have a positive effect on some children.

Common central nervous system stimulants include Ritalin, Cylert, and Dexedrine. The effectiveness of these medications with children and youth with autism is currently a matter of debate. Some physicians contend that these drugs have little therapeutic effect on children with autism. Others view these drugs as potentially beneficial, especially for higher functioning individuals. Side effects of these medications tend to be minimal, although there have been reports of appetite loss, irritability, anxiousness, and insomnia.

Antidepressant Medications

Tricyclics are the class of antidepressant drug most commonly prescribed for children, including those diagnosed with autism. This class of medication includes Elavil, Norpramin, Pamelor, Anafranil, and Tofranil. Tofranil is considered to be the most commonly used pediatric medication.

Antidepressants are prescribed for a variety of problems, including attention deficits, hyperactivity, enuresis, school phobia, sleep disturbance, and aggression. Anafranil is also commonly used to treat individuals with problems related to obsessions. Side effects of these drugs include nausea, loss of appetite, dry mouth, irritability, insomnia, and fatigue.

Antianxiety Medications

Problems related to anxiety and stress may be treated with medications such as Librium, Valium, Xanax, Atavin, Atarax, and Equani. These drugs are also sometimes used to induce sleep. Antianxiety drugs are occasionally associated with the following side effects: fatigue, drowsiness, and loss of coordination. There tend to be fewer side effects associated with antianxiety medications than with neuroleptic tranquilizers.

Opiate Antagonist Medications

The drug Naltrexone was originally developed to treat persons addicted to opiate drugs, such as heroin. This medication, which works by reducing naturally occurring opiate levels in the brain, has been associated with some experimental success, including in facilitating social interests and reducing aberrant behavior. However, this drug remains experimental, and its utility in treating children with autism is unknown.

Other Medication Treatments

One medication that has been used experimentally with children and youth with autism is *fenfluramine*. Originally designed to treat obesity in adults, this drug is thought to reduce serotonin levels (children and youth with autism sometimes demonstrate elevated levels of serotonin, a neurotransmitter thought to affect sleep, cognitive ability, and appetite). By reducing serotonin levels in children with autism, fenfluramine was believed by some to be able to improve behavior. Results of the use of this medication are mixed (Tsai, 1998). Although some initial reports were positive, more recent investigations have shown the drug to be generally ineffective in improving the behavior and learning of children with autism.

Beta blockers decrease blood pressure and heart rate, and have been suggested to be effective in treating severe aggressiveness. The usefulness of beta blockers with individuals with autism is unclear, and a number of side effects are associated with this drug.

Lithium has been used to treat aggressiveness and hyperactivity. Although side effects of this drug are typically minimal, the utility of this medication with children and youth with autism is unknown.

Risperdal is a relatively new medication developed to treat schizophrenia. Its effectiveness with children with autism is unknown.

Megavitamin therapy, including large doses of vitamin B, vitamin C, and various minerals, have been used to treat children and youth with autism for decades. Although claims of improvement have been associated with these supplements, there is no solid scientific evidence to suggest they have significant beneficial behavioral and cognitive effects. Research in this area continues.

Role of Drug Intervention Methods

Medications can have profound impact on health and behavior. Accordingly, drug treatment must be considered a viable option for treating children and youth with autism. However, drugs are not a cure for autism and must, therefore, be used only to support other treatments, such as behavior modification and education. Additionally, drugs are not appropriate or effective with all children and many drugs are in experimental stages. Consequently, any drug treatment effort must be systematically evaluated and monitored. For every child or adolescent treated with medications, medical personnel, therapists, educators, psychologists, and families must work closely together to determine the drug's benefit.

PSYCHOTHERAPY

Psychotherapy refers to any type of psychological or psychiatric treatment that is based on verbal and nonverbal communication. Although different types of psychotherapy exist, they generally rely on a discussion or interaction process; that is, they aim at improving behavior and mental health by having the person talk about personal issues and concerns. Thus, individuals are treated through discussions of their behavior, feelings, and motivations. Discussions may take place in individual sessions with a therapist or in groups of individuals having similar problems. With children or youth for whom talking does not come easily or who are too young to discuss their problems, play is used to allow them to express their feelings, conflicts, and concerns. With some forms of psychotherapy, therapists attempt to help children and youth gain insight, that is, to recognize, understand, and accept their feelings and motivations, including unconscious urges and drives, and thereby gain improved emotional health and behavior. To achieve such insight and understanding, children and youth examine past emotional experiences, sometimes experiences of which they may not be conscious.

A basic prerequisite of psychotherapy is that individuals have the potential for self-understanding and insight. Therefore, attention is focused on making children and youth aware of who they are and why they engage in certain behaviors, including responses considered to be maladaptive. Based on the underlying assumption that positive change can occur only with accurate self-understanding, children and adolescents are helped to understand their relationships with significant individuals in their lives, including parents and family members. Self-understanding and insight, however, require cognitive, language, and social skills that are not always present in children and youth with autism. As a result, most experts believe that psychotherapy has a limited role in treating children and youth with autism. In fact, it is most appropriate with higher functioning children and youth who have the skills needed to benefit from counseling and psychotherapy, and who need such treatment as a result of being aware of their disability. Indeed, as they become more aware of the differences between themselves and their normally developing peers, children and youth with autism may need to discuss their feelings and concerns with a therapist.

CONTROVERSIAL INTERVENTIONS

Controversial therapies and interventions have been a significant part of the history of children and youth with autism, more than any other disability. Perhaps this is because children and youth with autism have so many unique characteristics, including highly advanced splinter skills and other distinctive abilities that sometimes give them the appearance of having skills and knowledge that exceed their actual abilities. Whatever the reason, parents and professionals involved with persons with autism have been exposed to a never-ending stream of purported cures and unvalidated treatments. Indeed, autism appears to be fertile ground for even the most implausible of treatments.

We use the term *controversial treatments* to refer to unvalidated methodology or treatments (i.e., unproven methods), especially those promising extraordinary results. Included among controversial treatments are facilitated communication, auditory integration training, rhythmic and music-based treatments, vitamin interventions, vision therapies and tinted lenses, homeopathic remedies, and so forth. It is important to note that the term controversial treatments does not necessarily mean that the above-mentioned examples are ineffective or even fraudulent. Rather, the term means that the intervention lacks scientific support and validation. In some instances, these methods may prove to be effective treatments.

It is not surprising that some parents and professionals are willing to consider or use unproven interventions in an effort to improve the lives of persons with autism. As observed by Oliver Wendell Holmes, "There is nothing people will not do, there is nothing they have not done, to recover their health and save their lives." Indeed, there is evidence that people are willing to try any one of a number of untested medical treatments. Trachtman (1994), for example, reported that one of every three persons living in the United States uses unvalidated medical treatments, and that over $14 billion is spent on unproven interventions. In keeping with this trend, it is no surprise that many professionals and parents are willing to use unvalidated interventions, which typically offer hope for improvement that is far beyond that of traditional, scientifically valid methods. Indeed, the history of programs and treatments for individuals with autism is characterized by a never-ending search for methods that will lead a person with autism to normalcy.

Facilitated Communication

Facilitated communication is the best known recent example of an unvalidated intervention. Biklen (1992) is best known for his claim that facilitated communication (FC) permits individuals with autism to demonstrate unanticipated, and sometimes even extraordinary communication. In FC a nondisabled person provides hand-over-hand physical support to a person with autism or other disability. This support, typically offered so that a person with a disability can type or otherwise communicate, has purportedly resulted in persons with autism being able to type highly advanced thoughts and ideas. Thus, even after only minimal experience with FC, nonverbal individuals with autism who are thought to be severely retarded, have reportedly typed that they are socially competent, that they have normal intelligence, that they are trapped within a body that prohibits them from effectively communicating with others, due to a condition known as global apraxia.

An Australian by the name of Rosemary Crossley is given credit for developing facilitated communication. Crossley, who worked at an institution in Australia with individuals who were thought to be severely retarded, encountered a young woman, Anne, who had athetoid cerebral palsy. Crossley believed that Anne, who was unable to effectively communicate, feed herself, or walk, had more ability than she was given credit for, and that under the right conditions she was capable of communicating with others. By supporting her index finger, Crossley discovered that Anne was able to assist her in communicating through pointing. By shaping this initial response, Crossley was able to help Anne read and write (Crossley, 1992). Several years later, Crossley became affiliated with the Dignity through Education and Language Communication Centre (DEAL), an organization committed to assisting individuals with severe communication disorders. While affiliated with DEAL, Crossley reportedly used FC successfully with clients whose alleged intellectual impairments and physical disabilities made it difficult for them to use sign language and other commonly used augmentative communication devices (Biklen, 1992; Crossley, 1992).

Biklen introduced FC in the United States, where it became known as "the miracle intervention" that would permit persons with autism to lead normal lives. However, because of its dubious interactive features and lack of scientific support, FC almost immediately became surrounded by controversy. Because the procedure required that a nondisabled person hold the finger of a person with autism, who then communicated on a keyboard, many individuals were suspicious that nondisabled persons were actually the ones doing the typing. Indeed, scientific investigations have confirmed that when facilitators lack information needed to respond to queries posed to the individuals being facilitated, the individuals are unable to independently communicate.

Facilitated communication also has a dark side, as revealed in the case of a 29-year-old Australian woman with retardation who was removed from her home after communicating through FC that she was being sexually abused by her family and that she wanted to leave home to escape the abuse (Rimland, 1992). When she became distraught after being removed from her home, an evaluation of her ability to communicate by means of FC was ordered by the court. The woman's FC-assisted reports of abuse were seriously questioned when she was unable to answer a series of questions to which she reportedly knew the answers. The questions were taped by the facilitator with whom she worked, and this person assisted the woman in answering 40 questions under four separate conditions: (1) both the person with the disability and the facilitator were permitted to hear the questions; (2) while wearing earphones the facilitator and the person with the disability heard the same questions; (3) while wearing earphones the facilitator and the person with the disability heard different questions; and (4) while wearing earphones the facilitator heard only music, while the person with the disability heard the questions. Under Condition 1 the person with the disability correctly knew 8 to 9 out of 10 items; under Condition 2 she correctly answered 4 of 10 items; under Condition 3 she was unable to correctly answer her own questions, but correctly answered four questions that only the facilitator heard. Finally, under Condition 4 the person with the disability incorrectly answered every question. Based on these results, it was concluded that the woman was unable to independently communicate.

Facilitated communication remains in use today; however, it is generally viewed as an ineffective procedure. Thus, although it was initially viewed by many families and professionals as offering the best hope for significant improvement for persons with autism, and was made an integral part of many students' educational programs, it was later determined to be ineffective.

Using Invalidated Treatments with Persons with Autism

Families and professionals understandably would want to use the most current and promising procedures with children and youth diagnosed with autism. At the same time, many professionals and families associated with persons with autism are committed to using well-validated procedures. Indeed, unvalidated methods are likely to continue as autism interventions, and tension is likely to continue between those who seek novel, unproven treatments and those who advocate that only proven interventions should be used.

We feel that unproven methods must undergo scientific validation prior to being widely used with individuals with autism. Indeed, we consider it inappropriate and even reckless for individuals to subject persons with autism to unvalidated and unproven methods when they are presented as a cure or significant treatment. Although we believe that scientific evaluation is necessary to determine whether a controversial procedure can be effectively and legitimately used with persons with autism, we acknowledge that the legacy of using unproven methods will likely continue.

We also support scientific validation of unsupported and other controversial interventions because we think such a process will help alleviate users' vulnerability to pressure to obtain desired outcomes and the social ostracism of persons who fail to demonstrate desired results. Simpson and Myles (1995) reported a number of situations in which individuals who had failed to obtain the same level of success with facilitated communication as others were "severely criticized for 'not believing,' 'not doing it [facilitated communication] right,' or otherwise being subjected to emotional blackmail for failing to demonstrate the same degree of success with the procedure as others" (p. 7). They especially noted the negative experiences of one teacher:

> She underwent a "gut wrenching" self-examination of her beliefs and procedures related to using facilitated communication with one of her students at home each evening for an entire semester, because she was unable to obtain the same degree of communication success as several of her colleagues and the students' parents. She went on to say that her colleagues and the students' parents questioning of her belief in facilitated communication and her utilization of "correct methods" did little to assist her in responding to this dilemma. (p. 7)

We also think that failure to objectively and scientifically evaluate unproven methods will delay the legitimate acceptance and use of those methods that ultimately prove to be effective. Failing to objectively evaluate an ineffective intervention might also persuade families and professionals to emphasize use of an ineffective method at the expense of one that has more utility.

SUMMARY

In this chapter, we have identified and discussed major ways in which children and youth with autism are treated. In spite of the value of each, no single approach is complete or adequate with every child. Instead, the best treatment results when a combination of procedures is used. This requires cross-sections of professionals (e.g., educators, mental health workers, medical personnel) using a variety of treatment approaches (e.g., education, behavior modification) based on children's needs. Additionally, to ensure optimal progress, parents and families must play an integral part in the treatment and education process.

Language Interventions for Individuals with Autism

7

Laura Zionts and Suzanne Shellady

In this chapter we provide an overview of language development in children and youth with autism. We also describe intervention approaches used to facilitate language and communication skill development in children and youth with autism. The goal of this chapter is to provide an overview of the primary issues and topics in language and communication skill intervention and a preliminary understanding of the advantages and limitations of five intervention methods that may be useful when discussing options for educational programming.

CHARACTERISTICS OF LANGUAGE DEVELOPMENT IN CHILDREN WITH AUTISM

The many characteristics associated with the development of language and communication skills in children who have autism should first be considered in terms of the definition of autism. It is important to understand that autism is, at this point in time, not a specific disorder, but a combination of several factors present in a child's developmental history. As stated in Chapter 1, the criteria listed in the *Diagnostic and Statistical Manual of Mental Disorders–Fourth Edition* (American Psychiatric Association, 1994) that most directly relate to language and communication skills are (a) obvious impairment in the use of nonverbal communication behaviors (e.g., eye-to-eye gaze, facial expression, body postures, and gestures to regulate social behaviors); (b) delay in or total lack of development of appropriate, meaningful spoken language; (c) echolalia (the repeated use of spoken language out of context); and (d) delays, prior to age 3, in at least one of the following areas—social interaction, language used to communicate socially, or symbolic play. The language profiles and characteristics presented by children and youth with autism need to be examined on an individual basis to identify the most appropriate language curriculum and intervention strategies to meet each child's unique needs.

Frequently children who have autism are initially "discovered" when parents begin to realize that their child is not developing speech at a similar pace to other young children. Depending on the type of autism, an appropriate diagnosis can be made anywhere between 3 to 4 months and 3 to 4 years of age. As a result, the implementation of interventions to facilitate the development of language and social abilities can vary considerably.

Many professionals believe that children who have autism have an under- or undeveloped repertoire of all types of symbolic behavior; language is only one area in which this deficit manifests itself. Indeed, language is a system of symbolic representations used to convey meaning about concrete objects, people, events, time, or emotion. Children and youth who have autism are frequently quite concrete in their understanding and use of language. Thus, for example, they frequently have difficulty comprehending idioms and abstract statements (e.g., "It's raining cats and dogs").

? *What language skills are most functional for my child to learn?*

There are no hard and fast rules to determine what is most functional for your child, because what is functional for one child may not be functional for another. However, you can ask yourself some general questions when considering speech and language priorities for your child:

- In what type of environment(s) is my child spending most of her time? (Consider special education program, inclusive general education class, family home, group home, or employment setting when applicable.)
- If my child did not perform a desired speech or language skill independently, is it something someone would have to do for him?
- Is this a communication skill that is required for my child to use in her everyday world (school, home, or community)?
- Is the language skill age appropriate? That is, is it a skill others his age are expected to use and will it facilitate his capacity to interact with others?
- Do we have support from family, friends, or professionals to help us teach this skill to our child? (If the answer is no, it does not mean it cannot or should not be taught, but perhaps the skill and the lack of organized support warrant additional reflection.)

? How much time should we devote to broadening our child's vocabulary?

The focus in developing language skills in children with autism is best placed on designing a communication system that is "usable" for the child. Some children may develop words, phrases, and responses through direct training; that is, a child is programmed, prompted, and reinforced for making a desired response. As a result, a child may not necessarily understand what is happening in a given situation and reply with an appropriate communication response; rather, the child may learn what to say when placed in a particular situation and respond from rote memory.

An example of the complexities of problems that can be encountered while developing a communication system can be illustrated using the *DISTAR Language Program* (Engelmann & Osborn, 1973). While beneficial overall, the program has potential pitfalls for children who (a) display echolalia or (b) have a lower level understanding of pragmatics (i.e., the social rules for using communication).

Before we discuss a possible problem that can occur when using this program, it will aid understanding to first explain how the program is structured. The *DISTAR Language Program* requires direct teaching and repetitive rehearsal of verbal social responses, which are typically taught intensively in a classroom or clinic (i.e., outside of contextual situations). Lessons in this program follow a routine, predictable format, which is often an instructional necessity for children with autism. The lessons are scripted, which means teachers are told exactly what to say during the lesson and what they should expect as the "correct" answer. The child is taught to identify or label objects that may or may not be present during instruction. The teacher will ask "What is this?" to which a student will answer, for example, "a plate." The teacher is directed by the curriculum to praise the child's correct answer and to ask the child to answer again, using a complete sentence, by telling the child, "Say the whole thing." The child is expected to reply, "This is a plate." One potential problem with use of the *DISTAR Language Program* for children with autism is that, due to their particular language characteristics, some children with autism become "script bound." This means that they cannot complete a language-based social interaction without using the scripted format taught during the lessons. The child may request a paper plate during a picnic by saying "plate" or "plate please" but may not be able to alter the format of her request into a question (e.g., "May I have a plate, please?") until someone prompts her in the same manner to "say the whole thing." Again, the *DISTAR Language Program* is effective for some children who have autism and other developmental disabilities. The problems some children experience using it can be controlled through careful attention to instructional practices and attention to generalization.

As demonstrated through the example above, an important aspect of creating a language or communication system for a child who has autism is to make certain the system fits well within the child's naturally occurring environment. This implies that the child needs to learn first how to communicate regarding things most important to him before other language areas are addressed. When one concentrates on the immediate needs and wants of the child that are present within his regularly occurring world, it can be expected that the child may be more motivated to communicate. His communication attempts will more likely be true efforts to label, request, or alter the actions of others. That fact alone will provide natural reinforcement (getting the reaction or change he desired), which may make the child more likely to repeat his language efforts again in the future. By facilitating language and communication within the naturally occurring environment, it is more likely to be used in other situations and settings and with other people.

? *So the idea would be to help our child learn to communicate with us better?*

Yes, the aim is actually to promote two-way communication and information exchange. Inasmuch as your child will hopefully learn effective ways to express her needs and wants, the selected intervention should be designed as a system that mutually benefits the other people in her world. Parents, teachers, and friends will need to become adept at observing her use of language or the use of the child's communication system, and correctly extrapolating her intent. To be effective, communication requires a mutual exchange of information between people, not only a message sender but a receiver as well. Accordingly, in learning to communicate with others, the "others" should be learning how to correctly understand and respond to a child's language or communication system, how to interpret the child's behaviors, and how to respond using signals, gestures, and language that she will comprehend.

? *To be honest, our child does have underdeveloped communication skills, but isn't it more important to work on his challenging behaviors first?*

It may be useful to know that some children who lack effective communication skills develop myriad aberrant behaviors that may actually serve as "inefficient" communication skills. Because he cannot directly communicate what he wants or does not want, he uses whatever behaviors are within his repertoire to change the actions of the people or things in his environment. At times the behaviors he chooses may be destructive to his environment, self-mutilating, or aggressive toward those around him.

Through careful use of observation by the people in his life, the child's attempts to make his needs and wants known can become clearer. It is especially important to attend to establishing or facilitating a communication system in situations where a child has many challenging behaviors. The communication system (verbal or non-verbal) must be based in functionality. In other words, it must be designed to enable a child to communicate effectively his personal needs and preferences, to limit the child's frustration. Of equal importance for a child who has autism is the idea that this system must be created in tandem with a concrete behavior management program. Through the use of both communication and behavior management programs, the more challenging behaviors are gradually curbed and replaced by more appropriate communication-based behaviors.

LANGUAGE INTERVENTIONS

Language intervention programs can take various forms and host many ideals and goals. When reviewing which program might be the best fit for a child, it is important to try to obtain nonbiased, research-based information about programs. It is also helpful to look for information about each program's potential for impact with children of similar age, type of autism or PDD, and other developmental characteristics, such as level of speech development in language skills or communication prior to intervention. In this section we share introductory information about five language intervention approaches currently being used with children who have autism: Milieu Teaching, Picture Exchange Communication System, Auditory Integration Therapy, Functional Communication Training, and Intensive Behavioral Intervention.

Milieu Teaching

Milieu Teaching (Hart & Rogers-Warren, 1978) is an approach to teaching children in a context-specific situation. It may entail facilitating language interactions in either a clinic or a classroom setting that has been modified to approximate the naturally occurring environment, or it may be used to provide specific instruction outside of the classroom or clinic and in the usual place(s) where the child would be expected to use the language skill(s). For example, in teaching life skills, such as grocery shopping, the youth would be instructed in the grocery store. Another example would be a child's learning to communicate through an experiential lesson such as show and tell, where the acquisition of language and communication skills, as well as nonverbal behaviors of listening and attending or asking questions, may be taught through participation in the activity of show and tell. In a more traditional approach to teaching language and communication skills, a child would be taught skills in a small group or one-on-one direct teaching session, emphasizing vocabulary development or a particular communication skill in isolation.

? How do I know if this approach is right for my child?

The benefits to using a milieu-based approach can be summarized as follows: (a) it provides instruction in a naturally occurring environment, thus limiting problems with generalization (getting the child to perform the skill in appropriate environments outside of the classroom or clinic where the skill was taught); (b) it readily incorporates the adults and others with whom the child is expected to use the language or communication system, allowing others to learn how to communicate effectively with the child; and (c) it allows the natural antecedents and consequences within the environment to stimulate and reinforce the child's use of the skills (e.g., a child uses a communication skill in order to have a parent engage in a desired response connected to a game).

Milieu Teaching can occur, as mentioned in the beginning of this description, in a clinic or classroom (set up to look like the natural environment) or in the actual environment. The largest limitation to teaching in a clinic or classroom is that, regardless of how effectively designed, contrived settings cannot entirely imitate the natural environment. However, given limitations, the strategy seems to be effective. Indeed, given the limitations of teaching children with autism in all situations, including the financial expense of such a process and the amount of time needed to facilitate mastery and independence, instruction within clinical and classroom environments is often a necessity, at least in part.

? What criteria are used for determining when and where to use Milieu Teaching, and what specific Milieu Teaching skills or activities to use?

Parents and professionals who assist a child's language development through use of a Milieu Teaching approach need to be mindful of several concepts that should be considered when selecting where, when, and with what activities instruction can best take place. It is important that this program be well structured. The events associated with language intervention need to be anticipated, and instruction should be carefully considered. For example, it will be much easier to stimulate language in a child who is participating in a situation or event that the child truly enjoys. There also needs to be sufficient stimulation within the event or situation to promote the child's use of language. Children must be actively engaged in the activity in order for this method to be successful. If high levels of involvement do not occur as anticipated, then a plan must be ready for how the adult can best facilitate the child's participation. For example, ideas about how to modify an activity (e.g., breaking it into smaller tasks or focusing on participating in one portion of the total activity) or how to reinforce participation in the activity (e.g., through lots of praise or spending time with a favorite person) should be available.

A second key feature in selecting sites or activities in which to use Milieu Teaching is that the activity should be something that can be repeated many times in order that the child has an opportunity to become proficient in the skills being taught. For example, attending a baseball game to practice social conversation should be initiated at the beginning of the season to allow the child to attend many games during which the social conversation may be practiced. A second example would be to teach a child to greet the occupants of a room upon entering. There may be many opportunities to rehearse the proper language and communication skills needed to complete this activity within a given day.

A third consideration for selecting environments in which to use Milieu Teaching relates to the activity done in the environment. Preferred activities for Milieu Teaching comprise multiple tasks, parts of which provide many opportunities for communication and language use. For instance, a child can find many opportunities to use language and communication skills when participating in a complex task such as setting the table (e.g., identifying the many items to be placed on the table, inquiring about which dishes are most appropriate for the meal, and asking for assistance in locating particular items needed to complete the activity).

As mentioned earlier, if the child does not show a high level of engagement in the selected activity, then the adult guiding the activity will need to intervene to prompt or facilitate the desired level of engagement. For example, when the child is setting the table, the adult may manipulate the environment to facilitate interaction among the participants in order that the task be completed (e.g., removing the plates from their usual location requires the child to use language to ask for them). The adult would then use the opportunity to assist the child in developing functional use of vocabulary, in forming questions, or in demonstrating appropriate nonverbal behaviors (e.g., making eye contact) that would be likely to accompany this request.

Finally, functionality of the desired behavior would be another important criterion for deciding when, where, and what to teach using Milieu Teaching. Again we underscore the importance of teaching functional, relevant skills to children who have autism.

? *What should the adults working with the child do when using this method?*

The easiest way to approach Milieu Teaching is to consider the child's existing environments. In this context, natural opportunities for language and communication skill development should be identified and taken advantage of. Missed communication opportunities can occur in several ways: (a) by making environments so accessible to a child that she can easily obtain any materials she needs without having to communicate with others; (b) by selecting the "perfect" project or activity based on the fact that the youngster can perform each portion independently without asking for help; (c) by anticipating the child's verbalizations and completing ideas or thoughts without allowing her to express her ideas or needs completely; or (d) by asking questions that require only brief, perfunctory responses or statements.

Picture Exchange Communications System

The *Picture Exchange Communication System* (PECS) is a system for communication skill development (Bondy & Frost, 1994). This approach uses an augmentative communication system that serves in place of spoken language, and it may lead to the development or enhancement of speech. A few features set this approach apart from other language interventions.

One element shared by various communication enhancement strategies is a belief that nonverbal prerequisite behaviors (e.g., attending to others, imitating motor and verbal responses) need to be present before a child can learn basic communication skills. Further, it is believed that typically developing children acquire these precursors to functional language primarily through social reinforcement. Bondy (1992) asserted that, because children who have autism are not easily engaged nor reinforced by social interactions, traditional communication prerequisite skills are not formed.

Because the skill of making requests is typically reinforced by the consequences of the request made (e.g., the request for a cookie is more likely to occur when the child receives a cookie after making the request), the PECS begins teaching communication through the use of requesting. Many other programs begin teaching language by teaching the child to label or name things in the environment. The basic gist of this intervention program is that children as young as 2 years of age are taught to select a picture of an object, included on a board of pictures, and hand it to someone in exchange for the physical item. This enables the child to communicate with another person in a way that produces a tangible result within the context of a social interchange.

? *I have seen other children use picture boards. Is PECS like those systems where children point to pictures to indicate what they want?*

Each augmentative communication device operates in its own way. The PECS is similar to other picture communication devices, wherein children are asked to select a picture of an object to communicate their meaning. However, the PECS differs from others in that children are taught to direct their communicative intent toward a person. In many picture pointing systems, children simply point to the picture (e.g., the teacher may say "Point to a picture of a cow," and the child points to the corresponding picture). Using the PECS, the child is taught to hand the picture of a desired item to someone in order to receive the item. The purpose of this variation in format is to base communicative actions within social contexts. It is possible that the child using a traditional picture point system may point to any number of items in the absence of a "listener." Therefore, the child's attempts at communication are nullified rather than reinforced, making it less likely that future attempts to communicate will be made. Another rationale for the PECS format is that the child must be actively engaged in the communicative effort, rather than merely pointing to a picture without making eye contact with the requester or otherwise engaging in an appropriate communication exchange.

? *Does teaching my young autistic child to use an augmentative communication device mean that he won't later develop speech?*

Not necessarily. About half of the children diagnosed with classic autism fail to develop speech communication. However, about 75% of those taught at the clinic where Bondy and his associates have developed the PECS, have been reported to eventually develop speech. Again, the value of this approach is that it enables a child to learn to communicate successfully with others in his world, thus positively reinforcing his communicative efforts and encouraging him to expand on them.

Auditory Integration Therapy

Auditory Integration Therapy (AIT) is a treatment developed for persons with autism (and other disabilities) who demonstrate a hypersensitivity to sound. It is a controversial procedure because, although it has been used for many years, there is no scientific proof that it has positive effects on behavior, learning, or listening abilities. Because of these controversies, two position statements and one technical report have been published to caution parents of the experimental nature of this therapy. The most recent position statement will be presented later in this section.

Of a variety of therapies called AIT, the most common is one developed by Dr. Guy Berard, a physician (ear-nose-throat specialist) from France. He developed a theory based on hypersensitivity of sound. He suggested that some persons have such good hearing abilities at some pitches that they experience discomfort from the sounds in their environment, resulting in learning, emotional, or behavior problems. By lessening the intensity of the discomfort experienced by children with autism, proponents of AIT purport that language (and other) learning can be enhanced. Thus, they contend that, through AIT, the child with autism is relieved, to a certain extent, of some of the autism symptoms, and therefore is able to acquire language, to learn, and to behave more efficiently and effectively. Berard believes that the auditory system can be "retrained" to be less sensitive to sounds through Auditory Integration Therapy.

In Berard's variety of AIT, a subject receives AIT treatment using headphones to listen to compact discs and audiocassettes of a wide variety of music, which is randomly distorted or "modulated" by some filters within Berard's specially designed equipment (the Audiokinetron). Treatment is provided for 20 half-hour sessions over a period of 10 days and multiple intervention sessions may be provided. Occasionally, a hearing test is done before and after the treatment to measure differences in hearing sensitivity.

Berard's therapy has been criticized primarily because his theory that the auditory system can be "retrained" has not been proven. Although there is abundant proof that muscles can be retrained with physical therapy, the same cannot be said of the auditory system. In addition, Berard has never answered the following questions: Why is the treatment 20 sessions, rather than 10 or 30? Why half-hour sessions? How are the modulations determined? Why use music—and virtually any kind of music—for the treatment? A scientifically sound therapy would test for and answer these concerns, but the settings for AIT appear to be arbitrarily selected and remain unexplained. Other concerns include these: Why would using headphones after the treatment (for hearing tests or for listening to music) "cancel out" the treatment, as is claimed by some treatment administrators? Considering the risk of actually hurting the auditory system with excessively loud sounds, exactly how loud may the treatment get?

This last question led the Federal Food and Drug Administration (FDA), in 1993, to ban the import of the Audiokinetron, determining it to be an unapproved medical device. The Audiokinetrons already in use in the United States were designated as investigational devices, to be used only by approved research sites. The manufacturers of the Audiokinetron have made no effort to obtain FDA approval.

Because the auditory system is complicated, it seems logical to assume that there is a link to this treatment and hypersensitivity to sounds. However, legitimate treatments are based on what researchers know, so when changes occur, they can explain why. There is no evidence that AIT benefits individuals with autism any more than that 20 sessions of X-ray treatment or 20 sessions of aromatherapy would—in fact, with the latter two examples, people would ask, "Why would they work? There is no connection between X-ray or aromatherapy and autism." Audiologists and other professionals around the world express the same skepticism about AIT. In this regard, the following position statement was developed by a group of audiologists (American Academy of Audiology, 1995):

> The mission of the Educational Audiology Association is to provide comprehensive management of individuals from birth to graduation from high school in all educational environments who have listening and/or hearing difficulties. Recently, audiologists in school settings have been approached by parents for information about Auditory Integration Therapy (AIT). This therapy was originally designed for individuals with autism; however, individuals with dyslexia, attention deficit hyperactive disorders, and other disabilities have also received AIT. The intended purpose of AIT is to reduce hypersensitivity to sounds;

therefore, since AIT attempts to remediate listening difficulties, educational audiologists are ethically responsible for presenting accurate information and a professional position about a therapy designed to improve listening abilities.

One position statement (American Academy of Audiology, 1995) and one technical report (American Speech-Language-Hearing Association, 1994) regarding the practice of AIT have been published in recent years. Both documents described the experimental nature of AIT therapy, including that it is not supported by controlled scientific studies. Although both papers called for such studies to be conducted, none have been forthcoming. Since the publication of these papers, the FDA has determined the equipment used for AIT to be Class 3 medical devices, which require FDA clearance prior to being used clinically. AIT equipment has not yet received this clearance, and use of said equipment could be considered a violation of law and the equipment subject to seizure.

The Educational Audiology Association (in press) supports the position put forth by both the American Academy of Audiology and the American Speech-Language-Hearing Association, to wit:

> Auditory Integration Therapy has not been proven to be a viable treatment for any disability. Only inconsistent, uncontrolled, anecdotal evidence has been provided to support claims of changes in listening, behavior, or learning. Educational audiologists must advise parents of the risks of experimental procedures such as Auditory Integration Therapy: specific to AIT, that the therapy may not result in measurable changes, and that without controls to protect against excessively loud auditory stimuli, the therapy may cause harm to the child's auditory system.

Functional Communication Training

Functional Communication Training (FCT) is a well-researched and accepted intervention approach used to systematically teach persons with autism (and other disabilities) useful communicative responses to obtain preferred objects, events, or outcomes in natural environments (Carr & Durand, 1985; Carr & Kemp, 1989; Durand, 1990; Maning & Katz, 1991). The premise of FCT is that any newly acquired communication strategy taught to an individual with autism should be functionally equivalent to and at least as efficient as a previously used strategy.

For example, an overstimulated child with autism at a grocery store may drop to the floor and begin screaming "no store," which results in the desired outcome of the parent and child leaving the store. Using FCT the focus would be placed on teaching the child to make a socially appropriate communicative request, such as saying "go please," which would be rewarded by the parent taking the child out of the store. The socially appropriate request of "go please" allows the child to efficiently gain the same desired outcome of leaving the store without exhibiting inappropriate behavior. This allows the child to begin to see that socially appropriate communicative attempts can be used to alter environmental events.

Scientific studies have shown that both parents and professionals have successfully implemented FCT. The first step in the intervention process is to identify a situation (context) in which inappropriate verbal or nonverbal behavior occurs on a regular basis. Next, an educated guess (hypothesis) is made regarding the communicative function (purpose) that the inappropriate behavior serves for the individual with autism. It is important during this initial assessment to take special note of any gestures or actions used by the child and the length of the communicative response used. This will assist in ensuring that the communicative strategy selected to replace the inappropriate behavior does not exceed the child's communicative skill level.

Using the above example (i.e., to teach a more socially efficient, appropriate response for a child wishing to leave a store), the adult trainer would provide the question and model the appropriate response "go please" for the child. The adult would prompt the child for the appropriate response, which would be then immediately reinforced by leaving the store. A common question that arises is, "What if my child with autism does not respond to the verbal prompt given by the adult?" In this instance, the literature has shown that it may be beneficial to add a visual cue (e.g., a picture of the car) or use a peer or sibling model to facilitate acquisition of the new communicative skill. Once the child with autism learns that it takes less energy and time to use the more socially appropriate response to get the desired outcome, the adult can gradually increase the wait time between the request and the reinforcement.

Intensive Behavioral Intervention

One of the best known approaches for teaching speech and language to children with autism was advanced by Ivar Lovaas. Lovaas developed the University of California, Los Angeles (UCLA) Young Autism Project, which is an intensive home-based intervention approach for preschool children with autism (also referred to as The Early Intervention Project). The UCLA Young Autism Project is a controversial intervention approach because of issues regarding the type of child with autism who would best benefit from this intervention, the nature of the intervention, required qualifications of therapists, and reported outcomes (Gresham & MacMillan, 1997; Lovaas, 1987; Smith & Lovaas, 1997).

As reported by Lovaas (1987), the UCLA Young Autism Project is an intensive (average of 40 hours or more per week) one-to-one behavioral treatment, which typically takes place over a 2- to 3-year period. The children who participated in the initial 1987 study were all younger than 4 years of age and had received an independent diagnosis of autism. Intervention goals focused on decreasing inappropriate behaviors (e.g., aggression, tantrums, stereotypy) and increasing language, attending, observational learning, imitation, appropriate independent play with toys, appropriate interactions with peers, and preacademic skills.

The instructional program employs a format that uses a specific curriculum modified to meet the child's unique needs. The instructional curriculum is intended to be followed in a specific skill sequence that requires the child to learn simple skills before progressing to more complex behaviors. The majority of the therapists who provided the one-to-one behavioral programming in the 1987 study were UCLA students who had advanced training in the theoretical and behavioral principles that served as the foundation for the intervention program.

Lovaas (1987) reported positive, long-term follow-up outcomes for the children who received intensive behavioral treatment (40 hours a week, 50 weeks a year, for at least 2 years). Indeed, Lovass reported impressive academic and social gains for children with autism. However, professional dispute remains regarding several issues: (a) whether certain child characteristics (e.g., level of language development, level of intellectual functioning, degree of developmental delay) differentially affect the responsiveness of the child to the intensive behavioral treatment program; (b) how the qualifications and training of those implementing the intensive treatment affect child outcomes; and (c) what type of expertise, resources, and monitoring are necessary to assess the integrity of the treatment and to document student outcomes. Finally, and most important, significant flaws in Lovaas's 1987 study preclude this approach from being considered a best practices method. Answers to these preliminary questions need to be addressed through additional research, and there needs to be solid empirical evidence that the results reported by Lovaas in 1987 are indeed valid. Until such time, the one point on which all professionals agree and that research supports is that early intervention is essential in maximizing the outcomes for children with autism.

SUMMARY

Enhancing the development and use of language in children who have autism is a complex and challenging task. The information contained in this chapter provides a preliminary explanation of the many issues involved in language intervention for children with autism. Readers are encouraged to do further reading and to discuss with professionals the various approaches for improving language and communication skills for children with autism. Such further exploration will likely be needed to fully understand the various processes we have described or to accurately make decisions about which intervention may be best suited for each individual child.

We would like to thank Dr. Kristina English for her contributions to the section on Auditory Integration Therapy.

Coping with Self-Defeating Feelings That Can Prevent Successful Dealings with Persons with Autism

8

The purpose of this chapter is to help parents and professionals understand and perhaps control some of the self-defeating feelings and behaviors that may prevent them from parenting or working well with children and youth who have autism. Clearly, parenting, teaching, and taking care of children are not easy tasks, even with children and youth who do *not* have disabilities. The characteristics and behaviors exhibited by children with autism are challenging even to the most learned professionals, who are with them only a fraction of the time. Further, and most important, professionals' emotional investment in the children's success or failure often pales when compared with that of most parents. Interestingly, this personal investment may inhibit the ability to succeed.

Too often speakers on television and authors of articles and books focus on descriptions and possible remediation techniques for individuals with autism. It is a common misconception among such speakers and authors that if they, the so-called experts, provide the information, then the laypeople and professionals should be able to follow their advice. Rarely do the media discuss one major factor that is crucial to success: the parent or professional who works with the child. We contend that scant attention has been paid to an important variable that is critical to success: the mental health of the caregivers.

The purpose of this chapter is to explore the feelings and behaviors that may evolve from working closely with individuals who have autism. Feelings that may prevent a person from being as effective as he or she would like are called self-defeating. In many cases, these negative feelings may be attached to not being successful as often as desired. In other words, sometimes it is not the behaviors of the children and youth that impede progress, but the attitudes of those who want to affect change.

? *What feelings might prevent me from effectively working with students and clients with autism?*

Any strong feeling or behavior may prevent you from achieving your goals. For example, emotions such as anger, frustration, worry, fear, sadness, and anxiety, when severe, can prevent you from thinking clearly and acting calmly when you most need to do so.

Research has suggested that there may be more stress on families of individuals with autism than any other disability group (Bouma & Schweitzer, 1990). Consequently, when feeling stress and strong negative emotions, a person's ability to react calmly in situations that require calmness is difficult at best.

▶ **NOTE:** It is critical that the reader understand that the negative feelings and behaviors discussed in this chapter have the potential to be extremely serious. These feelings and behaviors may become out of control, preventing the person from behaving in a desirable manner.

? *Isn't it normal to feel these emotions, especially when constantly faced with failure?*

It is common to have self-defeating feelings when confronted with disappointment or failure. However, not everyone reacts to failure in the same way. Some people have very deep emotional reactions that may result in helplessness, anger, or frustration, and they behave in ways that seem to create more problems. Other people seem to accept their lack of success and not perceive themselves as failures. Consequently, they do not let their lack of success block their attempts at progress. They do not believe that failing at something makes *them* failures.

The differences between these people and those with less productive responses are their personal philosophies regarding failure. Because each person has his or her own philosophy, each behaves in a way that is consistent with the way he or she thinks about things. Some people are better able than others to control harmful feelings, especially when those feelings get in the way of goals. The purpose of the remainder of this chapter is to present one way in which parents and professionals can learn to control harmful feelings.

? *How am I supposed to control my feelings when my son won't respond to me, or when he continually messes up? How can I not have these feelings?*

It is normal to experience negative feelings when negative events happen to you. It is the degree of these feelings that is of concern. In other words, it is understandable to feel disappointed when you become upset when your son does not respond to you. What needs to be addressed is the process that occurs within you that creates an out-of-control emotion from that disappointment.

For example, being *merely* disappointed probably means that you will not react in an excessively negative manner to your son when he does not respond to you.

However, if you are *excessively* disappointed (or frustrated), you may find it hard to think clearly and thus overreact in an attempt to get your son to respond to you. In other words, it is not your son's behavior that creates your ability or inability to be effective with him; it is your perception of and reaction to that behavior. The central theme of this chapter is that negative feelings are not caused by "bad" things; rather, they are caused by perceptions of those things. Again, it is critical to remember that people may react differently to the same event. In this regard, differences in reactions to situations are no different from differences in opinions about the same book or movie. However, in this case, we are referring to something dearer to people's hearts—children—and that makes the task of controlling feelings more important and more difficult.

Even though individuals have different reactions to negative events, that still doesn't make it clear to me that I cause such feelings as severe anger or frustration. Can you explain?

Before explaining how emotional problems can occur, we want to emphasize that we are not assuming that everyone who interacts with individuals who have autism has emotional problems. Nor do we believe that everyone reacts in the same way when a problem occurs. However, when a person is feeling very badly, it may be because she has been led to believe that when something bad happens to her, the natural consequence is bad feelings. It is as if an uncontrollable cause-and-effect process happens. However, believing that bad feelings must accompany difficult situations negates a very important component of human nature: the ability to think (often referred to as cognition).

Thinking and feelings are closely related. We believe that thinking causes feelings. If a person perceives (thinks of) something as being pleasurable, he will then feel "good." If the person perceives (thinks of) something as being obnoxious, he will then feel "bad." In other words, people feel what they think. The fact that not everybody thinks the same way about a particular event demonstrates why not everybody has the same feelings about the same event.

Does this explain why I feel so frustrated when I can't get my son to understand me, while my wife seems to feel only minor aggravation?

Exactly! The kind of thinking that you might be experiencing is called irrational. Irrational thinking is a dysfunctional thought process that may take the form of unrealistic demands, overgeneralizations, exaggerations, and unvalidated assumptions.

Irrational thinking occurs when a person's opinions about certain events become facts to that person. It is when a person's desires become needs, or aspirations become requirements, that problems occur. Opinions, desires, and aspirations are highly individual, and when they cause an extremely emotional (out-of-control) reaction, they are irrational.

For example, your wife may also not like it that your son cannot understand her. Yet, instead of her believing (thinking) that he *must* understand her, she probably *wishes* that he would understand her. She knows that, given his condition, it would be unrealistic to *expect* such understanding from him without training or other intervention.

? *But this is not the way that I was raised. I was taught, and I believe, that it is not my fault if people treat me badly. Anger is a natural reaction. How can I change?*

Just because you were raised to think certain ways does not mean that you are destined to always think that way. With hard work, you can learn to think in new ways. Consequently, this new thinking will create new feelings. Let's look at a model for how we feel known as the ABC model. This model was developed by Albert Ellis (1996) as part of a psychological intervention program that is now called *Rational Emotive Behavior Therapy (REBT)*.

A = Activating Event

The A in the ABC model is called the Activating Event, which when negative is what we believe to be the source of our negative feelings. Many people believe that it is Activating Events (e.g., a child seems unable to understand us or cooperate with us) that cause our unhappiness. Although the Activating Event does *contribute* to our feelings, it is more likely that our perceptions or opinions about the Event actually *cause* our feelings.

C = Consequences

The feelings or behaviors (e.g., anger or frustration) that some regard as the result of the Activating Event is the C part of the model, or the Consequence(s). The consequences that are of concern in this chapter are those that are so severe that they prevent us from thinking and rationally meeting our goals. We are referring to such feelings as anger, as opposed to aggravation; depression, as opposed to sadness; frustration, as opposed to annoyance; and fear, as opposed to apprehension. Consequences of such feelings include such behaviors as eating too much or too little, sleeping too much or too little, and experiencing an inability to concentrate.

Many people believe that when something bad happens to them, the "natural" reaction is to feel bad ("Who wouldn't feel bad if a child continually refuses to cooperate?"). This is when the most important aspect of problem solving comes into play: Your commitment to change your feeling. In REBT we ask, "How can you change your feelings of anger?" Note that this question is not, "How do you want to change the Activating Event?" (e.g., the behaviors of others). Rather, the ABC model puts the responsibility for emotional growth squarely with the individual who experiences the emotions.

? *Aren't the differences in how people react based on the way they were raised?*

Perhaps. But regardless of the way we are raised, by recognizing response differences, we acknowledge that there are different reactions to what we sometimes believe can elicit only one natural reaction. These different reactions make up the major component of the ABC model—the B, or the Belief System. Belief systems refer to our perceptions or reactions to Activating Events.

B = Belief System

One way of understanding the concept of Belief Systems is to think of them as organized patterns of thought. They take the form of self-talk, that is, the specific things that we say to ourselves that create our feelings. For example, your perception seems to be that "it is not your fault when people treat you or your child with autism unfairly or badly." Yet, you seem to be taking the responsibility for others' behaviors. In other words, why is it *your* responsibility that other people act in a particular way? Surely, there are others who do not react to you in the same manner as others. Some people *might* be more sensitive to your needs, yet others may perceive your (or your child's) behavior in a negative manner (individuals do perceive things in their *own* way) and feel justified feeling and behaving the way that they do.

? *Hmmm. Belief Systems? There are more than one?*

Yes, hundreds of Belief Systems have been identified that create our feelings. However, people tend to use the same Belief System when they are confronted with a wide range of Activating Events.

❓ *Do you mean that when I get angry, depressed, or frustrated about my son's condition, I am not frustrated about his autism?*

Correct! You are likely to react in a similar fashion (anger, depression, or frustration) with other Activating Events that you cannot control. The theory of REBT suggests that we think in almost ritualistic ways when "bad" things happen. Further, we contend that you are frustrated because you are demanding that your son not be the way that he is. This frustration may also occur in other areas of your life when people or things do not live up to your expectations. The key concept here is the word *expectations*. If you *expect* people to behave in a certain way and they do not, then the consequence may be frustration. When you would *prefer* (less intense than expect) people to behave in a certain way, and they do not, then the consequence would be disappointment. Frustration may prevent you from trying new alternatives with your son. Disappointment may not be as debilitating. You may be operating in a Belief System called *Demanding*.

The Demanding Belief System encompasses an attitude by which you require, rather than prefer, things to be a certain way. Thus, the self-talk that occurs in a demander's thinking process includes words such as these:

should

must

have to

need

got to

These words become sentences that leave the thinker with little choice but to be distressed:

1. He shouldn't be autistic!
2. He must learn specific skills!
3. I have to be perfect as a caregiver!
4. He needs to be different!
5. I know the way he has got to be educated!

Although these above statements express understandable goals, when stated (and believed), they leave little option (when unfulfilled) except for the person to be distressed. If your son stays autistic and if he cannot learn skills you would like to see him develop, and if you make mistakes as a caregiver, and if he cannot be normally developing, and if you are not the best parent or professional, then you have the "right" to be disturbed! And, of course, in most cases, these realities do not readily change. However, your reaction to these realities *can* change.

? *What are my choices?*

Your choice is to carefully evaluate your Belief System (i.e., examine what you say to yourself). Your task is to *prove* that the statements you make (to yourself) are true. For example, "should" people behave the way you demand? That would be *nice*, but is it realistic? Given all of their "unique" life experiences, would you really expect them to behave differently (even if it is the correct thing to do)? If people have spent their lives being rude, inconsiderate, or inattentive, do you *really* have a right to expect them to be different because you have determined it so? We contend that although these statements may be preferable, they are not true. They are not facts and rarely get people anywhere except to produce unhappiness.

Your extremely negative feelings are created by the unrealistic beliefs evidenced in your statements. An examination of each of the "demanding" comments above reveals how inaccurate they are. This examination is called D for Disputation.

D = Disputation

Disputation is a process that can be both cognitive (thinking) and behavioral. Its object is to minimize your harmful feelings by attacking untrue self-talk. For example, with regard to the destructive self-talk used in the demands stated previously, the following evaluations could be used.

1. He shouldn't be autistic!

Dispute: Provide evidence to support your thinking. Can it be proven that your son "shouldn't be autistic"? This is preferable, of course, but not proven because, for whatever reason, he has autism. Your demanding otherwise will not change his condition. You can either accept this reality and be less angry, or not accept it.

2. He must learn specific skills!

Dispute: Must he "learn certain skills"? Given your son's personal history, it may be extremely unlikely that he will learn certain skills (e.g., learn to talk). Getting angry with your son because of his inability may create a problem with your relationship with him.

3. I have to be perfect as a caregiver!

Dispute: Do you have to "be perfect as a caregiver"? Can you, or anyone, be perfect as a caregiver, or at anything else for that matter? Demanding that you cannot make mistakes creates ripe territory for anger. Few, if any, people are infallible. The fact is that you will make errors, as will others, and if you accept them (not like them, but accept them), you can have less anger.

4. He needs to be different!

Dispute: Does he "need to be different"? Most parents and professionals would probably wish for individuals not to have autism, but they do not need to be "different." They have lived their lives being "different," or unique as individuals, just as you and I have.

5. I know the way he has got be educated!

Dispute: Do you really "know the way he has got to be educated"? You may be qualified to provide input about a particular student's education given everything you know about him. Yet, it is highly unlikely that anyone knows for sure what will absolutely, positively work for any individual, and what that individual needs.

The emotional consequences of these statements based in the Demanding Belief System create unhappiness. In addition, failure to examine the reality of these statements maintains that unhappiness.

? *It sounds good, but isn't it easier said than done?*

Absolutely! Again, the purpose of this chapter is not to suggest that change is easy. It is very difficult! However, the alternative is to continue believing things that simply are not true, and the consequence of this practice is often unhappiness. Self-defeating feelings and behaviors are created by beliefs that cannot be validated.

? *What other Belief Systems do we have?*

The *Awfulizing* Belief System also involves gross negative exaggerations. Thus, people who awfulize have self-talk that reflects evaluations that are "totally bad" or "absolutely horrible." In other words, they make a practice of "making a mountain out of a mole hill." Awfulizers tend to be "whiners." Rather than dealing with problems, they prefer to believe that the world is too difficult to deal with and that, therefore, they have to endure it (no matter how difficult). The self-talk that is part of their vocabulary includes the following:

awful

horrible

terrible

unbearable

catastrophe

poor me

These words become a working philosophy, and drive emotions toward unhappiness. The following are examples of unrealistic sentences using these words:

1. It's awful that he is autistic.
2. It's horrible that I had an autistic child.
3. It's terrible that he won't do what I ask.
4. My life is now unbearable.
5. Each time that a problem occurs, it is truly a catastrophe.
6. Poor me! Why does this always have to happen to me?

People who are awfulizers consider disappointments not merely as disappointments, but as indicators of the worst things that could possibly happen. For example, "My son with autism refuses to do what I ask. I can't believe anything worse can happen!" Certainly, for most people, this experience is not *the worst thing* that can happen.

? *Can't some things be absolutely, totally bad?*

Some things can certainly be very unpleasant, but probably not absolutely, totally bad because the worst thing that can happen to anyone can usually be topped by something worse. No matter how bad an Activating Event, it can always be worse. Can you *imagine* how things could be worse? Although this may not be a major comfort, it does reflect reality.

Many people who have disabilities, terminal illnesses, or other unfortunate problems do not feel and act as if their world has been taken apart. If Activating Events *caused* hardships, all of these people would react similarly to them. More likely, these people believed that events were extremely unpleasant, but tolerable.

Let's now examine some possible disputations for the awfulizing statements listed previously:

1. It's awful that he is autistic.

Dispute: Is it *awful* that he has autism? Although it certainly is not always pleasurable for him or you, it cannot be proven that it is 100% awful. Both you and the person with autism have and will experience many "unawful" and occasionally pleasurable times. This certainly minimizes your opinion that his condition is totally awful.

2. It's horrible that I had an autistic child.

Dispute: "It's horrible that I had an autistic child" is also an overexaggeration if by *horrible* you are describing the "worst thing that could have happened to you." Instead, you can perceive it as a less than desired event. Clearly, worse things could have happened. Your child could have more severe disabilities, your other children could have severe disabilities, or you could have died during childbirth. These are all events that could have been more horrible. The purpose of presenting such realities is not to be macabre. Rather, it is to make you look at the possible events that could have occurred to make your life more "horrible."

3. It's terrible that he won't do what I ask.

Dispute: It is not terrible that he will not do what you ask. He has not always done (and we imagine that others have not always done) what you have requested in the past and it has not been terrible. You have lived through the disappointment, even though you may not have thought that it was possible, *and* you adapted to the situation.

4. My life is now unbearable.

Dispute: That one's life is "unbearable" is a common awfulizing remark. Is it so unbearable that you would commit suicide over it? If you are seriously considering suicide, we recommend that you seek professional help. If not, how do the catastrophes in your life compare to those of others? Think of those with incurable diseases, the homeless, or those who have lost their homes because of financial difficulties or storms. Are the lives of all those people unbearable? How do you account for many of the survivors of concentration camps whose lives are not unbearable? How does the condition of your life compare?

5. Each time that a problem occurs, it is truly a catastrophe.

Dispute: When one believes that each time a problem occurs, it is truly a catastrophe, one obviously uses the word catastrophe very loosely. Unpleasant events, such as not getting your way all the time, do not fit the definition of catastrophe. You are simply choosing to use the word incorrectly.

6. Poor me! Why does this always have to happen to me?

Dispute: The "poor me's" are usually overreactions to unpleasant events. Bad things do happen. Because they happen to you does not make you worthy of pity. Clearly there is little evidence of the other overgeneralization, "everything always happens to me." Everything does not happen to anyone, including you!

? *But these events always seem so important when they occur. Is there a way that will help me look at the realistic side of things?*

One technique that might help is to ask yourself how you will feel about the event tomorrow, next week, next month, or next year. The answer is that you will probably feel that it is less "terrible." Why is that so? It is because when you distance yourself from a negative event, you gain a more realistic perspective about it. It may certainly still be unpleasant, but it will not take on the major proportions that it did when it occurred.

Think of some previous "horrible" events that no longer seem so disastrous. How do you describe the event now? Can you say the same things *now* about the current event rather than wait for time to elapse?

? *Sometimes when I feel bad, I tend to avoid unpleasant events. Is that normal?*

It is very normal to want to avoid negative events. However, avoiding events rarely solves problems. In fact, doing so might lead to more negative feelings because the problems may not go away.

? *But sometimes it is easier to avoid dealing with my autistic son and to avoid working so hard when I know that the results are most likely going to be less than what I want! Don't you see?*

It is easier, but is that what you want? Are you satisfied that you no longer spend the time you would like to with your son? Is the avoidance of work getting the desired results? Even if you are successful at avoidance, what are your feelings regarding the lack of progress? Are you creating more problems by this avoidance?

? *What can I do to overcome this avoidance?*

Choose to do the needed but undesirable behavior! Interestingly, most people report that when they engage in the uncomfortable behavior, the emotional results are rarely as "horrible" as they imagined.

In fact, whereas some believe that the way to approach an undesired event is in small doses, others suggest that the best way is to force yourself to fully confront the event. They believe that by doing it little by little, you are reinforcing the notion that it is a horrible event and that the only way to deal with it is with trepidation.

? *In my situation, I don't think I demand or awfulize. I just feel like a terrible parent (teacher, friend, whatever) when things don't go right.*

The reaction you describe is not uncommon. Some people attach worth to their behaviors. Others blame and attach worth to others, including teachers, school staff, and so forth. Both of these ways of dealing with a child with autism are indicative of the *Rating* Belief System, which involves evaluating human worth, whether or not you own the resources of others.

The Rating system suggests that when an event (a behavior or set of behaviors) occurs, people may inaccurately attach it to one's essence or worth. In other words, people do something "bad," then they are "bad." Or, if you do not do as well as you would like, you perceive yourself as "inadequate."

? *But isn't that what self-concept is all about? Doesn't it involve the way that we are perceived by others?*

We believe that it is an unhealthy approach to evaluating self-concept or self-worth when you base it on the perspectives of others. Who is to say that their evaluations, or yours for that matter, are accurate? Many times, these evaluations are based on a behavior, a mistake for instance. When this occurs, the evaluator is denying that human beings are fallible and that making a mistake is not a conclusive indication that one's worth is faulty. It is important to remember that almost all people are fallible; consequently, they do make mistakes.

When individuals blame themselves or others for a misdeed, they are taking a self-righteous role. They are saying (believing) that they or others do not have the right to err. To them, to err is not human, and to forgive could only be divine.

? *I don't understand. I know that I feel good when I do something well. Isn't it natural that I also feel good when my autistic child does something well? And, doesn't this also apply when my child or I do something poorly?*

It is appropriate to feel good when good things happen, but it is different when you think that you are a good person because you do a good thing. (We certainly know that people who do good things may also do "bad" things.) Further, it cannot be proven that if you do something bad, you become a bad person. To suggest that a person is good or bad based on a few behaviors is to overgeneralize. The following are some of the relevant self-talk words related to this type of thinking:

worthless

retard (or other name)

stupid

irresponsible

rotten

When these words are used to describe you or others, they will probably result in debilitating feelings, including depression, guilt, shame, or anger. They might be used in the context of the following self-talk:

1. Bobby hasn't improved at all. That teacher is absolutely worthless!
2. She is such a problem. She doesn't know how to behave.
3. I didn't do that well. I am so stupid.
4. She's late again. She is totally irresponsible.
5. What a rotten guy. He is so mean to my son!

Although it is understandable that we become disappointed when unpleasant events occur, there is little evidence to support the above self-talk evaluations. For example, consider the following disputations:

1. Bobby hasn't improved at all. That teacher is absolutely worthless!

Dispute: Is the teacher's worth based entirely on his ability to work with Bobby? Does he do well with other students? Have others been more successful with Bobby? Can one accurately evaluate the teacher's worth based on his interactions with Bobby? Even if he is not as successful with Bobby as is possible, will this faulty evaluation of his worth facilitate good communication with this teacher, which may very well improve Bobby's skills?

2. She is such a problem. She doesn't know how to behave.

Dispute: To describe an individual as a problem (even if the individual has been clinically assessed as having autism) because of inappropriate or certain other behaviors is a hasty and unfair generalization. It unfairly places the person in an unattractive category and contends that if people are different, they should be degraded. It also may lead one to treat that person unfairly because of the stereotypes that may follow the description.

3. I didn't do that well. I am so stupid.

Dispute: People who say they are stupid when they do not do well are suggesting that they must do well in everything not to be stupid. Do they become smart when they do some things well? This attitude takes away the reality of fallibility that is integral to our humanness. Can anyone honestly claim to be infallible?

4. She's late again. She is totally irresponsible.

Dispute: To suggest that somebody is totally irresponsible because of lateness (again) ignores or minimizes other qualities. Even if the person is not very responsible, does that make her a horrible human being?

5. What a rotten guy. He is so mean to my son!

Dispute: It is tempting to think of somebody as "a rotten guy" because he is mean to your son. The fact that your son has autism might add ammunition to your emotional arsenal. Not everybody knows how to effectively interact with individuals with autism and, while that is unpleasant, it gives little credence to the evaluation that a human being who may be ignorant is also "rotten."

? *I work very hard at what I do. I carefully plan activities for my child, and I can honestly say that I am at least adequate in everything that I do, or I just won't do it. So?*

It is too bad if you avoid what could be pleasant events because you are less than adequate at them (we wouldn't get out of bed, if we had to assure ourselves that *everything* we will do that day will be done in an adequate fashion). Keep in mind that the evaluation of adequacy means different things to different people. For example, adequacy for some golfers might be 100; others might define it as 75 and consider quitting the game if they score in the 80s. Another person who normally scores in the 100s and shot a 90 might be so happy that she would think of becoming a golf professional.

It is not inappropriate to strive for excellence. However, placing the pressure of perfection on yourself may severely limit your opportunities for progress and enjoyment (and of your child).

? *Okay, but does all of this understanding about what creates my upset feelings help me with my problem(s)?*

Simply understanding your problem does not stop your feelings from occurring. You have to practice the Disputations when the Activating Events occur. Actually working on your new thinking, which will then result in new feelings and behaviors, is called the E, or the Effect.

E = Effect

The Effect is your commitment to change your negative feelings. It will take hard work and practice to make the desired change. Behavioral principles such as positive reinforcement can often help ensure that your realistic self-talk is practiced. That is, rewards or punishments are applied when the self-talk is used (or not used).

? *How can I apply the ABC process?*

On a sheet of paper, apply the components of the model presented in this chapter. List your answers to the A, B, C, and D sections. Practice your D statements when you feel distressed. Ask yourself the following questions in order to facilitate the process:

A = *The Activating Event (What happened?)*

C = *Consequences (What emotions or behaviors do you want to change?)*
How does the feeling affect you?
How do you want to change this feeling?

B = *Belief System (List the self-talk that makes you . . .)*
What Belief System (Demanding, Awfulizing, Rating) are you using?

D = *Disputations (Give evidence that your Beliefs are true.)*

E = *Effect (How are you going to make needed changes?)*

Let's examine two damaging emotions: anger and frustration. They are damaging because they interfere with one's long-term goals of creating an active, loving, exciting, and enriching learning environment for children and youth with autism. Once a self-defeating feeling (behavior) is exhibited, it is extremely difficult to regain the composure necessary to achieve one's goals. A realistic goal would be to lower the level of intensity of our feelings so that we can express our displeasure without inflicting damage.

A number of events may make us feel upset under any circumstances. These events may be especially troublesome because of the added responsibility of being faced with the arduous task of continually dealing with an individual who has a disability. We have met with parents who reported to us that the following are only a few of the things that make this relationship difficult:

- Family members who do not understand the parent's situation
- Behavior of children (at parties, stores, etc.)
- Teacher's lack of knowledge about autism
- Fighting to get adequate treatment
- Slow progress
- Family stresses (lack of recreation times with spouse, less intimacy)
- Self-abusive behavior
- Caregivers who are "unprofessional"
- Doctors (who are ignorant, who ignore parents' feelings, or who even cast blame)
- Sibling issues (time, jealousy)
- People who do not care
- The future of the child (dating, dependency, employment)
- What happens after parents die?

Caretakers who are not parents, including teachers, have reported the following slightly different problems:

- Lack of support from administration and others
- Lack of client (child) progress
- Bad behavior of clients
- Inability to help certain youth

These problems can be debilitating if a person's Belief Systems (self-talk) are unrealistic.

PUTTING THE MODEL TO WORK

The following are descriptions of how Susan, and later Frank, used the ABC model to help them with their problems.

Susan's Problem: Handling Frustration

Susan has been attempting to help her son Joe learn some simple communication skills. The program involves training gestures that will allow Joe to make some of his needs known. At first, Joe seemed to be fairly successful at learning the program, but he continually regressed, sometimes to the point of losing all his skills. Susan feels she can't work with Joe. It seems that no matter what she tries, her efforts fail. She is very distressed at her inability to solve this dilemma.

A = The Activating Event (What Happened?)

"Joe is just a constant failure. He cannot learn to communicate. No matter what I try, he still fails to learn."

C = Consequences (What Emotions or Behaviors Do You Want to Change?)

"*Frustration*." (In this case, Susan had only one feeling about the Activating Event.)

How Does the Feeling Affect You?

"I find myself spending too much time trying to solve this puzzle. I find myself wanting to avoid Joe. This is getting in the way of relationships with my other family members, my social life, even my job. I would rate my frustration as a 75 out of 100."

How Do You Want to Change This Feeling?

"I would like to lower my frustration to 40. I want to be able to continue helping Joe and regain perspective on the other aspects of my life."

B = Belief System (List the Self-Talk That Makes You Frustrated.)

"I can't stand the fact that he isn't learning from me. This is the worst thing that has happened to me. Maybe he needs a better parent."

"He should know how to communicate by now!"

"*Everyone* can learn."

"There must be a way for me to reach him."

What Belief System Is Used?

Awfulizing, Demanding, and Rating, but mostly Demanding.

D = Disputations (Give Evidence That Your Beliefs Are True.)

"First and foremost, I seem to be telling myself that Joe, a severely autistic boy, should know better. Common sense would indicate that if he did know better, he wouldn't have autism. I'm not accepting conditions the way they are."

"I seem to be putting an awfully big responsibility upon myself. I would prefer to be successful in all of my endeavors, but it seems grandiose to expect that I am some sort of supermom."

"I know from my experiences, and the experiences of others, that everybody doesn't learn at the same speed or using the same program."

"This is really an unfortunate time that I am going through, but it certainly isn't the worst thing that has ever happened to me."

"There might be (not necessarily 'is') a way to teach Joe. I am going to continue to try."

"Joe isn't doing this 'to me'; rather, this situation is occurring because he can't help it."

E = Effect (How Am I Going to Make These Changes?)

"Even though it is frustrating for me to watch Joe slip each time, I will try to be more tolerant and accepting of him and myself. Since my goal is to teach Joe, my previous unrealistic feelings were only getting in the way of that goal (which may never be met). As a 'punishment,' if I find myself getting very frustrated again, I will offer to invite my in-laws over for Thanksgiving. However, if I can manage my frustrating feelings, I will go buy that sweater I have been admiring, but have been reluctant to buy!"

Frank's Problem: Managing Anger

Frank is a special education teacher who works with students with severe disabilities. He is considered to be good with his students, and has been highly evaluated by his superiors. During the last school year, Frank's principal, Mr. Smith, placed three students over the state's limit in Frank's classroom. The additional students put an unfair burden on Frank, which was detrimental to his students' education. Frank protested and Mr. Smith promised that if Frank did not "make waves," he would hire another special education teacher, which would mean underenrollment for Frank the next year. Frank agreed not to cause any problems.

This year, Frank's class is still three students over the maximum and there is little indication that it will change. Frank complained to Mr. Smith, who responded that he had not been able to get the necessary funds. "Besides," he added, "since you did such a nice job last year with your class size, I didn't think it would be a problem this year." Frank reminded Mr. Smith of their agreement, to which Mr. Smith responded that Frank should stop whining and that if he did not like his job, he could look for another one. He also reminded Frank that he agreed to the extra numbers the previous year, and that "Nobody put a gun to your head." Frank became extremely angry. He could not concentrate on preparing his lessons and he became short-tempered with his students and family. He could not sleep well. He began to consider quitting his job.

A = The Activating Event (What Happened?)

"Mr. Smith broke an agreement with me. He promised to reduce my class size. Heck, I wouldn't even mind if he just lowered it to meet the state regulations."

C = Consequences (What Emotions or Behaviors Do You Want To Change?)

"*Anger.* Also, resentment, frustration, and depression." (Frank chose one emotion to work on: Anger.)

How Does the Feeling Affect You?

"I can't sleep, can't concentrate. I feel like hitting Mr. Smith or telling him what a creep he is. It seems like I lose my temper too quickly with my students. I'd rank my anger at 90 (out of 100). I'm 'losing it,' and this is just not like me."

How Do You Want to Change This Feeling?

"This is tough. I know I'm right. I just can't do anything because of these feelings. I would like to be able to control myself, to lower my anger to a 60. I don't want to stop caring about this, but I'm also not getting anything done and I'm being a jerk with my students and family. They don't understand me."

B = Belief System (List the Self-Talk That Makes You Angry.)

"The jerk lied to me. He has no right to do that!"

"Principals shouldn't do that!"

"I'm going to do what I can to get that bum fired!"

"Poor me. I can't stand this job anymore." [Not appropriate for this problem! Does this statement make you angry or depressed?]

"Everybody should stand up and support me on this one! They don't care and they deserve what they will get." [Frank gives no realistic beliefs.]

What Belief System Is Used?

Demanding. Some Rating, but primarily Demanding.

D = Disputations (Give Evidence That Your Beliefs Are True.)

"How provable is it? Well, he did lie to me. I guess others have lied to me before and I've handled it. I'm old enough to realize that people do lie, even teachers! I wish they wouldn't, but that's the way it is."

"Principals are people, and many people do look out for their own best interests. I don't know why I let him sucker me. He's done it before. I'd prefer that he be honest."

"Maybe he was looking out for his own best interests, maybe even the students'. I wish he knew a better way to communicate, even though I know that he's always been this way."

"It would be nice if he would uphold his end of the bargain, because I upheld mine. Unfortunately, things don't always work out that way."

"Even though he *could* have acted differently, I really have little evidence that he *should* have. I don't know his pressures. Maybe he was telling me the truth, and he simply doesn't have the communication skills to effectively tell me."

"I guess I'm really asking *him* to be a better person because *I* want him to be one. Sounds like I'm doing the same thing he's doing. Maybe *I* can't have what I want all of the time, even though it was promised!"

"I could probably get others to agree that I was wronged, yet does that prove it without a shadow of a doubt?"

"I could probably be reasonably happy in my job with the extra kids. If I can't be happy, I might look for another job. What choices *do* I really have? To let him destroy my home life and job, or for me to tolerate his behavior?"

"My anger is not getting me what I want! My job and relationships are suffering. Mr. Smith is avoiding me. In fact, if I get my way through a demonstration of anger power, *he* just might figure out a way to get back at me!"

E = Effect (How Am I Going To Make Needed Changes?)

"I am going to try to accept my principal's dishonesty. I do not like it, but I do like my job and this community. His lies are really only an annoyance. I am going to try different avenues, in an assertive yet nondemanding way to get my class size lowered." (Notice that Frank is first trying to calm down and he will try to get the Activating Event altered.)

"The next time he lies, I am not going to be surprised. I will simply not react with great expectations to his statements. I will try to avoid future agreements with him. If I fail to accept his dishonesty and get angry with him again, my *punishment* (because I am not practicing my rational thinking) will be to ask him if there are any committees or extra work he would like me to do for him."

SUMMARY

The ABC model can be a very effective way to manage self-defeating feelings. It provides a process for examining and disputing the cause(s) of emotional and behavioral problems that limit one's opportunity for positive mental health. It involves analyzing one's perceptions about the events that contribute to unhappiness. In the two case studies, both Frank and Susan demonstrate how they can manage their negative feelings so that their *goals* can be met. They neither “gave in” to the negative events, nor passively accepted them. Instead, by examining the reality of their situations, they were able to temper their harmful feelings. This process requires hard work and diligence and, in some cases, the help of a health care professional such as a counselor or psychologist.

Parents and Families of Children and Youth with Autism: Strategies for Support, Management, and Involvement

9

Professionals are increasingly recognizing the benefits of supporting parents and families of children and youth with autism. This recognition derives from two main reasons. First, because family members and family activities (e.g., roles, functions) are interconnected, events and circumstances that affect one family member will affect other members as well. Thus, a child or youth with autism will influence and be influenced by his entire family, necessitating the focus of attention on more than only the child with autism. Failure to consider parent and family needs may result in overinvolvement by parents and family members with their child with autism (i.e., other family members' needs are overlooked as a result of excessive attempts to satisfy the needs of a child with autism), parent and family frustration, and poor communication between professionals and families. With more and more individuals with autism residing at home, these considerations are increasingly taking on importance.

A second major reason for involvement and support of parents and families of children and youth with autism is related to the extensive training and intervention needs of most children and youth with autism. As noted throughout this book, individuals with autism have significant needs in a variety of areas (e.g., social, language, medical, behavioral, cognitive). As a result, professionals are often unable to satisfactorily meet the needs of children diagnosed with autism without assistance from parents and family members. Such assistance, in the form of effective parent–professional communication and use of home-based management and training programs, has been shown to be an effective way of assisting children and youth with autism. Thus, to the extent that they are interested and able, parents and families should be involved in training, education, and treatment programs.

In this chapter, we discuss support measures and programs available to parents and families of children and youth with autism. Thus, this chapter is designed to assist parents in working with their children in home settings and in better advocating for their offspring with autism. We also identify ways parents and families can be involved in the education and treatment of family members who have been diagnosed as having autism. The emphasis is on understanding and working with educational and training programs, although other aspects of support are discussed.

TYPES OF SUPPORT PROGRAMS

Because families of children with autism differ widely, their support and other needs also vary. As a result, professionals must be able to individualize services and programs for parents and families, just as they do for children. Most parent and family needs fit into five major categories: education, training, and other programs for a family member with autism; information exchange opportunities; advocacy, legal/legislative, and partnership training; home program application; and counseling and support services.

Education, Training, Intervention Services, and Other Programs

Virtually every parent and family needs appropriate services for the family member diagnosed with autism. Parents and families want to know that the family member with autism is receiving appropriate educational, training, medical, vocational, or other types of services, whether it be through a public school, state-supported program, or private facility. No other need is as basic as this; therefore, until this need is met, other parent and family needs will be secondary.

Information Exchange Programs

Information exchange programs involve reciprocal needs for information between parents and families and the professionals working with them. Through two-way communication, professionals must obtain relevant facts about children and families (e.g., developmental history, school history, family expectations), as well as provide appropriate information, including progress reports, to parents and families.

Professionals should include assessment results in the information given to parents and family members, and provide opportunity to discuss these findings. Even though parents and families may have received an interpretation of autism following an assessment of their child, most likely they will benefit from a review of the information and from discussing issues associated with the disability and subsequent recommendations. Parents and families should also be given a description of the educational, training, vocational, medical, therapeutic, or other program to be provided the child, including the training methods, behavioral remediation, and other therapeutic and intervention programs scheduled.

Advocacy, Legal/Legislative, and Partnership Training

Parents are the primary case managers for their children, and are ultimately responsible for their well-being. Although parents have been granted significant authority in determining the programs, procedures, and treatments to be used with children with autism, few provisions have been made for training parents in how to serve in this case manager role. Thus, in spite of participation in school conferences and other parent–professional meetings and attempts to work cooperatively with professionals, parents have not been trained in how to do so effectively. Accordingly, if parents and family members are to be expected to function at a level consistent with their case manager role and assigned rights, they must be provided appropriate training.

First, parents and family members should be given information on how to participate in conferences and meetings and on their rights and responsibilities as parents and families of children with autism. Second, they should be informed about how they can serve as advocates and case managers for children with disabilities, and as effective consumers of community, school, and agency services and resources. Although it cannot be assumed that all parents and families need or desire partnership, case manager, and advocacy training, many families will make use of such preparation if offered.

Home Program Application

Both as tutors and behavior managers, parents and family members of children and youth with autism have proven to be valuable in extending professional intervention programs beyond classroom and clinical settings. For example, under professional direction, parents and family members can be trained to implement individualized tutoring and training programs with their own child. Such tutoring serves both to involve these individuals in a child's school or vocational program and to positively structure interactions between the family and child.

Parents and families have also been trained to employ behavior management and training procedures with children and youth with autism. This approach has allowed parents and families to effect planned behavior changes in the home and thus to extend the therapeutic influence of professionals.

Although some parents and families may be unmotivated or unsuited for this role, others will be highly appropriate. Training of parents and families to serve in this capacity provides a vehicle for extending problem-solving efforts into nonprofessional environments and for coordinating parents' motivations for involvement, participation, and case management. Accordingly, professionals should be willing (and able) to train parents and family members so that they can work with children and youth with autism at home.

Counseling and Support Services

A small percentage of parents and families of children with autism will need in-depth counseling and therapy. Furthermore, many parents and families will benefit from participating in support groups. Such groups are designed to assist families to discuss and accommodate members with disabilities, including those with autism; provide useful information regarding persons with disabilities; and give nondisabled family members a chance to discuss issues related to living with an individual with a disability. Support groups may be sponsored by schools, mental health agencies, or organizations such as the Autism Society of America (specific support resources are identified in Chapter 10).

Professionals should be able to provide interested parents and family members information about support groups, and parents and families should be able to correctly identify their support group needs. Although not every family will want or use them, support groups can be extremely valuable in assisting individuals to successfully live with and support family members with autism.

INDIVIDUALIZING PROGRAMS

Parent and family needs vary and must, therefore, be planned for individually. Much of this individualization can occur through development of effective Individualized Education Programs (IEPs) for school-age students, Individualized Family Service Plans (IFSPs) for young children, and Individualized Transition Plans (ITPs) for students preparing for the transition from school to work and adult life. Professionals should not assume that every parent and family member of a child with autism will have the same needs, and every family should not be expected to follow a rigid plan of involvement. Parents and families not only have different needs relative to children and youth with autism, but are unique in terms of time, resources, motivation, skills, commitment, and interests. For example, some parents and family members wish to interact and communicate with professionals frequently; others may prefer to be actively involved as advocates for a family member with autism; others may wish to serve as home tutors and behavior managers; and still others may have relatively little interest in training their child with autism at home.

It is important for parents and family members to select, through discussions with professionals, a level of involvement and participation that fits their needs, style, and interests. Thus, parents and family members must not feel guilty because their level of participation and involvement differs from that of other parents and families. Professionals must respect these decisions and assist parents and family members with implementing programs corresponding to their participation and involvement interests and abilities.

It is also important that both families and professionals recognize that involvement and participation levels do not remain constant, but depend on parent and family circumstances at a given time. For example, a parent who actively serves as a home tutor for a child with autism may be required to reduce her level of involvement after a divorce or the death of a spouse. Thus, parents, family members, and professionals must be flexible and willing to vary their support of a family member with autism according to family circumstances. The underlying consideration is that family members must be able to identify and satisfy their own needs in order to successfully support a family member with autism.

IMPORTANCE OF PARENT AND FAMILY INVOLVEMENT

All children and adolescents, including those with autism, are influenced by their parents and families. In fact, no other single experience impacts so profoundly on the way a person reacts to the world and its people. An individual's values, attitudes, and unique ways of behaving are often a direct result of parent and family influence. Although children and adolescents do develop behaviors that are uniquely their own, and they may be influenced by others, such as peers, teachers, language pathologists, and so on, parent and family support is necessary for children's optimal growth and development. The role of parents and families may include acting as (a) referral agents, (b) support agents, and (c) case managers for their children. As noted earlier, the degree of parent and family involvement will vary; however, it is important to recognize the influential role that parents and family members can play in the lives of children and youth with autism.

Parents and Families as Referral Agents

Parents occasionally find that the professionals they respect the most and have the most contact with do not share their concern over their children's behavior. In response to a parent's concern about a child's behavior, a pediatrician or a family physician, for example, may suggest that the child is going through a phase or that a given concern is unfounded. One mother observed that every time she attempted to talk to her family doctor about her son's problems, the doctor wanted to write her a prescription for tranquilizers. Thus, some parents find it difficult to find suitable professional help for their children.

Parents can take a number of steps to ensure that pediatricians, other physicians, and other professionals with whom they have contact (e.g., public health nurses, social workers) note their concerns. Make it clear that you are not asking your doctor (or other professional) to personally solve the problem. Explain that you are concerned about your child's behavior and are seeking an assessment by a professional trained and experienced to work with children and adolescents with disabilities, including autism. Physicians and other professionals sometimes lack the time and expertise to deal with children with developmental delays and problems.

Second, document your concerns. Rather than telling a professional from whom you are seeking assistance, "My child prefers to be by herself," attempt to identify precisely what it is your child is doing. For instance, does "prefer to be by herself" mean that she likes to play by herself in the same room as other family members, or that she actively avoids being near others, or that she engages in self-stimulatory behaviors (e.g., hand flapping) to the extent that she becomes unaware of the presence of others? Further, report how often, how intensively, and how long the problem occurs. Specifying that your child daily engages in self-stimulatory behavior for extended periods of time to the exclusion of all other activities and that this behavior has occurred consistently over the past year is far more meaningful than simply relating that your child rocks. Early intervention is particularly important for children with autism, making it essential to find appropriate assistance as early as possible.

? *What should I do if my doctor doesn't share my concern?*

Seek help for your child's behavior even if your doctor does not share your concern. If you have observed unusual behavior patterns over extended periods of time (e.g., extreme withdrawal for a month or more), seek outside professional help. The best source of referral information is your community or county mental health agency. You may also wish to contact the Autism Society of America or your state's autism society. Your child's problem may turn out to be insignificant and temporary. However, if you consider it significant and if it is disruptive or bothersome to you and your family, contact an appropriate professional or agency.

? *Can referrals for service be made by and through public school personnel?*

Yes. Although most children with autism are diagnosed prior to the time they begin school, they occasionally are identified during their elementary school years. This is particularly true for students with higher functioning autism disorders such as Asperger syndrome.

School personnel may be the first professionals to contact parents regarding their concerns about a child. For instance, a kindergarten teacher may call a parent subsequent to observing that a child has poor social skills or after noticing that he displays unusual behavior patterns. Contacts of this type are usually designed to provide teachers and other school personnel background information (e.g., developmental history, diagnostic information); to seek guidance regarding problem-solving strategies (e.g., parents' behavior management suggestions); and to obtain permission to conduct evaluations. Parents should be aware that public school personnel cannot conduct evaluations of children thought to be exceptional without first gaining their approval in writing. Similarly, school personnel must obtain parental permission prior to placing a child in a special education program.

Parents may also seek assistance from school personnel regarding their children's behavior and development. As in dealings with medical personnel, teacher contacts are most productive when the parents' concerns are specific and documented. Tell your child's teacher exactly what your concern is; how frequently and intensively the problem occurs; and how long it has been going on. Public schools are required to provide assessment and educational services for children and youth with disabilities, including those with autism. Thus, you may secure an evaluation for your child at no cost to you. If it is agreed that your child has a problem that should be investigated, ask the teacher to initiate a referral for evaluation.

? *What do I do if a teacher doesn't agree that my child has a problem?*

If a teacher or other school professional (e.g., principal, counselor) does not agree that a problem exists, parents may still request an evaluation. Such a request should be made if a parent or family member has reason to believe a child has a serious problem. To request an evaluation, write the director of special education in your local school district. If you do not have the individual's name and address, call the board of education or school administration office in your city. Your letter should specify the basis for your concern; request a district evaluation; and be accompanied by copies of relevant background documents (e.g., evaluation reports, developmental charts). School districts are required by state and federal mandate to consider parental requests for evaluation.

Parents and Families as Support Agents

Children with autism make optimal gains when the meaningful individuals in their lives work together. Thus, parents cannot expect their child to significantly improve exclusively as a result of professionals' efforts. Rather, parents and professionals must work together. Although the parents' role in this regard will vary, it can be expected to include cooperation and support for agreed-upon plans. In many instances, professionals develop plans for parents and families to follow. For example, parents may be asked to establish and maintain certain rules, to take certain actions, or to collect or provide certain types of information. For children to benefit the most, parents must support agreed-upon decisions and recommendations. Not only should parents and families be involved in decision making, once a decision has been reached, they must also support it.

Parents and Families as Case Managers

A case manager advocates and represents or acts in support of another. In the case of parents of children and youth with autism, this means that children's interests receive priority status, and that parents and family members take responsibility for seeing that the various needs of a family member with a disability are met. Although this may lead parents to view their situation differently from professionals, it does not mean that parents should disagree with, distrust, or otherwise resist cooperating with professionals. Conversely, parents should not unthinkingly accept all recommendations and suggestions without considering child and family needs as well as alternative recommendations. Parents and professionals must strive for a partnership in which both parties have the right to voice their opinions and to disagree. Such an open relationship strengthens the partnership and ultimately improves services to children.

The parents of a 16-year-old youth with autism, for example, found themselves caught between loyalty to their local school district and their son's interests. The school district had historically been responsive to their child's needs, including starting an elementary program for students with autism. When the boy outgrew the elementary program, however, the district did not have available a suitable alternative. Instead, school personnel recommended that the boy be placed in a high-school learning disability program since that was the only service available. The parents found themselves in the uncomfortable position of wanting to support the school district but knowing that the recommended service was not in their son's best interest. Open discussion of concerns between school staff and parents led the district to contract for appropriate services from a neighboring district. Only by taking case management responsibility and advocating for their son were these parents able to secure a suitable program.

? *Can parents be effective case managers and advocates for their children and still cooperate with professionals?*

Parents, including those of children and youth with autism, must seek to cooperate with and trust professionals. However, cooperation and trust do not mean passive compliance with suggestions and strategies that may not be in a child's best interests, or an expectation that others will take total responsibility for meeting a child's needs. Thus, parents must trust and support the professionals with whom they interact while keeping their child's interests a priority. Moreover, they should be willing to actively work to make sure their child's needs are being met.

THE INDIVIDUALS WITH DISABILITIES EDUCATION ACT

Being an effective advocate and case manager for a child or youth with autism implies having available appropriate knowledge and information relating to persons with disabilities. In particular, parents and family members who expect to effectively represent or support a family member with autism must be familiar with legislation that relates to children with disabilities.

The most comprehensive and significant legislation yet proposed and enacted for meeting the needs of school-age children and youth with disabilities, including those with autism, originally was named the Education for All Handicapped Children Act of 1975. This law (amended and retitled the Individuals with Disabilities Education Act in 1990; and reauthorized and amended in 1997) is so significant and far-reaching that it dominates every prior piece of legislation that has been enacted for children and youth with disabilities. The impact of IDEA is complemented and expanded by Section 504 of the Rehabilitation Act of 1973. Although both laws share a similar purpose—that is, to promote the rights of persons with disabilities—Section 504 broadens the range of individuals affected by expanding the age and definition requirements.

The Education for All Handicapped Children Act of 1975 (EHA) was designed to ensure a free and appropriate public education for all handicapped children and youth. This law, signed into effect by President Gerald Ford on November 29, 1975, following nearly 4 years of legislative proceedings, provides guidelines for aiding states and individual agencies (including public schools) in offering suitable educational experiences to children and youth with disabilities and in ensuring that the rights of these individuals and their families are protected. Many of the specific procedures involved in EHA are contained in individual state plans, which are documents explaining the precise manner in which each state will provide educational provisions and alternatives for children and youth with disabilities, including those identified as having autism.

Specific elements of the act, including those connected to the 1997 Reauthorization of IDEA, include the following:

1. Nondiscriminatory assessment in diagnosis
2. The right to due process, which protects exceptional children and youth from erroneous classification and denial of equal education and protection
3. Placement of students with disabilities in an educational setting that is the least restrictive environment
4. Individualized program plans, which ensure an appropriate education
5. Involvement of parents in their children's education

Each of these provisions is discussed in the following sections.

Nondiscriminatory Assessment in Diagnosis

IDEA requires that testing and evaluation methods used to diagnose students with disabilities, including those with autism, not be racially or culturally discriminatory. Moreover, evaluation procedures must accommodate a student's native language. Thus, non-English speaking children being evaluated because of an alleged school problem must be tested using materials and procedures that allow them to use their native language. Further, the evaluation process must be designed to accommodate students' deficits. For instance, a student with limited spoken language must not be evaluated using tests that require extensive verbal responses.

Parents (or legal custodians, in cases where children do not live with their parents) are actively involved in the assessment process. Thus, parents of children being recommended for evaluation due to a school problem or alleged disability must give written permission before evaluations take place.

Also, according to IDEA, requests for evaluation can be made by parents as well as by schools. Hence, parents of a child exhibiting autistic-like characteristics may request an evaluation or reevaluation of their offspring at any time they deem appropriate. However, a school district has the choice of whether or not to conduct an evaluation. If the district agrees to the request for an evaluation, written permission still must be obtained from the parents prior to actually conducting the assessment. If the district takes the position that an evaluation is not needed, they must notify the parents, in writing, of that decision. This notice must also inform the parents that, if they desire, they can request a hearing to arbitrate differences of opinion between the school and themselves regarding the need for an evaluation.

As discussed in Chapter 3, evaluations of children and youth considered to have autism or other disabilities should be both multidisciplinary and comprehensive. Consequently, evaluations must provide information relating to the physical, psychological, sociological, and educational status of each individual being evalu-ated. Furthermore, these evaluations must be made by a variety of "experts" representing their respective fields as opposed to a single individual. Thus, with regard to evaluations conducted by school personnel, professionals other than school employees may be involved. For example, in instances where a child with autism requires an evaluation by a professional who is not on a school's staff (e.g., audiologist, neurologist), a school is required to privately contract for those diagnostic services.

Evaluation- and assessment-related procedural modifications associated with the 1997 Reauthorization of IDEA include provisions for more closely connecting assessments of students with purported special needs to the general education curriculum; giving IEP teams (of which parents are a part) greater flexibility in determining reevaluation procedures; and including students with disabilities, whenever possible, in state- and district-wide assessments.

The Right to Due Process

The primary due-process rights afforded parents and children under IDEA include parental access to records, independent evaluations, surrogate parents, parental notice, and right to a hearing.

Parental Access to Records. Parents or legal custodians are allowed to view all records pertaining to the identification, assessment, and placement of their child.

Independent Evaluations. Parents and legal custodians are entitled to obtain an evaluation of their son or daughter from qualified (licensed or certified) examiners not affiliated with the district or agency recommending the action. However, even though parents are entitled to seek their own independent evaluation and even though schools or agencies may be required to recommend appropriate individuals to conduct the evaluation, parents may be required to assume the costs of an evaluation.

Appointment of Surrogate Parents. In instances in which a child or adolescent is a ward of the state, or the parents are unavailable or unknown, the appointment of a surrogate parent may be made. Surrogate parents are commissioned to represent the child in all matters pertaining to evaluation, placement, and education. The criteria for the selection of a surrogate parent is that the appointee have the necessary competence to represent an exceptional child or adolescent (including an individual with autism) and that no conflict of interest exists. Thus, individuals employed by or affiliated with an institution or setting in which a child or adolescent is a resident should not serve as surrogate parents.

Right to Parental Notice. As discussed earlier, parents, legal custodians, or surrogates must be provided written notice whenever a school or agency proposes to conduct an evaluation or make a change in the educational program for an exceptional pupil, including a child or youth identified as having autism. This requirement also applies in instances in which parents request changes or evaluations.

Right to Hearing. Parents and legal custodians must be provided a formal opportunity to present complaints on any matter relating to the identification, evaluation, or educational placement of their child. This process is designed to afford parents, schools, and agencies the opportunity for an objective and impartial hearing, the outcome of which will hopefully lead to the most appropriate educational placement possible for a child. Hearings can be held by the state, intermediate, or local educational agency, depending on the situations and locale.

The provisions of due process are extended not only to parents and legal custodians but also to agencies and schools. Thus, a school or agency is entitled to a hearing on its recommendation or refusal to initiate evaluation or placement procedures.

It is important that parents and family members of children and youth with autism recognize their due process rights under IDEA. Without this information it is impossible to be an effective advocate and case manager. However, availability of this information must not be viewed as an alternative to communicating and working with professionals. As noted before, children and youth with autism make the best progress when parents and family members work jointly with professionals, and when parents and family members are actively involved in identifying and managing services.

The Least Restrictive Environment

According to the least restrictive environment provision of IDEA, school-age children and youth with disabilities, including those with autism, must be educated with students without disabilities to the maximum extent appropriate. Children and youth with disabilities can be provided placement outside the regular classroom environment only when the severity or nature of their disability demands a more restrictive setting.

Although regulations pertaining to the least restrictive environment advocate the use of the regular classroom as the desired location for instruction, this policy does not apply to children and youth whose needs cannot be met in that setting. Thus, children and youth with autism who require special education or a more restrictive setting (e.g., hospital or residential program) are assured of such a program. The identification of the least restrictive environment, which is reviewed and determined at least annually, must be based on each child's or youth's ability and performance, as translated through the IEP. Because parents or legal custodians are major participants in this decision, it is apparent that this decision cannot be made by school or agency personnel without family input.

Individualized Program Plans

An Individualized Education Program (IEP) must be provided for each child or adolescent identified as needing special education. This includes children and youth with autism. An IEP is a written statement outlining the manner in which each school-age child with a disability will have his or her unique needs met. For adolescents, Individualized Transition Plans (ITPs) are also included, which assist students and families in preparing for the transition from school to work and adult life, and assist in orchestrating community agencies that will provide services after a student leaves school. Each IEP and ITP is different from others because each student has different needs. The document is developed in a meeting attended by professionals, parents, and, when appropriate, the child or youth.

For each child, the IEP includes the following:

1. A statement of the child's strengths, weaknesses, and functioning level (e.g., language, social skills, behavior, cognitive, self-help abilities)
2. Annual goals, or statements of areas in which professionals will focus their attention (e.g., to improve self-help skills, to improve social interaction skills)
3. Short-term objectives, which are statements identifying the specifics of annual goals (e.g., "James will initiate at least one appropriate social greeting, as defined by his teacher, with a peer on the school playground, on 5 consecutive days")
4. A statement of the specific educational services to be provided (e.g., speech pathology, occupational therapy)
5. The extent to which a student will be able to participate in regular educational programs (e.g., "James will be scheduled for lunch in the cafeteria at the same time as his same-age peers")
6. Projected dates for initiation and duration of services (e.g., "James will be scheduled for individual occupational therapy 30 minutes two times per week between September 1 and May 15")
7. Objective criteria for determining whether objectives are being achieved (e.g., "James will achieve 80% accuracy, as judged by his teacher, on a 20-minute three-part vocational collating task for 5 consecutive days")

Although the IEP format can vary between states, school districts, and agencies, such as residential treatment programs for children with autism, certain basic components, as previously noted, must be included. The IEP is not intended to be a legally binding contract, whereby districts, hospitals, residential centers, and agencies are bound to demonstrate that progress specified in the annual goals and objectives has been met. However, professionals must use appropriate methods to achieve specified goals and objectives, including those stated in the IEP.

Individuals who should be involved in the IEP conference include a representative of the school, hospital, residential center, or agency providing the services (other than the teacher); the teacher(s) who will actually implement the IEP, including at least one regular education teacher if the student will or might participate in regular education; the parent(s) or legal custodians; the child or youth, when appropriate; and others, at the discretion of the parents or program. During the development of the initial IEP, the district or agency recommending the program modification should also have available someone who can interpret testing and diagnostic procedures to parents.

Because parents are considered such an integral part of the IEP conference, and because effective case management requires parent and family involvement, provisions exist for guaranteeing their participation. Specifically, parents must be provided advance notice of the IEP conference, including the purpose, time, location, and those individuals who will be in attendance. Districts, programs, and agencies must also hold conferences at times and places mutually convenient to both parents and professionals. Those individuals coordinating the conference must also ensure that parents will be able to comprehend and have input into the session. For example, interpreters must be provided for deaf or non-English speaking parents or, if parents are unable to attend the session, the school, program, or agency must use other methods to allow their participation (e.g., conference telephone calls). Although IEP conferences can be held without parental representation, the district or agency must be able to document that parents were provided an opportunity to participate.

The Reauthorization of IDEA in 1997 resulted in several significant IEP-related modifications. Included are provisions for specifying the manner in which each student's disability will affect participation in appropriate activities for same-age peers; provisions and steps for more closely connecting students with disabilities to the general education curriculum; positive behavioral supports for assuring students' success; modifications for allowing students with disabilities to participate in state- and district-wide assessments; and guidelines for revising an IEP to be maximally flexible, effective, and efficient. The Reauthorization of IDEA also outlines provisions for disciplining students with disabilities, especially those students who fail to respond to intervention attempts and those who are aggressive and violent. In this regard, the general theme of the current IDEA enactment is that schools are prohibited from expelling students with special needs, including those with autism. It does, however, give schools greater flexibility in using alternative educational settings, such as a hospital day-treatment program, if a student is judged to be a danger to self or others.

Similar in some ways to IEPs, Individualized Family Service Plans (IFSPs) are designed for young children. An IFSP is designed to identify and organize resources and services needed by families to serve children with disabilities, including those with autism. The required components of an IFSP include an identification of a child's current functioning level in major areas such as language, cognitive development, and so forth; an identification of a family's major strengths and needs; major outcomes for a child and his or her family, including a plan for assessing progress in achieving the outcomes; services needed and dates for their delivery; the service manager responsible for coordinating the plan; a schedule of when the plan will be reviewed; and a transition plan for moving the child to services available to children ages 3 to 5.

Involvement of Parents in Their Children's Education

IDEA guarantees not only the right to a free and appropriate education for all children with disabilities, including those with autism, but parents' right to involvement in decision making, educational planning, and implementation. Indeed, the 1997 Reauthorization of IDEA strongly endorses and strengthens the role of parents. Accordingly, parents are clearly afforded opportunities to be case managers for their children with disabilities. This policy of parent involvement represents a radical departure from past practices whereby parents and families were often blamed for conditions such as autism and isolated from professional decision making. In contrast, IDEA allows and encourages parent involvement and case management opportunities in educational and related service matters that affect their children. Thus, through IDEA, parents have been given participatory and case management rights with regard to their children. As previously discussed, these include parents' rights to be a part of the process for assessing their child; to challenge their child's evaluation, program, or placement recommendations; to give or withhold evaluation or placement consent; to have access to records; and to plan their child's education and treatment program.

Although mandated parental involvement is not sufficient to establish and maintain a productive professional–family relationship, IDEA does provide a legislative structure for the meaningful involvement of parents, families, and professionals. To be effective, family advocacy and case management on behalf of children and youth with autism require familiarity with this law.

MANAGING BEHAVIOR

Parents and family members of children and youth with autism often experience difficulty in managing behavior. Because success in this area is often basic to children's improvement and family tranquility, rule setting and behavior management are areas in which parents and family members may make a valuable contribution.

Setting Good Rules

Knowing limits and expectations is necessary and beneficial for all children and youth, particularly for individuals with autism who often have difficulty establishing their own structure. The following steps are involved in setting and implementing effective rules.

1. **Rules should be purposeful.** For instance, a rule may state that a child will not play in the street *because it is dangerous*, or that a child will not play in the toilet *because it is unhygienic and socially unacceptable*. Thus, each rule should be designed to

accomplish a specific goal, usually to protect a child or to maintain order. Such clarity requires that both a specific *target behavior* (e.g., complying with parent requests, as opposed to "not minding") and a specific *consequence* (loss of bicycle privileges for 24 hours, as opposed to "something you will regret") be identified. Rules also should specify rewards for following rules as opposed to negative consequences for noncompliance. Rules should not be designed simply to demonstrate control. Telling a child she cannot do certain things merely to show that you are in charge and can control her behavior is unacceptable. Additionally, children must not be expected to do things they cannot understand or perform. For example, it may be unrealistic to expect a nonverbal child with autism to talk in complete sentences before he is allowed to eat.

2. **Attempt to involve children.** Children tend to be more accepting of rules they have helped develop. Such involvement will vary with children's age and ability. Yet, many children, including those with autism, can be involved to some extent. In some cases, parents may simply explain why a rule is being implemented (e.g., "You cannot play in the street because you might get hurt"). Other situations require more discussion. Thus, a teenager with Asperger syndrome may be actively involved in rule setting discussions with her parents.

3. **Limit the number of rules.** "The fewer the better" is a good guideline for rule setting. Children and adults not only have difficulty remembering long lists of rules, but they tend to consider them meaningless and take them less seriously.

4. **Establish fair and appropriate consequences.** Children must understand precisely what will happen if they comply or fail to comply with rules (e.g., "If you are able to refrain from hitting at dinner, you may go for a drive with Dad"). Only when such understanding is assured can consequences be effectively applied. Additionally, parents must make sure that consequences are reasonable and enforceable. They must not be too light or too severe. Similarly, impulsive and unenforceable consequences must be avoided (e.g., "You must stay in your room the rest of the day"). Also, parents must be able to enforce established rules. For example, do not tell an adolescent with autism that he must interact with peers in the neighborhood when you have no means of enforcing such a rule.

5. **Be consistent.** A consequence must occur *every* time a rule condition is not met. This requires that adults or family members are willing to apply the consequence any time the target behavior occurs, even if it happens at a highly inopportune time. Additionally, in applying consequences parents should attempt to adhere to the following guidelines: (a) do not argue and negotiate—when a rule infraction occurs, apply the stated consequence with a minimum of explanation and without allowing an argument to develop; (b) avoid emotional displays when applying the consequence—do what you said you would do in a straightforward, business-like manner (demonstrating to children that you are hurt or upset has little positive effect); and (c) apply the consequence after rule conditions have been met, never before. Telling a child, for example, that you have decided to provide her an agreed-upon trip prior to her meeting the conditions for the trip often has a negative effect on the overall behavior management program.

6. **Use positive as well as negative consequences.** It is not unusual for parents (and children) to think of rules exclusively in negative terms. Thus, for example, fam-

ilies may think only in terms of what a child will lose after violating a rule. However, rules tend to work best when rewards (including praise and attention) are used. If negative consequences are applied, they should be used along with positive consequences (e.g., a reward for following a rule).

Establishing Schedules

Children and adolescents with autism tend to be positively influenced by structure and routines. For example, having set bedtimes and mealtimes often aids children in understanding and following schedules and parental requests. Problems may occur when children are unable to anticipate events and activities. This does not mean that parents and families must never vary their schedules—such a practice is neither realistic nor desirable. However, basic schedules and routines have been found to reduce management problems.

A useful management idea is to structure activities for children. This does not mean that something must be scheduled for every waking minute, which would be burdensome for parents and children. However, behavioral problems are most apt to occur during unstructured times. Thus, parents may discuss with their offspring which activities are available to them after school and on weekends (e.g., puzzle work, ball playing, bicycling, summer camp). Parents will probably discover that the more involved children become in structured and productive activities, the less likely they are to engage in undesirable behaviors.

Implementing Management Programs To Alter Behaviors

Rules and other general management techniques may fail to change some behaviors. In such situations more structured management techniques may be necessary. Such methods are best applied under professional direction. Although parents are usually able to successfully use behavior change methods, these stricter procedures should be set up and followed by a trained professional, preferably someone who is familiar in working with children and youth with autism.

As noted in Chapter 6, there are basic steps and principles associated with setting up and carrying out behavior management programs with children with autism. Because of the importance of these steps, they are discussed here, specifically as applied by parents and family members.

Step 1: Identify a Specific Behavior To Be Increased or Decreased.

Behavior management programs work best when applied to well-defined behaviors. For example, attempting to change a behavior such as hyperactivity or social immaturity is difficult because the target behavior may differ in the eyes of various people, including the child. For example, one parent might define social immaturity as failing to follow parental directions, whereas another may view it as avoiding peers. As a result, parents wishing to change a behavior must specifically define it.

Definitions of a behavior are most effective when they specify what the behavior is, where the behavior will be observed and dealt with, and when the behavior will be observed and dealt with.

- The *what* requires that parents precisely define a behavior. For example, hitting might be defined as a child making contact with another person with his fist, hand, or arm. In this definition no attempt is made to differentiate between soft and hard hits, or purposeful or accidental hitting. A hit is a hit!
- The *where* identifies settings, specifically those sites where the target behavior will be observed and dealt with. For example, a program for hitting might be applied at home or at the baby-sitter's, but not at the store, particularly if it is impossible to carry out the consequence in a store setting.
- The *when* specifies the times during which the program will be applied (e.g., 7:00 to 8:30 p.m. Monday through Friday).

It also is important that parents make sure that the behavior they wish to change is under the child's control; otherwise, it cannot be changed through this management system. Behaviors such as slamming a door, saying "thank you," and throwing rocks at the family cat are ordinarily under a child's control. In contrast, seizures, tremors, and tics are generally not under an individual's control, and thus not usually subject to change using these techniques.

Step 2: Determine the Settings and Situations Surrounding the Problem.

Parents should examine the conditions associated with the problem. Does the behavior occur only around certain people (e.g., mother, baby-sitter) or at certain times (e.g., dinner, bedtime)? Identifying these factors is helpful. For example, if it can be determined that a child has a certain problem only with his father, the solution may involve improving their relationship rather than developing a formal management program.

Step 3: Evaluate the Function of the Behavior.

Behavior is purposeful, including responses of children and youth with autism. Accordingly, understanding what a child or adolescent is attempting to achieve through his or her responses is essential in crafting an appropriate and effective management program. If, for instance, a nonverbal child engages in an aggressive response in an effort to communicate with her family or to obtain adult attention, then it would be inappropriate and ineffective to put the youngster in time-out when she demonstrates these behaviors.

Understanding the purpose or function of a response is not easy. However, professionals trained to work with students with autism should be able to assist parents and families in understanding their child's behavior and in designing programs. An example of this process involved a mother who was extremely concerned about her son's reluctance to play with other children. Based on results of a functional analysis, she realized that her response to this problem was maintaining it. With the assistance of a school psychologist, she observed that when her child came home from school she immediately began nagging him to go outside and play with neighborhood children. The functional analysis evaluation revealed that the child enjoyed his mother's attention, even though it was negative, because when the mother ceased nagging, the child became more interested in playing with other children.

Step 4: Select and Apply Suitable Consequences.

After defining a behavior and the circumstances surrounding it, including the function(s) of the response, apply appropriate methods for changing it. The length of time interventions should be applied will vary from situation to situation and from child to child; however, it is important to apply the chosen methods long enough for them to have a chance to work. Parents should not change programs without first consulting the professional responsible for setting up the program.

Four major types of consequences may be used by parents and family members to change behavior: positive consequences, ignoring, behavior reduction consequences, and environmental changes.

Positive Consequences. As noted in Chapter 6, positive consequences are events that increase a behavior. Two major forms of positive consequence are contingent activities and social consequences. *Contingent activities*, also known as "Grandma's law," are preferred activities that occur after a person demonstrates a desired behavior. For example, children or adolescents may be told, "You may watch TV when you finish your homework," "You may ride your bicycle after you take out the trash," or "If you avoid hitting your brothers and sisters this afternoon, you may go get ice cream with your brother." As illustrated, a desired activity is used to encourage a specific, desirable behavior.

Social consequences include praise, parental attention, smiles, and hugs for desired behavior. When used consistently, these forms of human contact and appreciation are powerful motivators, including for individuals with autism. Thus, parents may recognize their children for specific deeds (e.g., "I appreciate your following directions"), realizing that when such attention consistently follows desired behavior, the behavior will often be repeated.

Ignoring. Ignoring, also known as extinction, may decrease problem behaviors that occur as a result of attention. For instance, a child who throws tantrums to make her parents give in to her demands may cease this behavior if family members ignore her when she begins to cry.

When attempting to change a behavior through ignoring, parents should consider the following:

1. At first, ignoring may increase a behavior. That is, children may initially try to gain attention by increasing the problem behavior.
2. Ignoring works only if everyone involved is able to ignore. In instances where children are ignored only some of the time and by some people, the system usually fails.
3. To decrease a behavior through ignoring, you must give attention for acceptable behavior. Thus, you must ignore behavior you want to decrease while paying attention to behavior you want to increase. If you fail to give attention for suitable behavior, you probably will not be able to decrease a negative behavior through ignoring.

Behavior Reduction Consequences. Behavior reduction or negative consequences, sometimes referred to as punishment (see Chapter 6 for additional discussion), refer to undesirable events that follow specific behaviors. For example, children may learn they will lose privileges (e.g., getting to watch a favorite videotape) if they do certain things.

Of the possible behavor reduction or negative consequences, one technique frequently used by parents and families is *time-out.* Time-out involves placing a child in a chair in a corner (or similar spot) when he or she displays a certain unacceptable behavior. For example, a child may be required to sit quietly for 3 minutes in a chair in the corner of the living room if he throws things in the house. When used correctly, this popular consequence has often led to positive results.

Time-out is most effective if used with specific behaviors. Putting a child in time-out for a variety of unacceptable behaviors usually reduces the potential effectiveness of this management tool. Additionally, the time-out site should be clear of toys, TV, and other interesting things, including people. Thus, parents and family members must ignore children in time-out. Further, time-out sessions should be short: 3 to 5 minutes of quiet have proven best. If children are crying at the end of the specified time, time-out should be extended until the crying stops. Finally, parents or others using time-out should limit their comments to the child (e.g., "No kicking; go to time out") until the time-out period is over.

As with other management options, time-out may not work with every child with autism. Indeed, some children prefer being by themselves in time-out. Under such circumstances, time-out obviously does not decrease the behavior for which it was intended; hence, alternative interventions must be identified.

Environmental Changes. Changing the environment may take a variety of forms, including any change in conditions that may be causing problems. For example, one child with autism threw severe tantrums whenever a mealtime routine was broken. Because this was the only circumstance that provoked a tantrum, the parents tried to consistently follow established mealtimes. They also found that telling their child, well in advance, that there would be a change reduced the chances of a tantrum. Another parent of a preschool child diagnosed with autism solved her child's problem of throwing glass decorative objects (no other types of items were thrown) by moving these objects out of the child's reach. As suggested by these examples, simple methods are often sufficient for dealing with problems.

Step 5: Evaluate the Effectiveness of Your Management Methods.

The effectiveness of behavior management consequences and methods will vary depending on specific children and conditions. Thus, a technique may work with some children with autism and not with others. Therefore, it is essential to evaluate a program. Without such evaluation, parents may continue to use ineffective methods or drop an effective procedure.

Evaluation ordinarily requires daily or other frequent monitoring of a target behavior. Parents are advised to seek the help of a psychologist, educator, or other qualified professional when developing evaluation methods.

Making Behavior Management Programs Work

Behavior management programs do not work 100% of the time. The best results occur when the following basic steps are followed:

1. Apply a consequence only *after* a target behavior. Do not allow a child to engage in a desired activity because you have faith that she will complete an agreed-upon chore, for example. Rather, wait till she completes the chore. Similarly, do not apply a behavior reduction consequence (e.g., place a child in time-out) because she *looked* like she was going to engage in some undesirable activity.

2. Apply the consequence consistently. Carry out whatever you said you would do each time the behavior occurs.

3. Apply the consequence as soon after the target behavior occurs as possible. Waiting diminishes the strength of the consequence.

4. Make a commitment to apply a procedure over time. Behavior management programs sometimes work quickly; at other times, they take a while. Regardless, unless they are used consistently for significant periods of time, they will probably not be successful. Thus, do not stop using a program when it starts to work. It is

sometimes tempting to drop a procedure when the target behavior improves, but most programs stop being effective when parents stop working to apply them.

5. Seek professional guidance when setting up a behavior management program. Once a program has been decided upon, it is important that you follow the plan and not make changes in what was agreed upon.

Establishing a Relationship with the Child

Managing the behavior of a child or adolescent who has autism requires more than sound rules and management techniques. Parents and family members must be able to establish a relationship with their offspring. Moreover, as discussed in Chapter 8, attitudes of parents and family members are extremely important.

Like normally developing children and youth, children with autism need positive relationships with their families. That is, parents and family members must not simply be dispensers of reinforcers, tutors, social skill trainers, language developers, or advocates without also developing positive interpersonal relationships with their children. In this regard, it is extremely important that parents and family members set aside time to be with a child with autism. Such involvement is as much a part of being an effective case manager as making sure that a child is receiving all necessary services.

Developing a relationship takes time and effort. Thus, parents must spend time with their children doing mutually enjoyable things. In addition to peer tutoring, training, and similar activities, parents and family members are encouraged to participate in games and leisure pursuits with their children. Moreover, as much as possible, family members with autism should be included in family outings and events (e.g., going shopping, going to sports events), for social and learning reasons. In some instances children with autism will need to be prompted to engage in such activities (e.g., walking with a parent after dinner, looking at a book with a brother or sister, going grocery shopping); however, the trust, rapport, and experiences acquired through such activities often facilitate growth and development; enhance children's response to management and skill development programs; develop social, cognitive, and independent living skills; and establish more normalized family relationships.

SUMMARY

Parents and other family members play a prominent role in the growth and development of their children with autism. They are the primary case managers for their children. They serve as referral agents, advocates, and behavior managers. To adequately fulfill all these roles, parents must seek appropriate professional services; establish fair, yet firm rules; and use appropriate management techniques to deal with specific problems. The degree of success with which these roles are fulfilled will almost always influence the growth and development of children and youth with autism.

Resources for Autism and Pervasive Developmental Disorders

10

Laura Zionts and Paul Zionts

Much information is available in both print and electronic media in the area of autism. This chapter is intended to provide parents and professionals with beginning points for exploring available information related to autism and PDD spectrum disorders. Inasmuch as current levels of knowledge of autism within the professions limit us, we have included resources that will provide readers with a broad base of readings about autism and PDD. Some may contain information that is controversial and unproven. We have attempted to exercise judicious editorial concern, however, to provide a sampling of the resources that are relevant and may be worth exploring.

The listed resources have been arranged into print and Internet sections, and further categorized (to the extent possible) within the two sections. Please be advised that World Wide Web sites and Internet addresses tend to be fluid. If you find that a listed address is outdated, you may use a search engine, such as Excite or Yahoo, to find a relocated site.

RESOURCES IN PRINT

Handbooks for Parents and Other Professionals

Aarons, M., & Gittens, T. (1992). *The handbook of autism: A guide for parents and professionals*. London: Travistock/Routledge.

Anderson, W., Chitwood, S., & Hayden, D. (1997). *Negotiating the special education maze* (3rd ed.). Rockville, MD: Woodbine House.

Attwood, A. (1998). *Asperger's syndrome: A guide for parents and professionals*. London: Kingsley.

Autism Society of America. (1990). *How they grow: A handbook for parents of young children with autism* (new rev. ed.). Silver Springs, MD: Autism Society of America.

Azrin, N. H., & Foxx, R. M. (1989). *Toilet training in less than a day*. New York: Pocket Books.

Baron-Cohen, S., & Bolton, P. (1994). *Autism: The facts*. Cary, NC: Oxford.

Brantlinger, E. A., Klein, S. M., & Guskin, S. L. (1994). *Fighting for Darla—Challenges for family care and professional responsibility: The case study of a pregnant adolescent with autism*. New York: Teachers College.

Brill, M. T. (1994). *Keys to parenting the child with autism*. Hauppauge, NY: Barron's.

Catalano, R. A. (1998). *When autism strikes: Families cope with childhood disintegrative disorder*. New York: Plenum.

Cohen, S. (1997). *Targeting autism: What we know, don't know, and can do to help young children with autism and related disorders*. Berkeley: University of California Press.

Dalrymple, N. J. (1992). *Helpful responses to some of the behaviors of individuals with autism*. Bloomington: Indiana Resource Center for Autism.

Dillon, K. M. (1995). *Living with autism: The parents' stories*. Boone, NC: Parkway.

Frith, U. (1989). *Autism: Explaining the enigma*. Oxford: Basil Blackwell.

Harrington, K. (1998). *For parents and professionals: Autism*. East Moline, IL: LinguiSystems.

Harris, S. (1994). *Siblings of children with autism: A guide for families*. Rockville, MD: Woodbine House.

Hart, C. A. (1993). *A parent's guide to autism: Answers to the most common questions*. New York: Pocket Books.

Hartley, S., & Stewart, J. (1993). *The professional's guide to estate planning for families of individuals with disabilities*. Raleigh: ARC/North Carolina.

Hartley, S., Stewart, J., & Tesch, M. (1985) *Estate planning for families of persons with developmental disabilities*. Raleigh: ARC/North Carolina.

Janzen, J. E. (1996). *Understanding the nature of autism: A practical guide. San Antonio: Therapy Skill Builders.*

Maurice, C. (1993). *Let me hear your voice: A family's triumph over autism*. New York: Fawcett.

Maurice, C. (1996). *Behavior intervention for young children with autism: A manual for parents and professionals*. Austin, TX: PRO-ED.

Maurice, C., Greene, G., & Luce, S. (1996). *Behavioral intervention for young children with autism: A manual for parents and professionals*. Austin, TX: PRO-ED.

Myles, B. S., & Simpson, R. L. (1998). *Asperger syndrome: A guide for educators and parents*. Austin, TX: PRO-ED.

Naseef, R. A. (1997). *Special children/challenged parents: The struggles and rewards of raising a child with a disability*. Trenton, NJ: Carol.

Powell, S., & Jordan, R. (1997). *Autism and learning*. London: David Fulton.

Powell, T. H., & Gallagher, P. A. (1993). *Brothers and sisters: A special part of exceptional families*. Baltimore: Brookes.

Powers, M. D. (1989). *Children with autism: A parents' guide*. Rockville, MD: Woodbine House.

Powers, M. D. (1996). *Educating children with autism: A guide to selecting an appropriate program*. Rockville, MD: Woodbine House.

Schopler, E. (1995). *Parent survival manual: A guide to crisis resolution in autism and related developmental disorders*. New York: Plenum Press.

Schopler, E., & Mesibov, G. B. (1992). *High-functioning individuals with autism*. New York: Plenum Press.

Schopler, E., Mesibov, G., & Kunce, L. J. (1998). *Asperger's syndrome or high functioning autism*. New York: Plenum.

Schopler, E., Van Bourgondien, M. E., & Bristol, M. M. (1993). *Preschool issues in autism*. New York: Plenum.

Schulze, C. (1993). *When snow turns to rain: One family's struggle to solve the riddle of autism*. Rockville, MD: Woodbine House.

Siegel, S. (1996). *The world of the autistic child: Understanding and treating autistic spectrum disorders*. New York: Oxford University Press.

Sigman, M., & Capps, L. (1997). *Children with autism: A developmental perspective*. Cambridge, MA: Harvard University Press.

Simons, R. (1987). *After the tears: Parents talk about raising a child with a disability*. Boston: Harcourt Brace.

Sperry, V. A. (1995). *Fragile success: Nine autistic children, childhood to adulthood*. North Haven, CT: Shoe String Press.

Turnbull, A., & Turnbull, R. (1977). *Parents: Views from the other side of the two-way mirror.* Columbus, OH: Merrill.

Twatchtman-Cullen, D. (1997). *A passion to believe: Autism and the facilitated communication phenomenon.* Boulder, CO: Westview Press.

Weber Bell, E. (1986). *Autism: a reference book.* New York: Longman.

Wodrich, D. L., & Kush, S. A. (1990). *Children's psychological testing: A guide for nonpsychologists* (2nd ed.). Baltimore: Brookes.

Books for Children and Youth

Amenta, C. A. (1992). *Russell is extra special: A book about autism for children.* New York: Magination Press.

Autism Society of America. *Autism: Information written for kids only.* Bethesda, MD: Author.

Edwards, B. (1999). *My brother Sammy.* Brookfield, CT: Millbrook Press.

Gartenberg, Z. M. (1988). *Mori's story: A book about a boy with autism.* Minneapolis: Lerner.

Katz, K., & Ritvo, E. (1993). *Joey and Sam.* Los Angeles: Real Life Storybooks.

Lears, L., Mathews, J., & Ritz, K. (1998). *Ian's walk: A story about autism.* Morton Grove, IL: Albert Whitman.

Meyer, D. J. (1997). *Views from our shoes: Growing up with a brother or sister with special needs.* Rockville, MD: Woodbine House.

Mialaret, G. J. (1996). *Dancing with dragons: An entire family's insights into a disability.* Arlington, TX: Future Horizons.

Nollette, C. D. (1985). *Having a brother like David.* Minneapolis: Fraser Child and Family Center.

Siegel, B., & Silverstein, S. C. (1994). *What about me? Growing up with a developmentally disabled sibling.* New York: Insight Books.

Spence, E. (1976). *The devil hole.* New York: Lothrop, Lee & Shepard.

Thompson, M. (1996). *Andy and his yellow frisbee.* Bethesda, MD: Woodbine House.

Watson, E. (1996). *Talking to angels.* Boston: Harcourt Brace.

Books About Individuals Who Have Autism

Axline, V. M. (1967). *Dibs in search of self.* New York: Ballantine.

Grandin, T., & Scariano, M. M. (1991). *Emergence: Labeled autistic.* Navato, CA: Arena Press.

Greenfield, J. (1972). *A child called Noah.* New York: Holt, Rinehart & Winston.

Greenfield, J. (1978). *A Place for Noah.* New York: Holt, Rinehart & Winston.

Johnson, R. (1992). *Winter's flower.* Austin, TX: Raintree.

Kaufman, B. N. (1976). *Son-Rise.* New York: Harper & Row.

Martin, A. M. (1984). *Inside out.* New York: Holiday House.

Martin, A. M. (1995). *Kristy and the secret of Susan.* Milwaukee: Gareth Stevens.

McKean, T. A. (1994). *Soon will come the light: A view from inside the autism puzzle.* Arlington, TX: Future Horizons.

Sperry, V. W., & Provence, S. (1995). *Fragile success: Nine autistic children, childhood to adulthood.* North Haven, CT: Archon Books.

Watson, E. (1996). *Talking to angels.* San Diego: Harcourt Brace.

Werlin, N. (1994). *Are you alone on purpose?* Boston: Houghton Mifflin.

Teaching Individuals with Autism

Adams, J. *Autism–P.D.D.: Creative ideas from age eight to early adulthood*. Arlington, TX: Future Horizons.

Alvin, J., & Warwick, A. (1992). *Music therapy for the autistic child* (2nd ed.). Oxford, England: Oxford University Press.

Axline, V. M. (1947). *Play therapy: The inner dynamics of childhood*. Boston: Houghton Mifflin.

Bachrach, A. W., Mosley, A. R., Swindle, F. W., & Wood, M. M. (1978). *Developmental therapy for young children with autistic characteristics*. Austin, TX: PRO-ED.

Berkell, D. E. (1992). *Autism: Identification, education and treatment*. Hillsdale, NJ: Erlbaum.

California Department of Education. (1997). *Best practices for designing and delivering effective programs for individuals with autistic spectrum disorders*. Sacramento: Author.

Freeman, S., & Duke, L. (1996). *Teach me language*. Langley, British Columbia: SBK Books.

Fullerton, A., Stratton, J., Coyne, P., & Gray, C. (1996). *Higher functioning adolescents and young adults with autism: A teacher's guide*. Austin, TX: PRO-ED.

Harris, S. L., & Handleman, J. S. (1994). *Preschool education programs for children with autism*. Austin, TX: PRO-ED.

Jordan, R., & Powell, S. (1995). *Understanding and teaching children with autism*. New York: Wiley.

Koegel, R., & Koegel, L. (1995). *Teaching children with autism*. Baltimore: Brookes.

Koegel, L. K., Koegel, R. L., & Dunlap, G. (1996). *Positive behavioral support*. Baltimore: Brookes.

Koegel, R. L., Schreibman, L., Good, A., Cerniglia, L., Murphy, C., & Koegel, L. (1989). *How to teach pivotal behaviors to children with autism: A training manual*. Santa Barbara: University of California.

Lovaas, O. I. (1996). The UCLA young autism model of service delivery. In C. Maurice, G. Green, & S. Luce (Eds.), *Behavioral intervention for young children with autism* (pp. 241–248) Austin, TX: PRO-ED.

Olley, J. G., & Stevenson, S. E. (1989). Preschool curriculum for children with autism: Addressing early social skills. In G. Dawson (Ed.), *Autism: Nature, diagnosis and treatment* (pp. 346–366). New York: Guilford.

O'Neill, R. E., Horner, R. H., Albin, R. W., Sprague, J. R., Storey, K., & Newton, J. S. (1997). *Functional assessment and program development for problem behavior: A practical handbook* (2nd ed.). Pacific Grove, CA: Brooks Cole.

Parker, R. (1996). Incorporating speech–language therapy into an applied behavior analysis program. In C. Maurice, G. Green, & R. S. Luce (Eds.), *Behavioral intervention for young children with autism* (pp. 297–306). Austin, TX: PRO-ED.

Prizant, B. M., & Wetherby, A. M. (1993). Communication assessment for young children. *Infants and Young Children, 5*, 20–34.

Quill, K. (1995). *Teaching children with autism: Strategies to enhance communication and socialization*. Albany, NY: Del Mar.

Sasso, G. M., Simpson, R. L., & Novak, C. G. (1985). Procedures for facilitating integration of autistic children in public school settings. *Analysis and Intervention in Developmental Disabilities, 5*, 233–246.

Simpson, R. L., & Myles, B. S. (1998). *Educating children and youth with autism: Strategies for effective practice*. Austin, TX: PRO-ED.

Simpson, R. L., Myles, B. S., & Sasso, G. M. (1997). *Social skills for students with autism* (2nd ed.). Reston, VA: Council of Exceptional Children.

Simpson, R. L., & Regan, M. (1988). *Management of autistic behavior*. Austin, TX: PRO-ED.

Wood, M. M., Davis, K. R., Swindle, F. L., & Quirk, C. (1995). *Developmental therapy–developmental teaching: Fostering social–emotional competence in troubled children and youth*. Austin, TX: PRO-ED.

RESOURCES ON THE INTERNET

To access the following sites, simply type the address line when you are on the Internet. At the end of some of the categories, we provide resources called Listservs. Listservs are discussion groups that you may access (they normally send out email as people contribute to the Listserv). Please be aware that, for the most part, contributors to these Listservs provide support and shared experiences; they are not edited for factual content.

Asperger Syndrome

ASPEN of America
http://www.asperger.org/

Asperger's Syndrome—Another View
http://www.udel.edu/bkirby/asperger/as_another_view.html

Aspergers Syndrome Homepage
http://www.ummed.edu/pub/o/ozbayrak/asperger.html

AS: Through the Lifespan
http://www.udel.edu/bkirby/asperger/as_thru_years.html

A Collection of Resources for AS and Related Disorders
http://www.udel.edu/bkirby/asperger/

Assistive Technology (see also Augmentative and Alternative Communication)

Applied Science and Engineering Laboratories
http://www.asel.udel.edu/

Assis-TECH, Inc.
http://www.assis-tech.com

Assistive Technology Act of 1998
http://www-npnd.org/ATBill.htm

Assistive Technology, Inc.
http://www.assistivetech.com

Assistive Technology On-Line
http://www.asel.udel.edu/at-online/html

Center for Information Technology Accommodations
http://www.gsa.gov/cita/

Educational Technologies for Kids with Special Needs
http://members.aol.com/dreamms/company.htm

IBM Special Needs Solutions
http://www.austin.ibm.com/sns/snsaccesdos.html

iTech Center at Parents Helping Parents
http://www.php.com/itech.htm

KeyGuard
http://www.austin.ibm.com/sns/snskeyguard.html

LAB Resources
http://www.execpc.com:80/~labres/

Network for Education and Assistive Technology (NEAT)
http://www.asel.udel.edu/neat

Origin Instruments (products to adapt computers)
http://www.inet-usa.com/wca/

Screen Magnifier
http://www.austin.ibm.com/sns/snsscmag.html

Screen Reader
http://www.austin.ibm.com/sns/snssrd.html

SpeechViewer II
http://www.austin.ibm.com/sns/snsspv2.html

THINKable
http://www.austin.ibm.com/sns/snsthk.html

Virtual Assistive Technology Center
http://www.at-center.com

Augmentative and Alternative Communication

(see also Assistive Technology)

Augmentative and Alternative Communication
http://www.abacon.com/list/st0222.html

Augmentative and Alternative Communication
http://www.asel.udel.edu/at-online/technology/aac/

Augmentative and Alternative Communication, from ERIC
http://www.indiana.edu/~eric_rec/ieo/bibs/aug.html

Gus Communications, Inc., Speech Disorders and Augmentative Communication
http://www.gusinc.com./

LAB Resources
http://www.execpc.com/~labres/augment.html

REHAB Brief: Augmentative and Alternative Communication
http://www.naric.com/naric/rehab_b/rb-15-3.html

United States Society for Augmentative and Alternative Communication
http://kaddath.mt.cs.cmu.edu/scs/93-7.html

LISTSERV: ACOLUG—Augmentative Communication Online Users Group: To subscribe send mail to listserv@vm.temple.edu. In the body of the message, type "sub ACOLUG your name" without the quotes. Site: Temple University, Philadelphia, PA 19122. Human administrator: acolug-request@vm.temple.edu

LISTSERV: Illinois Network for Augmentative and Alternative Communication. To subscribe send email to listserv@listserv.uic.edu. In the body of the message, type "sub INAAC your name" without the quotes. Site: University of Illinois at Chicago, Chicago, IL 60612. Human administrator: inaac-request@listserv.uic.edu

Autism

Allergies in Autism
http://www.autism.org/allergy.html

American Association for Childhood and Adolescent Psychiatry (AACAP)
http://www.aacap.org/factsfam/autistic.htm

AskERIC InfoGuide on AUTISM from AskERIC
http://ericir.syr.edu/cgi bin/markup_infoguides/Alphabetical_List_of_InfoGuides/Autism-11.95

Autism and Asperger's Syndrome Resources
http://web.syr.edu/~jmwobus/autism/

Autism and Brain Development Research
http://nodulus.extern.ucsd.edu/

The Autism Channel
http://www.norwich.net/~kellysm/autism.html

The Autism Depot
http://home.ptd.net/~rjd/autism/

Autism Research
http://www.uth.tmc.edu/uth_orgs/pub_affairs/uthouston/mar_96/aut.html

Autism Society of America
http://www.autism-society.org/

Autistic Disorder Symptoms
http://www.cmhc.com/disorders/sx65.htm

Dave Nelson's Autism Page
http://www.mindspring.com/~dgn/

Dave's Autism Information Page
http://www.lancs.ac.uk/people/cpadak/autism/autism.htm

Links to the Center for the Study of Autism
http://www.autism.org/

- **Autistic Savant,** http://www.autism.org/savant.html
- **The Cerebellum and Autism,** http://www.autism.org/cerebel.html
- **Diagnostic and Statistical Manual of Mental Disorders,** http://www.autism.org/dsm.html
- **Genetics and Autism,** http://www.autism.org/genetics.html
- **Limbic System,** http://www.autism.org/limbic.html
- **Naltrexone and Autism,** http://www.autism.org/naltrex.html
- **Non-Internet Resources for Autism,** http://www.autism.org/noninternet.html
- **Self-Injurious Behavior,** http://www.autism.org/sib.html
- **Stereotypic (self-stimulatory) Behaviors,** http://www.autism.org/stim.html

- **Stimulus Overselectivity, Tunnel Vision in Autism,** http://www.autism.org/tunvsn.html

National Institute Neurological Disorders
http://www.ninds.nih.gov/healinfo/DISORDER/AUTISM/autism.htm

Society for the Autistically Handicapped (SFTAH)
http://www.rmplc.co.uk/eduweb/sites/autism/

Yale Autism and PDD Clinic Homepage
http://info.med.Yale.edu/chldstdy/autism/

LISTSERV: Autism and Developmental Disabilities Discussion list. To subscribe, send an email message to LISTSERV@MAELSTROM.STJOHNS.EDU. In the body of the message, type "subscribe AUTISM your name" without the quotes. Contact: Bob Zenhausern, drz@sjuvm.stjohns.edu

LISTSERV: Autism Network International. To subscribe send email to Listserv@Listserv.SYR.EDU. In the body of the message, type "subscribe ANI-L" without the quotes.

Pervasive Developmental Disorders

Healthtouch
http://www.healthtouch.com/level1/leaflets/aslha/aslha078.htm

Parents Helping Parents PDD webpage
http://www.php.com/autism.htm

PDD Support Page
http://www.geocities.com/HotSprings/9647/

National Institute on Neurological Disorders and Stroke
http://www.ninds.nih.gov/healinfo/DISORDER/pervasiv/pervasiv.htm

Special Education Information

Americans with Disabilities Act Document Center
http://janweb.icdi.wvu.edu/kinder/

Center for Effective Collaboration and Practice
http://www.air-dc.org/cecp/

The Council for Exceptional Children
http://www.cec.sped.org/home.htm

ERIC Clearinghouse on Disabilities and Gifted Education
http://www.cec.sped.org/er-menu.htm

Individual Education Program (IEP) Parent Preparation and Planning
http://planet-hawaii.com/7thwave/iep.html

Individuals with Disabilities Education Act (IDEA 97)
http://www.ed.gov/offices/OSERS/IDEA/index.html

Kids Together, Inc.
http://www.kidstogether.org/

National Information for Children and Youth with Disabilities
http://www.nichcy.org/

National Institute on Disability and Rehabilitation Research
http://www.ed.gov/offices/OSERS/NIDRR/index.html

National Parent Information Network
http://npin.org/

Office of Special Education Programs in the US Department of Education
http://www.ed.gov/offices/OSERS/OSEP/index.html

Special Education Resources on the Internet (SERI)
http://www.hood.edu/seri/serihome.htm

Transition Research Institute at University of Illinois
http://www.ed.uiuc.edu/SPED/tri/institute.html

What Does That Mean? (listing of key special education and other terminology)
http://planet-hawaii.com/7thwave/dys.abbrev.html

Methods, Treatments, Programs

General

Autism Society of America's Package on Treatment Options
http://www.autism-society.org/packages/treatment-options.html

Nutritional

Autism Network for Dietary Intervention (ANDI)
http://www.autismndi.com/

Lisa S. Lewis, "Understanding and Implementing a Gluten and Casein Free Diet"
http://members.aol.com/lisas156/index.htm

TEACCH

Division TEACCH Home page
http://www.unc.edu/depts/teacch/

Option Institute Web Site (affiliated with the "Son-Rise" Program)
http://www.option.org/

Facilitated Communication

American Association for Childhood and Adolescent Psychiatry
http://www.aacap.org/publications/policy/ps30.htm

Douglas Biklen, "Common Myths and Misunderstandings about Facilitated Communication"
ftp://ftp.syr.edu/information/autism/common_myths_and_misunderstandings_FC

The Facilitated Communication Institute's Page
http://soeweb.syr.edu/thefci/

Gina Green, "Facilitated Communication: Mental Miracle or Sleight of Hand?"
http://www.rtd.com/~lippard/skeptic/02.3.green-fc.html

Information on Autism in U of Wisconsin–Milwaukee Behavior Analysis Archive
ftp://alpha1.csd.uwm.edu/pub/Psychology/BehaviorAnalysis/disability-autism/facilitated-communication-claims-evidence-green_shane

Position Statement on Facilitated Communication by the American Psychological Association
http://web.syr.edu/~thefci/apafc.htm

Lovaas Method/Applied Behavioral Analysis/ Behavioral Therapy/Discrete Trial Training

Autism Behavior Therapy Alliance
http://www.autismbehaviortherapy.org/

The Center for Early Education
http://www.earlyed.com/

Institute for Child Development
http://icd.binghamton.edu/

The Recovery Zone (Applied Behavioral Analysis)
http://pages.prodigy.net/damianporcari/recovery.htm

Richard Saffron's ABA resources
http://members.tripod.com/~RSaffran/index.html

LISTSERV: ABA-PRO. Send message to listserv@maelstrom.stjohns.edu. In the body of the message, type "Subscribe ABA-PRO ⟨your name⟩" without the quotes.

Services

Autistic Children's Activity Program
http://www.autism.com/acap/

Autism Services Association
http://members.aol.com/autismasa/

Autism Treatment Services of Canada
http://www.autism.ca/index.html#ATSC

Community Services for Autistic Adults and Children (CSAAC)
http://www.csaac.org/

COSAC (New Jersey Center for Outreach and Services to the Autism Community)
http://members.aol.com/njautism/whatis.htm

Florida's Center for Autism and Related Disabilities (CARD)

- **CARD at Florida Mental Health Institute (USF)**
  http://card-usf.fmhi.usf.edu/CARDhp.html

- **CARD at University of Florida Brain Institute (Gainesville)**
  http://neurosci90.health.ufl.edu/card.html

The Hanen Centre
http://www.hanen.org/

Internet Mental Health
http://www.mentalhealth.com/dis/p20-ch06.html

Judevine Center for Autism–Southwest Missouri Project
http://web.getonthe.net/~rsanders/judevine/

Kansas Autism Foundation
http://www.kansasautism.com/

Kerry's Place Autism Services
http://aci.on.ca/KP_AutismServices/

Kind Tree: Autism Services
http://members.tripod.com/~KindTree/Autism_In_Depth.html

The Miller Method
http://world.std.com/~ArnMill

National Speech/Language Therapy Center
http://www.nationalspeech.com/

New England Center for Children
http://www.necc.org/

Socrates Program: Communication for Integration (collaborative effort to create communication tool)
http://callisto.worldonline.nl/~auti/

Academic and Research Programs

The Autism Research Foundation (TARF)
http://ladders.org/tarf/TARF.htm

Autism Research Institute
http://www.autism.com/ari/

Autism Research Unit of University of Sunderland, England
http://osiris.sunderland.ac.uk/autism/

Children's Hospital of San Diego Neuropsychology Research Lab
http://nodulus.extern.ucsd.edu/

The Indiana Resource Center for Autism
http://www.isdd.indiana.edu/~irca/

National Alliance for Autism Research
http://babydoc.home.pipeline.com/naar/naar.htm

The National Autistic Society's Information Centre
http://www.oneworld.org/autism_uk/research.html

University of California at Santa Barbara, UCSB Autism Research Center
http://education.ucsb.edu/~doniel/autism.html

University of Kansas Special Education (graduate program in autism)
http://www.sped.ukans.edu/spedprojects/graduate_autism/

University of Texas at Houston, Autism Research
http://www.uth.tmc.edu/uth_orgs/pub_affairs/uthouston/mar_96/aut.html

Yale Child Study Center Autism/PDD Clinic
http://info.med.yale.edu/chldstdy/autism/page21.html

Online Papers

Matthew Belmonte & Ruth Carper, "Neuroanatomical and Neurophysiological Clues to the Nature of Autism"
http://www.mattababy.dyn.ml.org/~belmonte/Publications/Papers/98_Garreau/

Dorothy V. M. Bishop, "Autism, Asperger's syndrome and semantic-pragmatic disorder: Where are the boundaries?"
http://www.jaymuggs.demon.co.uk/bishop.htm

Patrick F. Bolton, Margaret Murphy, Hope Macdonald, Beth Whitlock, Andrew Pickles, and Michael Rutter, "Obstetric Complications in Autism: Consequences or Causes of the Condition?"
http://www.aacap.org/journal/feb/273.htm

California Division of Education, "Best Practices for Designing and Delivering Effective Programs for Individuals with Autistic Spectrum Disorders"
http://www.feat.org/CABP/

James R. Cash, "Language Acquisition in Autistic Children: What Does It Tell Us?"
http://www.lifestories.com/papers/autism.htm

Coordinating Council for Handicapped Children, "Participating in Your Child's IEP"
http://www.hounet.com/autism/article4.html

Richard Eisenmajer, Margot Prior, Susan Leekam, Lorna Wing, Judith Gould, Michael Welham, and Ben Ong, "Comparison of Clinical Symptoms in Autism and Asperger's"
http://www.aacap.org/journal/november/1523.htm

Catherine Lord and Andrew Pickles, "Language Level and Nonverbal Social-Communicative Behaviors in Autistic and Language-Delayed Children"
http://www.aacap.org/journal/november/1542.htm

Barbara B. Montee, Raymond G. Miltenberger, and David Wittrock, "An Experimental Analysis of Facilitated Communication"
http://www.envmed.rochester.edu/wwwvgl/jaba_articles/1995/montee-full.htmlx

Paul Shattock, "An Assessment of Some of the Unorthodox Forms of Biomedical Intervention Currently Being Applied to Autism"
http://osiris.sunderland.ac.uk/autism/durham95.html

Vijendra K. Singh, Reed P. Warren, and Dennis Odell, "Immune Response to Brain Myelin in Autistic Children"
http://attila.stevens-tech.edu/spons_proj/pages/immune.html

Lorna Wing, "The Definition and Prevalence of Autism: A Review"
http://www.jaymuggs.demon.co.uk/wing.htm

Organizations

Canada

Autism Society British Columbia
http://www.enet.ca/autism/

Families for Early Treatment of Autism (FEAT) of British Columbia
http://fox.nstn.ca/~zacktam/FEATbc/

Autism Society Ontario, Sarnia–Lambton Chapter
http://home.tct.net/autism/

Autism Society Ontario, Windsor–Essex Chapter
http://www.mnsi.net/~cdelduca/

La Société de l'Autisme du Montréal Metropolitain
http://www.odyssee.net/~patboul/

Société Québécoise de l'Autisme (French and English)
http://www.phy.uqam.ca:2000/~sqa/sqa_home.html

Saskatoon Society for Autism
http://www.sfn.saskatoon.sk.ca/health/autism/

Europe

Autism Europe
http://osiris.sunderland.ac.uk/autism/eur.html

United Kingdom

Allergy-Induced Autism Support and Research Network
http://www.demon.co.uk/charities/AIA/aia.htm

InternAUT (International Autism Self-Advocacy Organization)
http://www.inlv.demon.nl/internaut/

Liverpool & Lancashire Autistic Society
http://www.mersinet.co.uk/~lalas/

The National Autistic Society
http://www.oneworld.org/autism_uk/

National Autistic Society (Surry Branch)
http://www.jaymuggs.demon.co.uk/welcome.htm

Parents and Professionals and Autism (Belfast, Northern Ireland)
http://www.ulst.ac.uk/papa/PAPA.html

Parents for Early Intervention of Autism in Children
http://www.peach.uk.com/

Society for the Autistically Handicapped
http://www.rmplc.co.uk/eduweb/sites/autism/

Somerset Autistic Support Group
http://homepages.enterprise.net/timstreet/sasg.html

United States National

Autism Network International (ANI)
http://www.students.uiuc.edu/~bordner/ani.html

Autism Society of America
http://www.autism-society.org/

The Center for the Study of Autism
http://www.autism.org/

Cure Autism Now (CAN)
http://www.canfoundation.org/

National Alliance for Autism Research (NAAR)
http://babydoc.home.pipeline.com/naar/naar.htm

Our Kids
http://rdz.acor.org/lists/our-kids//

United States Regional

New England

Asperger's Association of New England (AANE)
http://www.autocyt.com/aane/

Alabama

Autism Society of Alabama
http://www.autism-alabama.org/

Arizona

Greater Phoenix Chapter of the Autism Society of America
http://aztec.asu.edu/phxautism/

California

Families for Early Autism Treatment (FEAT) of Northern California
http://www.feat.org/

Inland Empire Chapter Autism Society of America Home Page (San Bernadino–Riverside area of Southern California)
http://w3.dcache.net/inlandempire/

PDD/Autism and Related Disorders Education Support Group (Santa Clara County)
http://www.php.com/autism.htm

Connecticut

Fairfield County Connecticut Support Group
http://pages.prodigy.com/CT/maggie/pdd.html

Florida

Reaching Potentials
http://www.reachingpotentials.org/

Illinois

Autism Society of Illinois
http://www.siue.edu/SWIFNET/cfhir/a60.html

Indiana

Riverbend Down Syndrome Parent Support Group
http://www.he.net/~altonweb/cs/downsyndrome/index.htm?pdddef.html

Kentucky

The Autism Society of Western Kentucky
http://www.dynasty.net/users/autism/

Nebraska

FEAT of Nebraska
http://www.top.net/nebfeat/

New Jersey

Asperger Syndrome Education Network
http://www.aspennj.org/

New York

Broome–Tioga Chapter of the Autism Society of America
http://members.aol.com/Autism3/

Pervasive Developmental Disabilities New York City
http://members.aol.com/PDDNYC/intro.htm

North Carolina

The Autism Society of North Carolina
http://www.stellar1.com/autism/

Chapel Hill Area Local Unit of the Autism Society of America
http://www.autism-info.com/CHALU.html

Wake County Local Unit of the Autism Society of America (Raleigh)
http://members.aol.com/WCAutism/

Oklahoma

Disability Links for Oklahoma Families
http://www.oil.tec.ok.us/dee.htm

Oregon

Families for Early Autism Treatment (FEAT) of Oregon
http://www.rdrop.com/users/feator/

Pennsylvania

The Autism Society of Pittsburgh
http://www.pitt.edu/~timq/asp.html

South Carolina

Emerald Center Multi-County Board for Disabilities and Special Needs
http://www.schsp.org/emeraldcenter/

Tri-Development Center of Aiken County
http://www.aikentdc.org/

Texas

The Denton County Autism Society
http://www.kidquest.com/asa/index.shtml

Families for Early Autism Treatment (FEAT) of Houston
http://www.neosoft.com/FEAT_Houston/

Families for Early Autism Treatment (FEAT) of North Texas (Dallas/Fort Worth)
http://www.neosoft.com/TRCA/

Fort Worth/Mid-Cities Autism Society
http://www.jjt.com/fwas/

Texas Gulf Coast Chapter of the Autism Society of America
http://www.kidquest.com/asa/index.shtml

Washington

Autism Society of Washington
http://www.olywa.net/autism/

Families for Early Autism Treatment (FEAT) of Washington
http://members.aol.com/featwa/

Wisconsin

Autism Society of Wisconsin
http://www.asw4autism.org/

SUMMARY

At a glance, the number of resources listed in this chapter can seem overwhelming. Yet, we have listed only a fraction of currently available resources. We have tried to offer a representative sample and do not necessarily endorse the resources assembled here.

References

American Academy of Audiology. (1995). Auditory integration therapy: Position statement. *Audiology Today, 5*(4), 21.

American Psychiatric Association. (1994). *Diagnostic and statistical manual of mental disorders* (4th ed.). Washington, DC: Author.

American Speech-Language-Hearing Association. (1994). Auditory integration therapy. *ASHA, 36*(11), 55–58.

Anderson, G., & Hoshino, Y. (1987). Neurochemical studies of autism. In D. Cohen & A. Donnellan (Eds.), *Handbook of autism and developmental disorders* (pp. 166–191). New York: Wiley.

Autism Society of America, Inc. (1995). Definition of autism. *Advocate, 27*(6), 3.

Bayley, N. (1993). *Bayley Scales of Infant Development* (2nd ed.). San Antonio: Psychological Corp.

Baron-Cohen, S. (1991). Do people with autism understand what causes emotion? *Child Development, 62*, 385–395.

Berard, G. (1997). *Auditory Integration Training packet*. San Diego: Autism Research Institute.

Berkell, D. E. (1992). *Autism: Identification, education and treatment*. Hillsdale, NJ: Erlbaum.

Bettelheim, B. (1967). *The empty fortress*. New York: Free Press.

Biklen, D. (1992). *Typing to talk: Facilitated communication*. Circle Pines, MN: American Guidance Services.

Bondy, A., & Frost, L. (1994). The Picture Exchange Communication System. *Focus on Autistic Behavior, 9*(3).

Bouma, R., & Schweitzer, R. (1990). The impact of chronic childhood illness on family stress: A comparison between autism and cystic fibrosis. *Journal of Clinical Psychology, 46*, 722–730.

Carr, E., & Durand, M. (1985). Reducing behavior problems through functional communication training. *Journal of Applied Behavior Analysis, 18*, 111–126.

Carr, E., & Kemp, D. (1989). Functional equivalence of autistic leading and communicative pointing: Analysis and treatment. *Journal of Autism and Developmental Disorders, 19*, 561–578.

Clark-Hall, M., Collier, H., Fayman, K., Grinstead, J., Kearns, P., Robie, D., & Rotton, M. (1976). *Responsive parent training manual*. Lawrence, KS: H & H Enterprises.

Cohen, D. J., Riddle, M. A., Laor, N., Young, J. G., & Shaywitz, B. A. (1983). Neurobiological perspectives on neuropsychiatric disorders of childhood. In H. Hoppius & G. Winokur (Eds.), *Psychopharmacology: Vol. 1, Part 2. Clinical psychopharmacology* (pp. 53–73). Amsterdam: Excerpta Medica.

Crossley, R. (1992). Communication training involving facilitated communication. In DEAL Communication Centre (Eds.), *Facilitated communication training* (pp. 1–9). Melbourne, Australia: DEAL Communication Centre.

Durand, M. (1990). Severe behavior problems: A functional communication training approach. In R. Horner, G. Dunlap, & R. Koegel (Eds.), *Generalization and maintenance: Life-style changes in applied settings* (pp. 221–241). Baltimore: Brookes.

Education for All Handicapped Children Act of 1975, 20 U.S.C. § 1400 *et seq*.

Educational Audiology Association. (in press). Position statement on auditory integration therapy (AIT). *Educational Audiology Association Newsletter*.

Ehlers, S., & Gillberg, C. (1993). The epidemiology of Asperger syndrome: A total population study. *Journal of Child Psychology and Psychiatry, 34*, 1327–1350.

Ellis, A. (1996). *Better, deeper, and more enduring brief therapy: The Rational Emotive Behavior approach*. New York: Brunner/Mazel.

Engelmann, S., & Osborn, J. (1973). *DISTAR language program*. New York: SRA–McGraw-Hill.

Folstein, S., & Rutter, M. (1978). A twin study of individuals with infantile autism. In M. Rutter & E. Schopler (Eds.), *Autism: A reappraisal of concepts and treatment* (pp. 219–241). New York: Plenum.

Freeman, S., & Duke, L. (1996). *Teach me language*. Langley, British Columbia: SBK Books.

Grandin, T. (1988). Teaching tips from a recovered autistic. *Focus on Autistic Behavior, 3*(1), 1–8.

Gresham, F., & MacMillan, D. (1997). Autistic recovery? An analysis and critique of the empirical evidence on the early intervention project. *Behavioral Disorders, 22*, 185–201.

Happe, F. (1995). *Autism*. Cambridge, MA: Harvard University Press.

Hart, B., & Rogers-Warren, A. K. (1978). A milieu approach to teaching language. In R. L. Schiefelbusch (Ed.), *Language intervention strategies* (pp. 193–235). Baltimore University Park Press.

Hobson, R. P. (1993). *Autism and the development of mind*. Hillsdale, NJ: Erlbaum.

Individuals with Disabilities Education Act of 1990, 20 U.S.C. § 1400 *et seq*.

Kanner, L. (1943). Autistic disturbances of affective content. *The Nervous Child, 2*, 217–250.

Krug, D. A., Arick, J. R., & Almond, P. J. (1993). *Autism Screening Instrument for Educational Planning* (2nd ed.) Austin, TX: PRO-ED.

Lambert, N., Nihira, K., & Leland, H. (1993). *AAMR Adaptive Behavior Scales–School* (2nd ed.). Austin, TX: PRO-ED.

Leiter, R. G. (1948). *Leiter International Performance Scale*. Chicago: Stoelting.

Lovaas, O. I. (1987). Behavioral treatment and normal educational and intellectual functioning in young autistic children. *Journal of Consulting and Clinical Psychology, 55*, 3–9.

Lovaas, O. I. (1996). The UCLA Young autism model of service delivery. In C. Maurice, G. Green, & S. Luce (Eds.), *Behavioral intervention for young children with autism* (pp. 241–248) Austin, TX: PRO-ED.

Maning, A., & Katz, K. (1991). Facilitating functional communication with echolalic language users. *Focus on Autistic Behavior*, 6(3), 1–7.

Mesibov, G., Schopler, E., Schaffer, B., & Landrus, R. (1988). *Adolescent and Adult Psychoeducational Profile*. Austin, TX: PRO-ED.

Mitchell, P. (1997). *Introduction to the theory of the mind*. New York: St. Martin's Press.

Rehabilitation Act of 1973, 29 U.S.C. § 701 *et seq*.

Rimland, B. (1964). *Infantile autism*. New York: Appleton-Century-Crofts.

Rimland, B. (1992). A facilitated communication "horror story." *Autism Research Review*, 6(1), 1, 7.

Rimland, B. (1994). The modern history of autism: A personal perspective. In J. L. Matson (Ed.), *Autism in children and adults: Etiology, assessment, and intervention* (pp. 1–12). Pacific Grove, CA: Brooks/Cole.

Schopler, E., & Mesibov, G. B. (1992). *High-functioning individuals with autism*. New York: Plenum.

Schopler, E., Reichler, R., Bashford, A., Lansing, M., & Marcus, L. (1990). *Psychoeducational Profile-Revised*. Austin, TX: PRO-ED.

Schopler, E., Van Bourgodien, M. E., & Bristol, M. M. (1993). *Preschool issues in autism*. New York: Plenum.

Simpson, R., & Myles, B. S. (1995). Facilitated communication and children with disabilities: An enigma in search of a perspective. *Focus on Exceptional Children, 27*(9), 1–16.

Simpson, R., Myles, B. S., Sasso, G. M., & Kamps, D. (1997). *Social skills for students with autism*. Reston, VA: Council for Exceptional Children.

Simpson, R. L., & Regan, R. (1986). *Management of autistic behavior*. Austin, TX: PRO-ED.

Smith, T., & Lovaas, O. I. (1997). The UCLA Young Autism Project: A reply to Gresham and MacMillan. *Behavioral Disorders, 22*, 202–218.

Sparrow, S., Balla, D., & Cicchetti, D. (1984). *Vineland Adaptive Behavior Scales*. Circle Pines, MN: American Guidance Service.

Strauss, A. A., & Lehtinen, L. E. (1947). *Psychopathology and education of brain-injured child*. New York: Grune & Stratton.

Stutsman, R. (1948). *Merrill-Palmer Scale of Mental Tests*. Los Angeles: Western Psychological Services.

Trachtman, P. (1994, September). NIH looks at the implausible and inexplicable. *Smithsonian*, 110–123.

Tsai, L. (1998). Medical interventions for students with autism. In R. Simpson & B. Myles (Eds.), *Educating children and youth with autism*. Austin, TX: PRO-ED.

Wechsler, D. (1981). *Wechsler Adult Intelligence Scale–Revised*. San Antonio: Psychological Corp.

Wechsler, D. (1989). *Wechsler Preschool and Primary Scale of Intelligence–Revised*. San Antonio: Psychological Corp.

Wechsler, D. (1991). *Wechsler Intelligence Scale for Children–Third Edition*. San Antonio: Psychological Corp.

Wood, M. M., Davis, K. R., Swindle, F. L., & Quirk, C. (1996). *Developmental Therapy Objectives Rating Form–Revised*. Austin, TX: PRO-ED.

Index

About the Authors

Richard L. Simpson is professor in Special Education and School Psychology at the University of Kansas. He also has worked as a teacher of students with behavior disorders, school psychologist, clinical psychologist, director of a program for students with severe emotional disturbance and autism, and administrator of a mental health organization's prevention and support program. Simpson is senior editor of *Focus on Autism and Other Developmental Disabilities*, as well as author of numerous books, articles, and book chapters dealing with parents and families, children and youth with emotional and behavioral disorders, and children and youth diagnosed with autism and Asperger's syndrome.

Paul Zionts received his PhD in educational psychology from the University of Connecticut and is a professor of special education at Central Michigan University. He has taught and applied the principles of Rational Emotive Behavior Therapy in his roles as a teacher in a reform school and in an inner city high school, a program director, consultant, and teacher educator. He has lectured and provided training in local, state, and national events and has conducted hundreds of workshops that have included teachers, counselors, psychologists, social workers, administrators, parents, secretaries, and bus drivers. He has written over 20 articles and chapters; authored *Teaching Disturbed and Disturbing Students* (now in its second edition) and *Understanding Children and Youth with Emotional and Behavioral Problems*; and edited a book titled *Inclusion Strategies for Students with Learning and Behavior Problems*.

Laura Zionts is an assistant professor at Central Michigan University in the Department of Counseling and Special Education. She received her PhD from the University of North Texas, Denton. She taught early childhood and secondary level special education to diverse students in public and nonpublic settings. During her position as an early childhood education teacher at The Institute for Effective Instruction in San Diego, California, she taught young children with autism and pervasive developmental disorders emphasizing development of communication skills and behavioral intervention. Her research interests are in the areas of early childhood assessment and intervention, behavior disorders, and diversity issues in education.

Suzanne Shellady is currently an associate professor in the Department of Counseling and Special Education at Central Michigan University. She received her PhD in special education from the University of Iowa in 1994. Her research interests include inservice and preservice training issues in the areas of behavioral disorders, oral language and social skills development, and autism.